Agricultural Exports and Economic Growth

Economic Growth

A Study of the Botswana Beef Industry

Agricultural Exports and Economic Growth

A Study of the Botswana Beef Industry

Michael Hubbard

KPI

London, New York and Sydney

First published in 1986 by KPI Limited
11 New Fetter Lane, London EC4P 4EE, England

Distributed by
Routledge & Kegan Paul, Associated Book Publishers (UK) Ltd.
11 New Fetter Lane, London EC4P 4EE, England

Routledge & Kegan Paul Methuen Inc.,
29 West 35th Street
New York, NY 10001, USA

Routledge & Kegan Paul
Methuen Law Book Company
44 Waterloo Road
North Ryde, NSW 2113
Australia

Set in Times
by HBM Typesetting Ltd, Chorley, Lancashire
and printed in Great Britain
by Dotesios Printers Ltd, Bradford-on-Avon, Wiltshire

ISBN 07103 0121–9

Contents

Contents

Contents

Tables in the text

x

Tables in the appendix

Figures in the text

Figures in the appendix

For Petra, Patric and Richard Luc.

Glossary of Abbreviations, Terms and Conventions Used

Abbreviations

AAC	African Advisory Council
ACP	African, Caribbean and Pacific countries, so called because the countries involved in the Lomé Convention with the EEC are situated in these regions
BAMB	Botswana Agricultural Marketing Board
BECCAT	CDC's northern ranches at Bushman Pits, Nata and Pandamatenga
BMC	Botswana Meat Commission
BNA	Botswana National Archives
BP	Bechuanaland Protectorate
BPA	Bechuanaland Protectorate Abattoirs Ltd., the semi-nationalized forerunner company to BMC
CAP	Common Agricultural Policy of the EEC
CDC	Colonial (later Commonwealth) Development Corporation
CDW	Cold Dressed Weight
CD and W	Colonial Development and Welfare Fund
CELF	Cattle Export Levy Fund
CET	Common External Tariff of the EEC

CSC   Cold Storage Commission of Southern Rhodesia
DVS   Director of Veterinary Services Department
EAC   European Advisory Council
ECCO   Export and Canning Company
EDF   European Development Fund
ELAKAT   Compagnie d'Elevage et d'Alimentation du Katanga
f.o.r.   free on rail
FSAMI   Federated South African Meat Industries
HC   High Commissioner
ICS   Imperial Cold Storage and Supply Company
JAC   Joint Advisory Council
KMC   Kenya Meat Commission
LAB   Livestock Industry Advisory Board (forerunner to LIAC)
LIAC   Livestock Industry Advisory Committee
NAC   Native Advisory Council (former title of AAC)
NCEA   Ngamiland Cattle Exporters' Association
RC   Resident Commissioner
RC(BP)   Resident Commissioner (Bechuanaland Protectorate)
RCC   Rhodesian Cooperative Creameries Ltd
SACUA   Southern African Customs Union Agreement (originally 1910 revised 1969) between South Africa and the High Commission territories (Bechuanaland Protectorate, Basutoland and Swaziland)
TGLP   Tribal Grazing Lands Policy

Terms

administration   the colonial administration of the Bechuanaland Protectorate; used interchangeably with government.
breeder   used here to mean a herder or producer of cattle from their birth to slaughter. It is used in this sense (for want of a better term) to distinguish such producers from fatteners and speculators. It does not here mean a producer who specializes in

	the breeding stage, selling off the progeny, unless the context indicates this clearly.
chilled beef	beef stored at a temperature just above freezing point, consisting usually of the more valuable cuts.
fattener	one who buys lean stock and adds weight to them by feeding. In Botswana the fattening function should more properly be termed growing out i.e. buying young stock and adding weight to them by letting them mature on natural pasture.
fifth quarter	the offal and by-products of beef production.
fresh beef	newly slaughtered beef, as distinct from chilled and frozen beef (in accordance with the current usage in FAO Trade Statistics).
government	used interchangeably with administration to refer to the colonial government of the Bechuanaland Protectorate at Mafeking. The two higher tiers of British imperial government in Southern Africa (the High Commission based in Cape Town and the Dominions office in London) are referred to specifically as such.
herder	used interchangeably with breeder.
prices	all prices mentioned are current money values unless specified as real values.
Pula	Botswana's currency from August 1976. One Pula is treated as equal to one South African Rand and half a South African pound (the South African currency until 1961).
'smuggling'	this term is used in inverted commas since it deals with import of cattle from the Protectorate into South Africa in contravention of South African import controls which were (and are) themselves in contravention of the letter of the SACUA.
speculator	one who buys cattle for immediate resale i.e. without fattening.
trader in cattle	similar to speculator but cattle buying takes place at trading store.

Conventions

Place names   referred to by their name at the time of the event. Thus:
Bechuanaland Protectorate is modern Botswana
Congo is modern Zaire
Nyasaland is modern Malawi
Northern Rhodesia is modern Zambia
Southern Rhodesia is modern Zimbabwe
South West Africa is modern Namibia

References to publications in the text   books, articles, papers, pamphlets, consultancy reports and theses are referred to by name, date and page, e.g. (Smith 1969:101) in the text and listed in the select bibliography;

government publications and other official publications are cited in footnotes. They are listed separately in the select bibliography.

Republic of Botswana

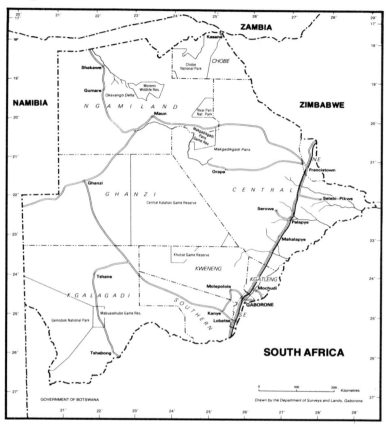

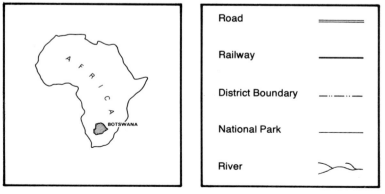

Preface

By the late 1970s Botswana had become the largest regular exporter of beef on the African continent. This study examines the affairs of Botswana's beef export industry from its early twentieth-century beginnings in supplies of cattle for the meat requirements of the growing mining complexes of the Witwatersrand and Copperbelt, through its period of suppression and disruption in the depression years, to the post-war establishment of a viable export abattoir, nationalization, rapid growth and association with the EEC, and their link to the problems and possibilities which the expansion of cattle production is bringing for rural people.

The study was motivated by the lack of a comprehensive history of the industry which has been at the heart of the colonial and post-colonial economy. It was facilitated by the availability at the Botswana National Archives of a vast quantity of catalogued colonial records dealing with cattle and beef exports. Once embarked on the work I soon found that the industry in colonial times had been so exposed to the machinations of foreign meat companies and governments and so heavily influenced by events in regional and world markets, that in order to disentangle the threads linking events a considerable amount of background information was needed on the meat industries and markets of South Africa (mainly) and colonial Zimbabwe, Zambia, Namibia and Zaire, and on the world beef trade. At the South African Library in Cape Town the collection of catalogued twentieth-century newspaper cuttings proved invaluable. The documents section of the University of the Witwatersrand library, the Johannesburg Public Library and the Meat Board library in Pretoria were the sources of most of the reports of commissions of inquiry cited and of historical statistics for countries of the region. The library of the Institute of Development Studies at the University of Sussex provided most of the material on the world beef trade.

On cattle production and marketing in Botswana the collections of the Botswana National Archives, the Ministry of Agriculture and the National Institute of Research were supplemented by an informal survey among farmers of Bokaa and Gabane villages (December 1977) and by interviews with farmers and cattle traders in the Molopo, Ghanzi, Tuli and Tati blocks and in Maun (July–August 1978). The information on the Botswana Meat Commission was obtained directly from them and also from the Ministry of Agriculture.

The main limitations of the study are twofold. Firstly, there is a dearth of secondary material on the political economy of the meat industry in South Africa and in other countries of the region. I was able to find only a single article (Phimister 1978, on Southern Rhodesia to 1938). The result is that my interpretations of foreign events and ascriptions of motives to foreign companies and governments are based almost entirely on the necessarily limited primary research on these countries which I was able to carry out myself. But perhaps the present work will provide some points of departure and dispute to stimulate further study elsewhere. Secondly, there is a difference in the type and quantity of historical information available on the colonial and post-colonial periods. For the colonial period from 1923 there are carefully kept sets of files of the various government departments, by and large complete, which supply a detailed record of policy, communications with the High Commission and the Dominions Office, with other governments and with firms and individuals. But there is little statistical material or information on cattle production and internal marketing. By contrast, for the post-colonial period archival records of policy matters regarding the industry are as yet very limited, but there is a relative wealth of statistics on all its aspects. This difference in material is inevitably reflected in the work itself: the writing on the colonial period is mainly narrative and concerned with policy deliberations, while that on the post-colonial period is more quantitatively based. This bias may have been increased by my lack of access to the minutes of meetings of the Botswana Meat Commission. Whatever the case, the main benefit of access for the study would have been to confirm or deny general observations concerning BMC decision-making gleaned from government files and consultancy reports. I did not lack any statistics on BMC, and am grateful for the cooperation received.

As is usual in any length empirical study, the number of people who deserve thanks for assistance is very great – too great for all to be acknowledged. I am particularly grateful to: George Akafekwa, Roy Behnke, Aina Bergstrøm, Manfred Bienefeld, Christopher Colclough, David Cooper, Michael Crowder, Pauline Cuzen, Louise Fortmann, Binks and Ginny Glover, Sandy Grant, Kimberley Griffin, Charles Harvey, Bob Hitchcock, Derek Hudson, Jan Izaksen, Raphael Kaplinsky, Masisi Lekaukau, Tebogo Leshona, Sheila Letshwiti, Iain McDonald, Valentin von Massow, Freddy Modise, Richard Morgan, Stephen Morrison, Nelson Moyo, Gilbert Mpolokeng, Emery Roe, Kevin Shillington, James Simpson, MG Singh, Tony Williams. None of them is responsible for any errors.

Additionally, acknowledgement for financial assistance must be made to the Research and Publications Committee of the University of Botswana and to the Norwegian Agency for International Development (NORAD).

Finally, without the care and patience of Petra Hubbard in the face of her partner's dereliction of marital duty, this work never would have reached its end – and our marriage might have instead.

Michael Hubbard
University of Birmingham

Part I
Introduction

Chapter 1
Hypotheses and Concepts of the Study

This chapter looks first at the theories relevant to the field of study and then presents the hypotheses arrived at by the study and the principal concepts used.

Theories relevant to the field studied

The objectives of the study are, firstly, to identify the role of the cattle and beef export industry in the evolution of Botswana's economy and, secondly, to relate this experience to that of other beef exporting countries.

Two strands of theory concerning exports and economic growth can be identified. Firstly, there are hypotheses which can loosely be termed neoclassical because they portray the relation between export growth and economic development as a 'cumulative and harmonious process . . . initiating modernization and more rapid development in other sectors' (Baldwin 1966:4); failure of accumulation of a diversified nature to take place in the underdeveloped country is attributed to social and cultural factors.

Under this heading fall:

A.   Classical ideas of trade stimulating growth through (i) being a 'vent for surplus' production (Smith:416), (ii) providing a higher standard of living to all trading partners by enabling them to specialize in the type of production to which they are best suited (Ricardo: 83) and (iii) encouraging inflows of capital and manpower to the underdeveloped country (Mill's view of trade between imperial power and colony as an extension of domestic trade) (Mill:685–6).

B.   Neoclassical 'factor proportions' theory (Hecksher-Ohlin) of gains from trade dictated by specialization according to resource endowment; Pearson & Cownie's study (1974) of the 'Net Social Gain' conferred by African export industries was based on this theory.

C.   The 'induced innovation' theory of agricultural development, propounded by Hayami and Ruttan (1971). Technological innovation is induced by scarcity of a factor of production. Hence innovations which enhance the productivity of land and thereby enable intensive cultivation (irrigation, plant breeding, improved management) are only induced historically once land becomes scarce and production cannot be increased by extending the amount of land cultivated. The theory has its roots in Boserup's hypothesis (1965) in which agricultural land productivity increases historically with increased population density.

D.   'Staple theory', which originated in the hypothesis that the export of staples has been the chief historical source of Canadian economic growth (Innis 1930), from which it has been developed into a set of hypotheses concerning economic growth (Watkins 1963).

(i)   Within a given environment (factor endowment and prices, infrastructure, markets) the spreading of diversified growth (through backward, forward and final demand linkages) from a staple industry is determined by the production function of the staple. Linkages are maximized where they require resources and technology locally available.

(ii)   The character of the staple is the focus of the analysis: '. . . the emphasis is on the commodity itself: its significance for policy; the tying in of one activity with another; the way in which a basic commodity sets the general pace, creates new activities and is itself strengthened or perhaps dethroned, by its own creation' (Fay 1934).

(iii)   In the long term the achievement of diversified growth depends on the ability 'to shift resources at the dictates of the market' (Watkins 1963: 149) to alternative exports and domestic production.

(iv)   A 'staple trap' awaits the economy which is unable to develop 'a capacity to transform' (ibid.); further investment in the staple industry then results in perverse, or immiserising, growth – because of diminishing returns to further expansion of staple production or adverse shifts in demand.

(v)   The probability of successful diversification for the 'staple economy' (i.e. newly settled countries, such as Canada and Australia, in which the indigenous mode of production has been all but eradicated) is raised through its low man/land ratio and absence of 'inhibiting traditions', resulting in an institutional structure open to change.

(vi)   The probability of failure to diversify (the 'staple trap') is greatest 'where export production is superimposed on a pre-existing subsistence economy' (ibid.) since linkages are likely to be very weak and staple growth will fail to raise real wages owing to disguised unemployment; a strong and rigid institutional bias to staple export may develop; imports may serve only to destroy existing subsistence production.

Baldwin's analysis of the copper export industry and economic development in Northern Rhodesia 1920–60 (Baldwin 1966) is based in staple theory through the primacy he gives to changes in the production function for copper in explaining linkage development. So too is Thoburn's study of tin and rubber export linked development in Malaysia (Thoburn 1977).

The second strand of theories concerning exports and economic growth can loosely be labelled Marxist in their orientation, since they portray a negative relation between foreign trade and economic growth of colonized or dominated territories as a feature of global capital accumulation. They include structuralist arguments ('dependency', 'centre and periphery' and secularly declining terms of trade) as well as arguments which lay claim to more direct descent from Marx's law of value – especially Kay's hypothesis (Kay 1975) concerning the importance of merchant capital in underdeveloped countries, Emmanuel's 'unequal exchange' (Emmanuel 1972) and Amin's 'unequal development' (Amin 1980).

Existing studies of beef export industries span the full spectrum from the explicitly political (Smith 1969) through the political economic (Hanson 1938, Roux 1975, Feder 1980, Shane 1980, Raikes 1982) to the strictly economic (Simpson 1974). None focuses on the testing of any particular theory.

The theory advanced

The theory put forward in this study takes from both the Neoclassical and Marxist strands. Staple theory is drawn on for (i) its emphasis on linkages to the staple industry, (ii) the possible relevance of its hypothesis that the character of the staple itself is important in determining the spread effects from its production, (iii) the concept of the 'staple trap', in which failure to diversify is accompanied by continued investment in the staple, resulting in growth which is perverse in its impact on social welfare. The structuralist concept of centripetal 'centre-periphery' relations is included as a likely fundamental determinant. Finally, merchant capital is given an important role in the 'centre-periphery' relation.

In summary, the theory consists of the following eight hypotheses:

(1)   That the territory that came to be Botswana evolved during the last hundred years to be periphery of South Africa for imperial, nationalist, ecological and, ultimately, self-reproducing economic reasons.

(2)   That during the first half of the twentieth century the cattle and beef export industry reflected these characteristics in being bound to a role as cattle reserve for the two major regional markets: the Witwatersrand and ˊ ˋCopperbelt, and in being dominated by trading interests.

(3)   That the post World War II commodity shortages, British decolonization and the new international demand for lean beef resulted by the late 1960s in Botswana's beef industry (like those of several other previously marginal beef exporters) breaking away from its peripheral status as a regional cattle reserve. This was achieved, in Botswana's case, through the establishment of a successful processing sector free of foreign domination, through forward integration into its main markets and (most crucially) through the ascendancy of breeding interests both within the industry and within government. A priority was thereby given to the interests of the industry which had always been lacking under the colonial government.

6

(4) That during the post-1970 mineral export led phase of the economy, the beef export industry has continued to be the country's major growth industry accessible to domestic investment. Furthermore, it is a growth industry which households find compatible with full-time employment. It has thus continued to be the main investment outlet for the increased personal savings generated since independence.

(5) That deepening conflict has emerged between expansion of the beef industry on the one hand and social welfare on the other, with regard to: (i) Resource use: overcrowding and possible degradation of grazing lands; (ii) Resource distribution: rising assetlessness and inequality in income distribution; (iii) Fiscal incidence: the major growth industry funded by domestic investment bears no net fiscal burden.

(6) That these conflicts of economic growth are, in part, symptoms of a 'staple trap' in cattle production.

(7) That Botswana's arid climate together with the labour extensive nature of its cattle production make unlikely a change in land use away from cattle production in response to further income growth.

(8) That whether the future social costs of rural specialization in cattle production are lessened or increased will depend on the impact which the growing scarcity of grazing land is allowed to have.

Since this theory of the role of the beef export industry in Botswana's economic development brings together disparate theoretical strands the pitfall of eclecticism must be avoided by ensuring that the components brought together are not contradictory. The key concepts used must therefore be defined at the outset:

Peripheral Economy   The terms 'periphery' and 'centre' or 'core' are theoretically neutral in their description of the observed agglomeration of manufacturing production, innovation and political and economic control in some areas (the 'centres') and not in others ('the peripheries'). But they have become controversial through their prominent use in structuralist writings on development (notably Frank 1971), which are criticized by some Marxists (e.g. Kay 1975:104) as a-theoretical in their preoccupation with structures rather than with the nature of accumulation that underlies the structures.

Yet past capital accumulation on a world and regional level has shaped the conditions of present capital accumulation: conditions manifest as structural differences within and between nations and regions. Thus even analyses adhering closely to Marx's law of value are obliged to import a structural determinant into their explanations; either implicitly in the case of Kay[1] or explicitly in the case of Amin's theory of the peripheral capitalist economy (Amin 1980:131 et seq.). In southern Africa the use of the 'centre periphery' concept has particular point owing to the polarizing effects of the Southern African Customs Union (SACUA) on industrial development – acknowledged in the agreement itself.

Staple Trap   For the 'staple trap' (as defined above p.5) to be avoided or escaped from it is necessary that the primary sector leading the economy possess 'a capacity to transform' and thereby, ultimately, to 'dethrone itself' from its leading role. To do so it must through its own growth and the growth it induces in linked industries raise the real price of the resources it employs in order (i) to create growing incomes and therefore an enlarged market as a basis for expansion of manufacturing; (ii) to transform itself into an increasing cost sector, thereby both reducing its comparative advantage and inducing technological innovation within it.

Reserve Industry   By a 'reserve industry' is meant a sector exhibiting extreme peripheral characteristics through being located in a reserve: its conduct dictated by external interests, its product exported in the crudest form, its revenues subject to volatile and uncontrollable (by the government) fluctuations and its marketing dominated by the reserve trading system (see definition below).

Growth Industry   The 'growth industry' contrasts with the 'reserve industry'. It is a relatively robust and stabilized sector. On the basis of the experience of Botswana's beef industry the transition from 'reserve industry' to 'growth industry' requires: a wider market, development of the product and of marketing capability to reach beyond the regional market; breaking of the dominance of the 'reserve trading system' in the industry; acquisition of adequate resources by the state to stabilize and subsidize where necessary; acquisition of political power by those standing to benefit from the industry's growth, to direct public resources to it and give it an importance in international bargaining which it previously lacked.

Reserve Trading System   The 'reserve trading system' (selling manufactured goods from the regional centres in South Africa and Southern Rhodesia and buying livestock, grains etc. and even labour – until this function was specialized in the South African Chamber of Mines' recruiting organizations) formed the principal economic link between the 'periphery' and the 'centres'. In the Bechuanaland Protectorate the freehold farming blocks were largely part of this trading system, acting as holding grounds for cattle export trading, with many farmers owning trading stores in addition. The 'reserve trading system' was characterized in its cattle dealings by external control exerted through purchasing-credit provided by livestock auctioneers and agents in Johannesburg and by Northern Rhodesian butchers.

The main function of this 'reserve industry' within capital accumulation in Southern Africa was herein reflected: namely as a supplier, when needed, of cheap meat to feed mine workers on the Witwatersrand and the Copperbelt. The reserve trading system in cattle was effectively the instrument of external capital (buying cattle only when needed and demanding them in the most convenient form for its market i.e. on the hoof because their value to the buyer was then maximized). As a result a further characteristic was its ambiguous relation with the colonial administration: on the one hand the trading system was relied upon for export marketing and internal marketing, on the other hand trading interests obstructed efforts by the government to stabilize the industry and to set up a meat processing sector.

Marx argued that: 'The independent development of merchant capital . . . stands in inverse proportion to the general economic development of society' (Capital III:328). The parallel is clear in the present study: to turn the beef cattle export sector from being a 'reserve industry' into a 'growth industry' (the crucial stage in which was the establishment of a viable export abattoir in the 1950s) required the defeat of cattle export trading interests.

Chapter 2
The International Beef Trade

Through its heavy orientation to export, Botswana's beef industry has been shaped in its historical development by the changing nature of the world beef trade.

The examination of the development characteristics of the world beef trade in this chapter was designed to provide guidance for the case study of Botswana by answering two questions. Firstly, what is it in the nature of beef demand and production conditions in a particular historical period which locates export supply in some areas and not others? Cattle in large numbers are found in several different regions of the world, but relatively few regions (and not

Table 2.1: *World meat production 1974/76—1983 (000 tonnes)*

	1974–76 (yearly average)	1981	1983
Beef and Buffalo	43,703	44,808	45,600
Pigmeat	40,970	51,843	54,000
Sheep and Goat meat	6,811	7,793	8,197
Poultry	18,548	27,112	28,624
Horsemeat	505	489	513
TOTAL	113,160	135,021	139,933

Source: FAO Production Yearbook 1983 Tables 96, 97.

always those with the largest herds e.g. India) have become geared to beef export supply. Secondly, how can the experience of supplying countries in beef export development be categorized? Part I of the chapter identifies the features of the world beef trade and secular changes therein. Part II examines the factors governing location of beef export supply historically and Part III the comparative experience with beef export development of the supplying countries. Part IV concludes.

I: Features of the world beef trade and secular changes

(a) Present Features

Production and Consumption　Pigmeat and beef are the principal meats produced worldwide, but poultry meat production shows the most rapid growth (Table 2.1). Meat is a luxury form of protein owing to the greater amount of energy required to produce it

Table 2.2: *Protein production from some common agricultural systems*

Source of production	Typical yield of protein per annum (kg/ha)
Crop	
Wheat	225
Potatoes	450
Vegetables	500
Non-ruminant livestock	
Pigs	66
Eggs	100
Broiler	100
Intensive ruminant (crop and grass)	
Milk*	95
Intensive beef	55
Extensive ruminant	
Sheep	27
Beef Cows	32

*Milk data corrected to allow for replacements.
Source:　FAO The State of Food and Agriculture 1982 p.81, adapted from Holmes, W. 'The Livestock of Great Britain as Food Producers', *Nutrition*, London, 29 (6) 331–336, 1975.

Table 2.3: *Estimated elasticities of expenditure on meat and fresh milk: differences between countries by income level*

	Per caput GNP (current $ US)	Elasticities Meat	Fresh milk
Germany FR 1978	10,300	0.54	0.61
Mexico 1977	1,160	1.02	1.03
Tunisia 1974/75	680	1.08	1.09*
Indonesia 1978	340	2.18	1.93**
Sri Lanka 1977	160	1.23	1.20
Bangladesh 1973/74	90	3.25	3.81

*Milk and Dairy Products
**Milk, Dairy Products and Eggs
   Source: FAO The State of Food and Agriculture 1982 p.98, drawing on FAO calculations of elasticities and World Bank GNP per caput figures

Table 2.4: *Livestock numbers and productivity in developing countries (figures indicate percentage of total world numbers and production)*

	Per cent of world's animals in developing countries 1982	Per cent of world's production in developing countries 1982
Cattle and Buffalo	68	Beef 34
		Milk 21
Sheep and Goats	65	Mutton 50
		Wool 26
Pigs	58	Pork 37

Source: FAO The State of Food and Agriculture 1982 p.87

compared to vegetable proteins (Table 2.2). Therefore the income elasticity of demand for meat (and other animal products) tends to be higher than that of vegetable proteins, particularly at low to middle income levels (Table 2.3). Less developed countries contain over two thirds of the world's cattle and buffalo but produce only one third of the world's beef (Table 2.4). However, the most rapidly increasing consumption of meat has recently been in less developed countries with high rates of economic growth, particularly the major exporters of oil and manufactures.

Trade Beef enters international trade in three forms, namely, live, refrigerated (chilled and frozen) and precooked (packaged, canned and bottled). The live trade (still large internationally) is now carried on only between adjacent countries owing to unfavourable transport economies of livestock relative to meat and disease control regulations. Imported beef destined for the butcher's shop or supermarket ('butcher's meat'), and for caterers, is generally chilled (i.e. maintained just above freezing point). The higher-priced cuts (mainly hindquarters) are usually disposed of in this way. Lower-priced cuts (forequarters etc.) are usually frozen and increasingly destined for manufacturing into hamburgers, frankfurters etc. Lower-priced cuts and lean meat have become increasingly important in world trade owing to growing deficits of manufacturing grade beef in the industrialised countries (see page 22). The bulk of all refrigerated beef imported now comes in deboned form, vacuum sealed and packaged. The beef entering the precooked trade often consists of the by-products (off-cuts etc.) of deboned beef production for the refrigerated trade (Fig. 2.1).

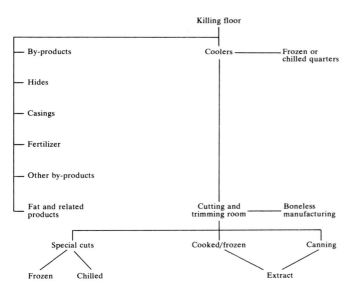

Source: Simpson and Farris 1975:11

Figure 2.1 *Flow diagram of beef processing in a model integrated packing plant*

13

Only a very small proportion of total meat production (4% to 8%) enters international trade. The proportion is slightly higher for beef alone. Fresh, chilled and frozen beef is the principal meat in international trade, accounting alone for 34% of volume and 41% of value of all meat traded internationally in 1983 in whatever form (FAO Production Yearbook and Trade Yearbook 1983).

Exports and imports of beef are concentrated regionally. Europe (including the USSR), North America and Japan are the principal net importers and Australia and New Zealand and temperate South America the principal net exporters.

Leaving out the heavy inter-European trade (which is principally a 'quality exchange' to obtain an appropriate balance of grades in each country), the principal long-distance trade lines in refrigerated beef are clear-cut. North American and Japanese imports come mainly from Australia and New Zealand and Europe's from South America. This pattern is dictated by the harsher US and Japanese veterinary import regulations which exclude South American (and African) refrigerated beef because of endemic Foot and Mouth disease on these continents.

State interventions in the form of strict veterinary and hygiene regulations, import quotas and tariffs, subsidized exports and administered domestic prices, channel, limit and often destabilize international trade in meat, refrigerated meat particularly. Accordingly the trade lines in precooked beef (not subject to such strict veterinary regulations) are more diverse, with a strong link from South America to the US in particular. Import controls limit the volume of meat traded internationally: 'consumer prices of beef in importing countries are as much as 2.5 times c.i.f. import prices which severely restricts consumption in these countries' (Valdes & Nores 1978: 5). The end result of the numerous market imperfections is that, strictly speaking, there is no 'world market' in beef as there is for grains and metals, rather a network of bilateral trade lines.

The notorious instability and unpredictability of the international beef trade, revealed in alternate gluts and shortages, is also caused by: (i) the beef production cycle and its unsynchronized phases in the major supplying countries. The beef production cycle is particularly long since calves take from two to four years to reach slaughtering age, far longer than pigs, sheep and especially poultry. The 'cattle cycle' is subject to sudden disruptions through drought or grain price increases bringing about precipitous liquidations of investment in calves and breeding stock, in the form of greatly increased slaughterings (Simpson 1979); (ii) secondary effects of price changes. During production gluts import restrictions are tightened and the major importing countries (which are also the major beef producers) dump their surpluses onto export markets in order to prevent domestic prices falling. The net exporting countries, which generally export a large proportion of their total production, therefore experience a disproportionate collapse of prices, further destabilizing their production.

(b) Secular Changes in the World Beef Trade

Two 'long waves' are apparent in the modern history of the world meat trade, running through the short cyclical fluctuations. The first rises in the 1880s, peaks in 1919 and declines to the late 1940s. The second rises in the 1950s, climbs steeply through the sixties and seventies and flattens out in the early eighties.

The shape and timing of these 'waves' follow the long trend of income changes in industrialized western economies and are, therefore, no doubt, characteristic of many internationally traded commodities. Most importantly (relating to heavily grain-based beef production in developed countries during the second 'wave') the trade in grains follows this pattern too (Berlan: 1980).

First Period   The main characteristic of the first 'wave' in the beef trade is the degree of geographical concentration at both ends of the trade. Import demand was concentrated in Britain and export supply first in the US and then (after 1910) in Argentina (Table 2.5). In 1934–38 the UK accounted for 81% of all imports of refrigerated beef with the balance for Continental countries (mainly Germany and Italy) and a small amount to Japan. South American countries supplied 69% of all exports (Argentina 56%) and Australia and New Zealand only 21%. The picture for trade in canned meats at this time is similar. This highly concentrated trade system was already fixed by 1910 and remained in place until mid-century.

Second Period   The second 'wave' is characterized by a greater diversity of both import demand and export supply, although it remains highly concentrated. On the demand side, owing to increases in domestic production and slower rates of income increase, Britain has lost her predominance in Europe (France, Italy

15

Table 2.5: *Historical picture of world trade in fresh chilled and frozen beef 1918–1983*

Thousands of Metric Tons and Percentage of World Total
Source: FAO Trade Yearbooks and Hanson 1938: 201

Exports – Principal Exporting Countries (Selection)

	1918 Vol.	%	1934–38 Vol.	%	1948–50 Vol.	%	1957 Vol.	%	1970 Vol.	%	1981–83[4] Vol.	%
EUROPE	28	4	43				255	27	732	35	1786	52
Denmark	13	2	14	2			83	9	70	3	131	4
France									114	5	308	9
Germany (FR)									55	3	344	10
Hungary									27	1	48	1
Ireland					3		27	3	140	7	220	6
Netherlands									115	5	232	7
Poland									17	1	5	
Romania									22	1	82	2
Sweden									24	1	21	1
UK[1]	4	1			9	2			10		145	4
USSR							74	8	34	2	16	
Yugoslavia									48	2	34	1
NORTH AND CENTRAL AMERICA	285	25	7	1	56		62	7	158	8	223	6
Canada			5		46	8	22	2	39	2	60	2
Costa Rica									18	1	24	1
Dominican Rep.									3		4	
El Salvador											1	
Guatemala									12	1	12	
Honduras									12	1	18	1
Mexico					4	1	8	1	37	2	8	
Nicaragua									24	1	13	
USA[1]			2		2		32	3	9		78	
SOUTH AMERICA	743	66	507	69	329		414	44	598	29	483	14
Argentina			409	56	256	44	355	37	352	17	235	7
Brazil	57		43	6	18	3	27	3	98	5	87	3
Colombia									8		20	1
Paraguay									10		3	
Uruguay			54	7	55	9	32	3	131	6	139	4
AFRICA	14	1	23	3	8		15	2	72	3	39	1
Botswana[2]									5		32	1
Chad									14	1		
Kenya							1		2			
Malagasy	6		7	1	3		2		5		1	
South Africa	8		7	1			8	1	28			
Zimbabwe			8	1	1		2		10		3	
OCEANIA	180	16	155	21	145	25	278	29	506	24	798	23
Australia	74		107	15	82	14	161	17	328	16	554	16
New Zealand	106		48	7	63	11	117	12	178	9	243	7
ASIA											91	3
India											48	1
Mongolia											20	1
Turkey											9	
WORLD TOTAL[3]	1133	100	730	100	580	100	951	100	2088	100	3436	100

NOTES:
1. UK's and US's exports are largely re-exports.
2. Botswana's exports are included in South Africa's until 1970.
3. World and regional totals are greater than the sum of principal country exports cited.
4. The figures for 1934–38, 1948–50 and 1981–83 are annual averages.

Table 2.6: *Historical picture of world trade in fresh chilled and frozen beef 1918–1983*

Thousands of Metric Tons and Percentage of World Total
Source: FAO Trade Yearbooks and Hanson 1938: 201

Imports – Principal Importing Countries (Selection)

	1918 Vol.	1918 %	1934–38 Vol.	1934–38 %	1948–50 Vol.	1948–50 %	1957 Vol.	1957 %	1970 Vol.	1970 %	1981–83 Vol.	1981–83 %
EUROPE	1133	100	678	95	490	86	858	95	1241	62	1415	43
Austria									17		9	
Belgium–Luxembourg			11		24				19		29	1
Czechoslovakia					10						24	1
France	302	27	13				33		72	4	254	8
Germany DR			30						13		22	1
Germany FED							54	6	185	9	176	5
Greece									68	3	89	3
Italy	149	13	27		14		93	10	290	14	413	12
Netherlands					24		22		44		61	2
Poland											32	1
Romania											21	1
Spain					10		32		99	5	20	1
UK	683	60	572	81	367	64	465	51	265	13	176	5
Yugoslavia											34	1
USSR							90	10	82	4	378	11
NORTH AND CENTRAL AMERICA			7		42		70	8	611	30	667	20
Canada									61		56	2
USA					35		57	6	527	26	575	17
SOUTH AMERICA			3		18		5		25		79	2
Brazil											37	1
Chile									13		5	
Peru					11				10		19	
Venezuela											18	
ASIA			15		8		43	5	84	4	509	15
China											20	1
Hong Kong									5		23	1
Iran									6		57	2
Iraq											54	2
Israel									36		47	1
Japan			12				23		23		127	4
Korea (South)											57	2
Saudi Arabia											51	2
Singapore									5		12	
AFRICA			5		8		29	3	42	2	250	8
Algeria							11				21	1
Egypt											109	3
Ivory Coast											11	
Libya											15	
Nigeria											25	1
Zaire									14		2	
WORLD TOTAL	1133	100	710	100	570	100	905	100	2009	100	3313	100

NOTE: The figures for 1934–38, 1948–50, 1981–83 are annual averages

17

and Germany becoming as important), while Europe as a whole has declined relative to the US and Asia, which recently accounted for 17% and 15% respectively of world imports (1981–83) (Table 2.6). On the supply side, Australia has become the largest single exporter (16% of world exports 1981–83), Argentina's share has declined, Brazil's has increased and the EEC has become a major net exporter since the late seventies.

A feature of the second wave of growth has been the entry into beef exporting of a variety of countries – Central American, South American, African (including Botswana) and, very recently, Asian. These countries had previously been outside the mainstream of the world meat trade, either not producing beef (e.g. the forest zones of Central and South America) or confined to supplying cattle on the hoof to regional markets (e.g. Botswana). Their opening up for beef export production has not affected world beef export volume greatly but has been most important within the political economy of the countries concerned. The reasons why their entry took place, the impact thereof, and why (in most cases) they will not long remain beef exporters, are a focus of the remainder of this chapter.

II. Historical location of beef export supply

The three main factors governing the location of beef export supply historically have been the nature of the markets, the nature of the products demanded and the nature of supply conditions. These factors are discussed in turn for each of the two historical periods, followed by some observations concerning the general characteristics of multinational capital's interest in the beef industry.

(a) First Period[1]

(i) *Markets* In the last half of the nineteenth century rapid industrialization, urbanization and real wage increases in western Europe created an unprecedented demand for animal protein and grains. In the case of Britain this was satisfied by imports of cattle and sheep shipped live from the Continent and Ireland. Grains came from the US, Australia and Argentina in which British capital invested in railway construction was helping in the rapid expansion of colonial settlement.

While salting ('jerked beef') remained the only method of meat preservation there was effectively no substitute for the live trade. But with the long sought after answer to the preservation problem having been found in the French discovery of refrigeration, British (and later American) capital was enabled to develop a vigorous trade in chilled beef from the US rivalling and then surpassing the trade in live animals, particularly after diminishing Continental export surpluses and the Rinderpest outbreak of 1877 brought heavier reliance on US exports. From then until the late 1890s US beef made up over 90% of British beef imports while imported beef accounted for an ever-increasing proportion of total British beef consumption (over one third by 1900).

Refrigeration provided a bonanza of cheap protein. In Britain, meat prices led the 25% fall in the consumer price index between 1877 and 1899. Real wages rose 14% and the market for meat increased greatly among ordinary people. Britain was not unique in Europe at the turn of the century either in her rate of industrialization or potential access to cheap food supplies. But her degree of proletarianization was substantially higher and she was the only western European country to respond to the availability of cheap foreign-grown food with an open door. The main response on the Continent was harsh import regulations (mainly veterinary for meat) and tariffs. The result was that Britain had become the single substantial and steady import market by the turn of the century. Even during World War I, when import restrictions were relaxed by France and Italy to let in frozen meat for their troops, Britain still accounted for 60% of total imports. She reverted to 80% in the post-war period as Continental protectionism was re-asserted (Table 2.6). The US was self-sufficient.

(ii) *Supply Conditions* The concentration of beef export supply in Latin America and particularly Argentina during the first half of the twentieth century followed the decline of the US as an exporter by the turn of the century (owing to growing domestic demand). The principal contenders to take the place of the US in the British market were Argentina and Australia. In both countries colonization was well-nigh complete, there were large, lowly populated land tracts and, most importantly, a class of large landowners holding cattle on their estates and keen to organize production for the export market (having formed associations for that purpose viz. the Sociedad Rural d'Argentina). But a number of technical and political factors favoured Argentina, and, in the stagnant or contracting market conditions prevailing after 1919, Argentinian exports held the lion's share of the British market until mid-century, despite the attempts by Commonwealth interests to shift the balance at Ottawa in 1932. Writing in 1937, Hanson summed up the technical superiority of beef production in Argentina's temperate zone, compared to Australia at the time:

'The analyst of Argentina's position as a beef producer must inevitably be impressed by it. As one of them states: 'Among all the beef-surplus countries of the world there is none physically so well adapted to the production of so huge a surplus at so low a cost' (L. Edminster 'The Cattle Industry and the Tariff' p.147). In none is the preparing and distribution organization superior to that of Argentina. Export animals in the Argentine are produced in the temperate zone under conditions of equable humid climate and rich soil that permit year-round grazing; true, there are dry spells, but not the devastating droughts with which Australia is periodically afflicted.

Argentina has another advantage in internal transportation; railway facilities are good, distances are shorter, and gradients small . . . In Australia transport facilities in the interior are inadequate, herds often are driven long distances in heat which is trying on the animals, especially in times of shortage of water and feed. Location at a lesser distance from the consuming markets is another factor . . . Costs of transportation are much lower from the Plate.' (pp.256–8).

On the political level, the comparative ease with which foreign meat packing firms (British and, later, American) could establish themselves in Argentina and operate an oligopoly was important. Although the Argentinian *estancieros* had tried to establish their own meat packing and exporting industry in the 1890s it had failed through lack of marketing strength. In Australia, while the firms later to become the meat packing giants were setting up in Argentina in the 1900s, ranchers were still experimenting with numerous cooperative slaughtering enterprises (Hanson 1938: Ch. 3) and the doors were only opened to the packers after 1910 (viz. the land concessions to Vestey in 1913)[2].

During the period of stagnation and contraction of the market after 1919 the export trade was characterized by sharp oligopolistic struggles for export volume among the now highly concentrated packers (Swift, Armour and Vestey being the largest), expressed through competition for shipping space, speed and marketing facilities. Vestey (Union Cold Storage), the only British Firm among the giants, was well-equipped to fight the periodic 'meat wars' (e.g. 1925–27):

'Vestey packed beef in its own plants, shipped cargo in its own boats, insured voyages through its own company, deposited meat in its own cold storage rooms and sold it to the public through its own butchers'. (Smith 1969: 113).

The packers' price-fixing activities were the subject of state investigation in the US, Britain and Argentina and brought them into head-on conflict with Argentinian cattle breeding interests in the early 1930s. The result was the Argentinian Meat Laws of 1933, passed at a time when the state in most Western countries was intervening to support agricultural producers by instituting marketing control boards and encouraging cooperative marketing efforts. The age of unbridled control by the packing firms was closing; henceforth they would find their power increasingly circumscribed by marketing boards and producers' cooperatives in the major supplying countries, and, later, by the rising strength of retailing chains in the major importing countries (Harrington 1976: 415).

(iii) *Products in Trade* The imports of live cattle from the Continent, Ireland and the US with which Britain's rising import demand was at first satisfied were designed to supplement British beef, which was mainly high grade (i.e. fat) and consumed by the richer households. As refrigerated shipping became more economic than live, so chilled imports were designed to fill the gap left by the diminishing live imports at the upper end of the market. Frozen meat, by contrast, was regarded as an inferior product, and it was not until after the First World War (during which frozen meat was supplied to troops, and sold at a premium above chilled) that it was widely accepted, particularly on the Continent. Refrigerated beef was usually shipped 'bone-in' as sides or quarters and destined largely for the butchering trade (as distinct from the small manufacturing and catering demand). At the very bottom of the trade were the small imports of boneless beef (frozen) for manufacturing into sausages and pies. Only the most inferior beef was deboned, as an alternative to canning or boiling down for beef extract.

Ninety per cent of Argentina's beef exports were chilled for the British market and the rest frozen or canned for Continental as well as British markets. Southern African exports were all frozen and sent mainly to the Continent (particularly Italy), until the Ottawa concessions (1932) provided a guaranteed market for Southern Rhodesian and South African chilled beef.

(b) *Second Period* (post 1950)

(i) *Markets* The enormous increase in meat consumption in the developed countries (some 2% per caput per annum) since 1950, has been met principally by domestic production increases, but leaving a rising deficit to be covered by imports. The increase in the deficit has been most marked in manufacturing beef, reflecting both an increasing demand for manufacturing beef and a dwindling domestic supply. Manufacturing type beef (utility, cutter and canning) amounted to 18% of US production in 1959 but had fallen to 13% by 1973 (Feder 1978:65). The increased demand for manufacturing beef results from the rapid growth of the 'fast foods' industry (hamburgers, frankfurters etc.) for which cheap, lean beef is required. On the supply side, two factors have had a negative impact. Firstly, increased grain production since the 1950s in both Europe and North America, and the secularly increasing beef/grain price ratio (Crotty 1980: 29), have brought about increasing specialization of beef herds in grain-fed 'high grade' fat-stock production. Secondly, the chief source of manufacturing beef (and in Europe of all beef) has been cull dairy cows. But increased productivity of dairy cows and sluggish demand for dairy products have reduced dairy herds and this source of lean beef. Since dairy herds have also been a major source of male calves to fatten for slaughter, the relatively slow increase in dairy cattle numbers and the much increased demand for fattening stock have raised calf prices substantially in Europe and the US.

(ii) *Products in Trade* The changes in the form in which beef is shipped reflect higher veterinary hygiene standards, higher packing and transport technology and the growing trade in manufacturing-type beef (i.e. the kind of cuts demanded by manufacturers). Refrigerated beef is now shipped predominantly deboned – for veterinary reasons[3], convenience in later manufacturing and to keep down transport costs (lower weight and volume per unit value, easier handling). Increased precooked exports from South America reflect US veterinary import restrictions against South American refrigerated exports.

An idiosyncrasy of the modern trade has been the re-emergence of a significant amount of trade in live cattle internationally, between adjacent countries in Europe and the Americas. Much of this trade is in response to the structurally induced shortages of fattening stock.[4] The United States now imports about a million head of store and feeder cattle per annum. (FAO Trade Yearbook 1983, Table 7).

(iii) *Supply Conditions* The decline of Argentina's share of world exports, and the corresponding rise in Australia's and New Zealand's, reflect partly Argentina's increased domestic demand and much higher beef consumption levels per head, as well as much greater increases in overall herd productivity in Australia and New Zealand.[5] But a further important cause has been the rise of the lucrative US import market and the resulting stimulus to export production. The US gives veterinary access for fresh, chilled and frozen beef to Australia, New Zealand and temperate Central America, but denies it to South America because of endemic Foot and Mouth disease. The US beef deficit has been a principal cause of growing beef exports from Central America during the period.

The remaining 'new exporters' have been African (including Botswana, Kenya, Madagascar, Swaziland) and their overseas export trade has been based largely on the demand for lean beef in the British market, assisted in the 1950s and 1960s by Commonwealth Preferences and, since Britain's accession to the EEC, by the rebate of 90% of the EEC's 'variable levy' on beef import quotas granted to the ACP group of countries under the Lomé Convention of 1975 (renewed 1979, 1984). Exemption from the EEC's common external tariff of 20% was simultaneously granted.

The more sophisticated and hygienic slaughtering, preparation, packing and transporting of meat now demanded by the export market have, in important respects, aided rather than hindered the entry of new, more remote exporters by facilitating efficient and hygienic meat processing even under adverse conditions. Automated and standardized slaughtering processes facilitate high productivity and focus skill requirements on management rather than labour. Plastics, stainless steel, vacuum sealing and precooking enable higher hygiene standards to be maintained more easily. Deboning and boxing reduce transport costs of meat; together with improved refrigeration techniques they have made the up-country location of abattoirs more economic, freeing overseas exporting abattoirs from their prior coastal locations, provided transport infrastructure in the hinterland is adequate (Mittendorf 1978).

A major new feature in the world trade in beef and dairy products is the growing EEC surplus resulting from subsidized production and export under the Common Agricultural Policy. Increasing EEC beef exports have had a particularly severe effect on ACP beef exporters who now find themselves competing against EEC beef dumped on their alternative markets (the EEC has only very limited access to the major net importers, the US and Japan). In 1981–83 EEC net exports of fresh, chilled and frozen beef supplied 24% of world imports excluding the imports of the US, Japan and EEC itself (FAO Trade Yearbook 1983). The ACP beef exporters under these circumstances become increasingly dependent for export sales on their preferential access to the EEC. (This issue is taken up in Chapter 8.)

III. Generalizations from experience with beef export development

Firstly, beef production is a relatively poor generator of diversified growth, since backward, forward and final demand linkages from it are limited[6]. The implication is that beef production is relatively independent of growth in other economic sectors except in so far as it competes for resources (particularly land and capital, since cattle raising is not labour intensive).

Secondly, beef exporting countries have moved along a growth path involving investment in livestock production and export of meat, followed by a rise of the domestic market (through income and population growth), increasing competition for land use from arable production (which helps to induce productivity increases in livestock production – not least by providing increased stock feed), followed by continuing reduction in the exportable surplus and then change of status to net importer of meat.

Variations in the progress along this path have had several causes. A country may remain a net exporter of meat through having a particularly low ratio of population to land area and having achieved particularly great increases in productivity in meat production (viz. Australia, New Zealand), or may revert to net exporter status through heavy subsidization of livestock production (EEC). Alternatively, a country may become prematurely a net importer of meat, through increases in productivity of meat production being particularly low and/or through increases in domestic demand for meat being particularly high (several Central and South American exporters in the second 'wave' of growth of the world beef trade). Thirdly, the 'new exporting countries' (or parts of countries e.g. forest areas of Brazil) in Latin America and Africa, share several characteristics which have made their experience with beef export particularly socially problematic. These characteristics all relate to the peripheral nature of their economies – ecologically, agriculturally, industrially and internationally.

Land The second 'wave' has seen the increased opening up for beef production and export of *tropical* areas not previously heavily exploited, where soils and climate are inferior for both arable and livestock production (arid savannah, tropical forest) and over-exploitation carries a heavier desertification risk. The low private costs of exploitation of such land (there being no productive alternative private uses competing for it) worsens the risk of over-exploitation and creates a major task in social resource management – as in among others, northern Australia (Young 1979), parts of Latin America (Feder 1978, Shane 1980) and parts of Africa (see Chapter 9). It also makes unattractive those innovations (such as grazing management, land reclamation and seeding of pastures) which enhance the productivity of land. Inappropriate land tenure can further reduce the private costs of over-exploitation. Large estates under absentee ownership are one instance: cattle raising by *estancieros* in tropical Latin America has been described as 'scavenging' (Crotty 1980: 28) and Feder remarks:

'Enormous losses occur in various ways – through low fertility rates, high calf mortality, low weight gains etc. – as a result of the failure to control animal health, through lack of adequate nutrition because of poor pasture management, failure to provide food supplements or minerals and simply poor care. In Latin America ranching was and is in most important areas in a primitive state of affairs' (Feder 1978: 54).

25

Unregulated communal tenure of grazing lands is another instance, particularly evident in Botswana (see Chapter 3).

Agriculture Practically all the major beef exporters of the first and second 'waves' have also at the same time been net exporters of cereal grains (FAO Trade Yearbooks) whereas the small, new exporters of the second 'wave' are all substantial net importers. Their failure to be self-sufficient in food grains (and stock feed) is not simply a result of infertile land; none of the countries appears to have realised its food crop potential.

Industry The development of cattle and sheep production through private enclosures has always displaced peasants and hunter gatherers – whether in eighteenth century Britain, nineteenth century North and South America, Australia, New Zealand and South Africa, or in the present opening up of new beef production zones in Latin America and Africa. But with scant industrial development to provide alternative employment for displaced people, the social costs of ranch development in the new beef exporting countries has been particularly high[7].

International Trade and Payments By the outbreak of the First World War the United States and several industrialized West European countries were becoming net importers of beef (Tables 2.5 and 2.6). Except for the special cases of Australia, New Zealand and the EEC (see page 16 above), the pattern has been reproduced by other industrializing countries. In the 'new exporters' too there is now rapid change toward net importer status. It has already occurred in Kenya and Panama and forecasts indicate that, among others, Mexico, Ecuador, El Salvador, Bolivia, Paraguay and Guyana will be net importers by 1990 (Valdes & Nores 1978: 17). In these countries the main sources of the existing or impending deficits are population growth (which at 3% plus per annum virtually offsets the annual increase in Latin American beef production), relatively low increases in cattle herd productivity, and relatively high per capita beef consumption levels in Latin America. The result has been frustration of the hopes of policy makers who had intended that rising beef exports should provide a source of foreign exchange additional to their main exports (fruit and coffee), and frequent policy prevarication.

On the one hand, low incomes and low productivity in food production have caused some Latin American governments to pursue 'cheap beef' policies; 'since beef makes up the largest single share of family food expenditure, policy makers tend to treat beef as a "wage good" like rice, beans and maize. In most of Latin America, even low income families spend no less than 10% of their total income on beef' (ibid.: 18). The effects of a 'cheap beef' policy are to reduce beef export revenue – by increasing local consumption and decreasing production. On the other hand, foreign exchange shortages and attractive export opportunities have underlain occasional efforts to marry 'cheap beef' with higher exports through declaring 'meatless days' (e.g. Guatemala, Honduras, Argentina), designed both to reduce domestic demand and to increase the exportable surplus. This conflict between exports and the domestic market reflects the greater conflict between large landowners (the main cattle producers) and the landless poor, which is so strong a feature of much of Latin America.

Because the anticipated deficits in many 'new exporters' have their main source in population growth and low productivity, their impact on beef production may also be different from that in countries where the deficit is the result more of income increases. Where rising incomes have driven the domestic price up, absorbed the domestic supply and started to attract imports, a politically powerful farming lobby (seeing that its future lies in the domestic not the export market) has sometimes succeeded in forcing through import controls and marketing legislation to make for a 'captive' home market. The resulting higher prices and subsidies act to raise land values further, even of marginal land, by encouraging production. Examples are France and Germany in the late nineteenth century after they ceased exporting cattle to Britain and closed their markets to cheap US and Argentinian beef imports (Hanson 1938: 93), the US in the early twentieth century (ibid.) and South Africa in the mid-1930s when the state gave up trying to establish the country as a major beef exporter and turned to regulating and protecting the expanding internal market (see Chapter 5). By contrast, a beef deficit caused by growth of a low income population does not offer such opportunities for extracting higher returns from a captive market: the demand is for an increasing volume of production at given prices, whereas higher returns to beef production depend heavily on higher prices (if land is not privately costless and given the biological limits to cattle productivity) (see Preston 1976: 243). The impact might rather be to depress beef production, as a result of the 'cheap beef' policies which the growing low income population gives rise to.

Botswana's experience shares features of the other 'new exporters' except that to date she has suffered no overt conflict between domestic beef requirements and exports. A very low population/land ratio (the lowest among beef exporters) is likely to ensure that little conflict arises in the near future, despite a high rate of population and income growth and continuing low productivity in cattle production (Appendix Table A4, page 255).

In sum, the argument of this section is that the experience of beef exporting countries rising in the first and second periods differs broadly. The expansion of beef export production into predominantly tropical areas has not been accompanied by the same degree of industrial and agricultural growth as occurred in the major exporters rising in the first 'wave'. Besides the threat to the more fragile tropical soils and forest zones, the result has been that people have been displaced with little prospect for re-employment, productivity has remained low and there will be in many cases an early reversion to net importer status, owing largely to natural increase in population. No immediate prospect for change appears to be present within the dynamic of the economies themselves. Described in staple theory terms, the case is one in which staple-led growth has failed to transform the economies.

IV: Conclusions: Indications for the Present Study

The discussion above has indicated that the two 'waves' in the world beef trade are its main historical feature and should, therefore, underlie the detailed periodization (based upon regional events) to be constructed for the present study. The main characteristics of each of the 'waves' (price and volume trends, products in trade, trade lines, trade restrictions) have provided the framework within which each supplying country could manoeuvre. They acted to exclude small and relatively unproductive beef exporters in the first 'wave' and to admit them in the second.

Regarding comparisons with other beef exporters, the discussion has categorized Botswana as one of the 'new' supplying countries in which the growth of the beef export industry has led to unresolved conflicts. The suggestion was made that competition for domestic resources of capital, labour and land from other growth industries in the earlier generation of beef exporters tended to resolve the conflicts in resource use, allocation and distribution which result from the growth of a staple industry; lack of such competition has led to the non-resolution of these conflicts in the 'new' exporting countries, in the manner of the 'staple trap'.

Chapter 3
Cattle Production in Botswana

The purpose of this chapter is to examine the historical relation between the beef export industry and cattle production in Botswana. In order to do so it considers the main features of cattle production in the pre-colonial, colonial and post-colonial periods.

I. The Pre-Colonial Cattle Economy

Because of fragmentary evidence only a static picture of pre-colonial cattle production can be outlined, hoping to capture its main features but inevitably missing its historical dynamic and differences among Tswana states.

Describing the pre-colonial economy of the Ngwato kingdom Parsons (1977:114) outlines their system of cattle holding as follows:

'It was based on the *mafisa* system, characteristic of Tswana and Sotho societies, whereby the ruling class farmed out cattle to client clans or families, who became herdsmen holding royal property in a sort of feudal system. *Mafisa* cattle formed the constructural basis of political relations between the rulers and the ruled'.

This structure has led to the conclusion that 'unlike many other parts of Africa, where land has greater commodity value as means of production, here cattle was the particular commodity with the same significance in the feudal political economy . . . (W)hat elsewhere in Africa led to types of tenancy relations in land, here led to cattle owning. Usufruct to land here became access to loan cattle, in both cases, as means of production . . .' (Prah 1977:11).

Cattle were both a production good (draught, transport, calves) and a consumption good (milk, meat, hides) and an excellent form of savings for future consumption and production – savings which multiplied.

By comparison the products of labour in the fields were exclusively consumption items (except for seed), could not be stored for long periods without severe deterioration, and, given climate and soil, were far less reliable and more arduously obtained. Moreover, after the introduction of the plough (circa mid-nineteenth century) and the expansion of fields consequent upon it cattle became essential in crop production.

Trade in cattle outside the Tswana state seems not to have been significant. But cattle did change hands in large numbers between states as the booty of wars.

Cattle were integrally bound up in the domestic economy, providing a contrast with later developments in which both backward and forward linkages of the industry move increasingly outside the home and the country.

Cattle numbers fluctuated according to drought and disease incidence around a long-term average set by water availability and dispersion in the dry season. In the wet summer months, with water lying in river beds and pans, cattle could be trekked out to graze the abundant sandveld, retreating again to the perennial water places for the dry winter and spring. The poorer the winter pasturage within reach of perennial water the fewer the cattle which could survive to the next flush season.

Pre-colonial cattle management seems to have differed from that of the present day not so much in its practices as in the means (e.g. veterinary and water technology) used to carry them out. Kraaling (for milking, weaning, taming and herd formation), castration (for draught power), herding (for feeding, protection and watering) and herb medication, were the basic practices. Herds may have been large, as archaeological evidence of large cattle kraals currently suggests (Denbow 1982).

31

Institutional differences are more pronounced. The pre-colonial system of grazing land management based upon the *modisa* (grazing lands overseer) has all but disappeared (Hitchcock 1980:4) and the basis of the system of *mafisa* was altered with the transition to private ownership of cattle, which appears to have taken place in the mid- to late nineteenth century. Parsons (1977:119) notes in regard to Khama III of the Ngwato: 'To the royal herdsmen and to the *batlhanka* vassal herdsmen he renounced any royal rights to the ownership of the cattle that they held: the cattle (and therefore the serfs with them) were now "private" property'.

The nature and period of the transition in other Tswana states is not clear. But by the early twentieth century private ownership of cattle was apparently universal in the main Tswana states (cf. Schapera's discussion 1943: 30–31 of cattle post organization). The transition to private ownership did not mean that the *mafisa* system ended, but that it now became a loaning of cattle by individual owners instead of the chief alone.

Finally there is a systemic difference between pre-colonial cattle production and its later form which apparently enabled cattle to be kept in relatively large numbers for many centuries without evident long-term ecological deterioration. Production was historically mobile, with entire villages being uprooted and relocated to where water, grazing and soil fertility were more favourable. Long periods of regenerative fallow thus took place for both grazing and culti-vated lands. This is no longer the case as settlements are now relatively fixed.

II. Colonial and Post-Colonial Cattle Production

A marked increase in cattle population and offtake numbers (Table A1), in the number of waterpoints in the geographical spread of cattle across the country, and the fencing of the country into sepa-rate veterinary compartments – these have been the most visible changes on the ground in Botswana's cattle production during the colonial and post-colonial periods. Less visibly, the pattern of cattle ownership has changed as well as people's relations to cattle, crops and jobs.

The first part of this section presents an outline model of Botswana's cattle production in the colonial and post-colonial phases. The second part considers changes in the social relations within which cattle production takes place.

(a) An Outline Model of Cattle Production in Colonial and Post-Colonial Botswana

While the main justification for construction of the outline model is that relations of the export sector to cattle production assumed in later chapters should somewhere be made explicit and defended, a secondary objective is to reveal the complexity of the subject and the limitations of some current dogma concerning investment and offtake.

Problems of data availability and complexity of relations multiply with increasing breadth of a model. Since the model is broad and the data very limited in both quantity and quality, no attempt has been made to quantify relations; to have done so would be to create an impression that concreteness is possible where it is not. It is an outline model with no pretensions to exhaustive explanation.

An additional important limitation of the outline model should be noted. It is a model of fluctuating aggregate accumulation through geographical expansion of an essentially unchanged system of cattle management. As such its relevance is historical not predictive, since with the present ending of the 'frontier' of cattle production virgin grazing land will become increasingly scarce, thereby altering the economics of accumulation.

(i) *Cattle Numbers*

In the discussion above of the pre-colonial cattle economy the amount of dry season grazing around perennial water points was argued to be the long-term determinant of cattle numbers, with shorter term fluctuations induced by disease, epidemics and drought. The colonial period brought more waterpoints, unlocking the grazing wealth of unexploited lands for perennial use, and veterinary medicines – evening out previous fluctuations due to disease. Both served to reinforce grazing availability around perennial water points as the long-term constraint on growth in numbers, while enabling cattle numbers to trend upwards in the long term for the first time.

Figures 3.1 and 3.2 show absolute and percentage changes in cattle numbers annually between 1936 and 1984. No annual figures pre-1936 are available. Indications are that the cattle population

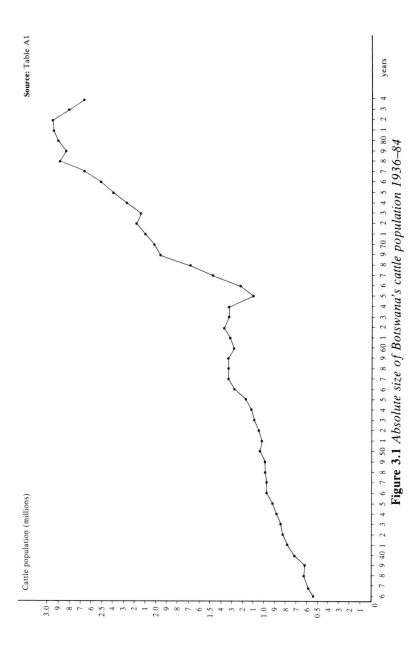

Figure 3.1 *Absolute size of Botswana's cattle population 1936–84*

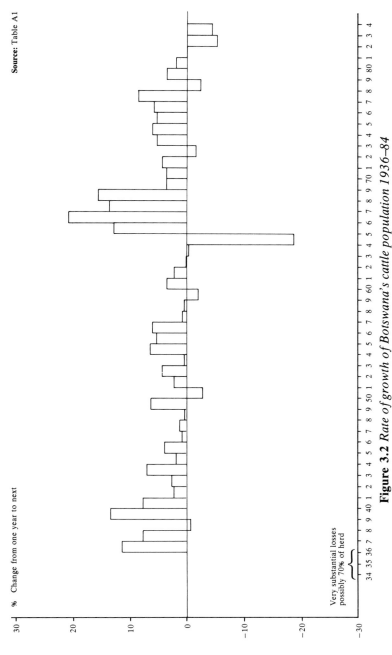

Figure 3.2 *Rate of growth of Botswana's cattle population 1936–84*

Source: Table A1

% Change from one year to next

Very substantial losses
possibly 70% of herd

may have been some half a million in the late nineteenth century, reduced towards 100000 by the Rinderpest Pandemic of the mid-1890s (Roe 1980: Table 1).

The graph in Fig. 3.1 shows the long-term upward movement in numbers while the histogram in Fig. 3.2 shows the fluctuations in herd growth rates.

The three main events are the great drought and cattle selling of the mid-1930s and the great droughts of the mid-1960s and mid-1980s. Despite the lack of annual statistics pre-1936, it is clear that cattle numbers fell drastically in all three cases as successive low rainfall years eliminated pasture and water reserves alike (with additional economic complications in the mid-1930s). The two earlier droughts were followed by marked increases in the rate of herd growth. As Raikes has argued for East Africa:

'. . . it is reasonable to assume that growth would be most rapid in the immediate aftermath of a disaster once all the secondary effects had worked themselves out. At such times, the range would be least heavily stocked and grass most abundant, the disease level would often be lower, in part because many of the weaker animals have succumbed to the effects of drought and the herders are more than usually concerned to build (or rather rebuild) their stocks'. (1981:92).

Four to five years after the end of each major disaster the herd growth rate subsided once more to fluctuate around its average level of some 4% per annum.

While the three major drought episodes provide the overall shape of changes in the herd growth rate the accelerated construction of water points (dams and boreholes) from the 1930s onwards, and increasing medication against fatal diseases,[1] underlie the upward population trend whereby numbers increased almost five-fold between 1936 and 1980. That this is not simply a cyclical increase is best demonstrated by comparing the 'troughs' of the two most recent complete cycles: after the mid-1930s disaster cattle numbers were some half a million compared to approximately one million after the mid-1960s disaster.

The cattle population data are variously based on livestock censuses and veterinary crush counts – probably interspersed with several estimates derived from assumed growth rates. Therefore fluctuations from one year to the next could be due as much to error as to changes in other factors. Nonetheless, two periods of high rainfall (mid-50s and mid-70s) stand out as periods with above average herd growth rates (Fig. 3.2) while the single drought seasons of 1972/73 and 1978/79 both registered population decreases. Together these reinforce the impression that major changes in rainfall remain crucial determinants of short-term changes in cattle population.

To sum up:

(i) Rinderpest (1896–97) and the three great drought episodes (1931–36, 1961–65, 1982–85 continuing) are the principal features in the colonial and post-colonial history of Botswana's cattle population. Together they stake out three phases.

(ii) The first phase (1898–1937) may have continued a pre-existing cyclical pattern whereby cattle numbers were severely cut back after a major drought or pandemic with no long-term tendency to rise on average from one cycle to the next, owing to no significant long-term increase in perennial water supplies and disease control. Sound statistical evidence for or against this suggestion is lacking.

(iii) The second and third phases (1937–66 and 1966–82) see a rising long-term population trend owing to construction of water points and increased medication.

The determinants of cattle population suggested in the discussion above are the number of water points and medication (long-term trend in population) and major deviations of rainfall from average (short-term fluctuations from the trend in population). Thus:

Cattle numbers: short term changes = f (Major deviations of rainfall from average) Link 1.

Cattle numbers: trend = f (Waterpoints, Medication) Link 2.

(ii) *Offtake: alternative explanations of net accumulation*

The tendency towards aggregate long-term net accumulation of cattle has been observed in other parts of East, Central and Southern Africa by students of pastoralism, and explained in various ways which can be classified broadly into those which emphasise ideological and material motives respectively.

Ideological explanations are epitomised by the so-called East African 'cattle complex' (Herskovits 1926) in which 'ideology was thought to be the only determinant in the relationship between man and animal' (Hedlund 1980: 17), with cattle accumulated primarily for their religious, ceremonial and aesthetic value. Thus the attitude of the Ila of Barotseland was characterized in the following way in the early twentieth century:

'Above all their possessions, above Kith and Kin, wife or child, the Ba Illa, with few and occasional exceptions, love and value their cattle. They prized exceptionally oxen, decorated them, praised them in songs and dancing. They sold few, and would not use them for labour, but then they slaughtered them in great funerals'. (Smith and Dale, quoted by Fielder 1973: Footnote 13).

Fielder's work shows that in fact cattle provided the material base for the traditional Ila economy and that their accumulation was essential to its reproduction and expansion, with taboos concerning cattle being adapted to changing material circumstances.

Material, or socio-economic, explanations of net accumulation of cattle have stressed both individual and social reasons. Stressing the microeconomic logic of cattle accumulation for the individual herder, a body of social anthropological writing emerged in opposition to the 'Cattle Complex' (Schneider 1964, Dyson Hudson 1966).

Economic motives to individual accumulation identified included insurance against drought and disease, creation of a herd of viable size and convenience as a form of savings. The economic benefits of accumulating cattle for each of these reasons have been widely documented in Botswana.

Large herders can more effectively preserve their cattle through a drought than can small ones. Devitt (1978:122–3) argues that smaller herders will have to sell off their breeding stock sooner than large ones, that the competition for milk between calves and people in poorer families makes calves vulnerable even in mild droughts and that the use of breeding stock for draught power by households with insufficient oxen reduces calving rates and lowers resistance. Small herds have also been shown to be less viable economic units than large ones, owing mainly to the level of fixed costs in cattle keeping (Farm Management Survey 1977/8, Carl Bro International 1982: Chapter 4, Bailey 1981: Chapter 5). A strong incentive exists to raise herd size to a viable level. Moreover most herds in Botswana are below estimated viability levels of some 20–25 head. The Rural Income Distribution Survey of 1974 found that 80% of rural households owned fewer than 21 head of cattle. With unviable small herds and an unproductive unreliable agriculture, the diversified economic strategy of Tswana households (employment, crops and cattle) is essential if the family is to survive, let alone prosper. With cattle being the savings and investment outcome of the diversified strategy their rate of accumulation measures the strategy's success. The 'banking role' of cattle is common to many African pastoral societies.[2] They are well-suited to the role, generating both income (through milk, draught power and natural increase) and capital gains (through price increases). On capital gains alone they have provided a good hedge against inflation in the period 1960–83 (see Fig. A2).

Material explanations of herders' individual behaviour have been extended in recent years to include price responsiveness, where the 'backward sloping supply curve' consistent with net accumulation had long been considered an example of a non-commercial orientation by herders and an exception to the market responsiveness of other peasantries. Studies by Jarvis (1974) and others indicate that a decrease in supply is the characteristic short-term response of cattle farmers in industrialized countries to an increase in price which is expected to be permanent – in order to accumulate additional breeding stock to increase sales volume in the long term.

A similar pattern is revealed by African pastoralists – albeit that their motive is net accumulation – with offtake numbers (i.e. supply) increasing in the longer term as a result of greater accumulation.[3] The result is that price-responsiveness data have come to be recognized as an inadequate indicator of the degree of commercial orientation of cattle farmers (Low 1980:20).

These observations can be built into a more comprehensive material explanation of net accumulation, as set out below. In sum, the hypothesis put forward is that net accumulation has made micro economic sense historically because of Botswana's peripheral status in southern Africa, expressed mainly in the very low elasticity of product substitution of the land used in cattle production i.e. the very low rate at which other agricultural products will be substituted for cattle in response to a fall in the ratio of cattle prices to other agricultural product prices.

The evolution to peripheral status (see p.7 above) has environmental, social, political and economic aspects, intertwined with each other in historical events. In the case of cattle accumulation, these diverse aspects have maintained the opportunity cost (private and social) of the use of land for cattle keeping at a low level historically.

With its emphasis upon the determination of type of production by relative resource costs the hypothesis falls within comparative cost theory – but modified by building in an historical dimension to provide for alteration of comparative costs over time, explicitly to avoid that theory's otherwise static and resource-mechanical nature. The argument relies upon distinguishing motives and means and individual and aggregate net accumulation.

Two related economic motives for accumulating cattle were identified above (p.38). The primary motive is that associated with the 'banking' role of cattle: the return in real income and capital growth to investment plus the high liquidity of the investment (i.e. the ease with which cattle can be converted back to cash). The secondary motive, flowing from the first, is to create a viable herd size i.e. one which generates a positive real income at least, and is also large enough for its breeding core to be sustained through a major drought.

While the first motive is basic to all net accumulation the second is of varying importance at different stages of accumulation. Firstly, there is the accumulation by small herders, including newly formed households at an early stage in their life-cycle, beginning perhaps with inherited fragments of their parents' dismantled larger herds. Typically at the present time even a small herd generates a positive real income (in milk, draught power and growth), despite costing more cash than it brings in directly through offtake (Carl Bro 1982:4, 131). In such small herds there is an urgency to build the herd to a cash-viable (not to mention drought-viable) size. Once the points of drought and cash viability have been passed this preoccupation may be less, until a level is reached where a major investment (e.g. in a borehole) is needed and raises costs drastically, making accumulation of more cattle urgent once more in order to cover the increased costs.

Figure 3.3 below depicts the cash-viable and drought-viable herd sizes and provides a basis for the rest of the argument.

Explanation of Fig. 3.3: OA is indicated as smaller than OB based upon Vierich's (1979) estimate of 22 head as the drought viable herd size in Kweneng compared to the 30 to 40 head indicated by

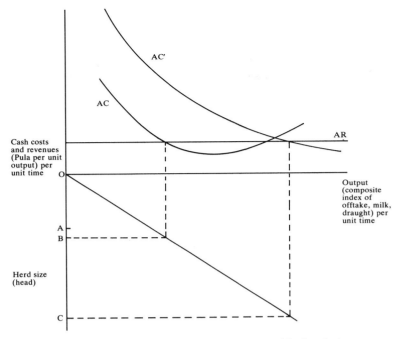

Figure 3.3: *Cash-viable and drought-viable herd sizes*

Notes to Fig. 3.3

AC   Average cash costs of maintaining a herd under conditions suitable for a small herd but not for a large herd: namely, at the lands or on the outskirts of the village, buying or begging water, with high grazing pressure from numerous small herds in the vicinity.

AC′   Average cash costs of maintaining a herd under conditions suitable for a larger herd: namely, on own or shared well or borehole on remoter grazing lands.

AR   Average revenue from the herd i.e.

       Total revenue
       ‾‾‾‾‾‾‾‾‾‾‾‾
       Units of output
       same as average price per unit of output sold.
       Assumed constant.

Diagonal line in lower quadrant   Reflects points within the upper quadrant onto herd size. Drawn as a straight line it indicates that the productivity of larger and smaller herds are similar.

OA   Drought-viable herd size

OB   Cash-viable herd size for small herd kept on village outskirts or at lands.

OC   Cash-viable herd size for larger herd kept on own or shared borehole or well.

Carl Bro International (1982:4.131) as the minimum level for cash viability.

AC slopes downward at first as fixed cash costs (particularly labour) are spread over a larger output with increased herd size. In both the case of the large and the small herder the ability of the household to realize the motive to accumulate cattle is limited by the means it has available to do so, namely, its investible cash relative to the costs of cattle accumulation. The small herder holding fewer than OA or OB cattle puts cash into the herd because of the expectation of being able to surpass OA and OB. With limited savings only, and poor access to credit, the small herder's investible cash available for putting into the herd will consist largely of current earnings from alternative sources. Lack of sufficient investible cash to surpass OA and OB results in the herd being run down when unusual cash demands or drought overtake the household – a frequent occurrence among small herders.

Should the small herder succeed in accumulating cattle a point will be reached beyond which increasing the herd kept on the outskirts of the village or at the lands will become increasingly difficult – owing to high grazing pressure and problems in finding sufficient water by begging or buying from council boreholes or neighbouring syndicates. Field observations by the author in Kgatleng indicate that this point may be reached within a herd size range of 60 to 100 head. Increased cash inputs into the herd are likely to result in diminishing herd increase and hence diminishing increase in outputs, causing AC to rise. There is a need to shift to better grazing and water – which usually has meant drilling a borehole or well, or buying a share in one. Thus the limit on the larger herder's ability to accumulate is set by the investible funds available (from credit, savings and other current earnings) to provide for the large capital outlays (particularly for waterpoints) which are unavoidable obstacles in the way of expansion beyond a certain herd size.

In terms of Fig. 3.3, after a certain herd size is reached large fixed capital outlays must be made which raise the average cost curve from AC to AC' thereby increasing the cash-viable herd size to OC and making accumulation to OC urgent[4].

To sum up: the primary motive for accumulating cattle is the income (kind and money) they generate. The ability of the individual herder to accumulate is dictated by access to investible funds in relation to the costs of cattle keeping. *Ceteris paribus,* a rise in costs raises the cash-viable herd size and thereby reduces net accumulation by making a cash-viable herd size more costly, and therefore more difficult, to attain.

It is left to point out that Botswana's peripheral status has kept down the costs of cattle keeping – most crucially in the case of land – thereby providing the basis for long-term net accumulation. The peripheral nature of most of Botswana's land resource is both an ecological and political matter. With poor rainfall and soils it is physically ill-suited to highly productive agriculture – which may in itself be an important reason why it was not more extensively settled by the British as was Kenya. As a collection of 'native reserves' channelled into becoming 'labour reserves', the territory was starved of the infrastructural investment (education, roads, marketing facilities) and private investment which would have made the return to agriculture more competitive with cattle, at least in the better-watered east and south.

As regards labour, its migrancy to South African mining, industry and agriculture probably further decreased the competitiveness of crops compared to cattle, since the labour extensive nature of cattle production helped to ensure that withdrawals of labour did not hinder expansion of the industry (see p.61) as seems to have occurred in the case of agriculture.

This lack of alternative forms of investment for the land and labour resources channelled into cattle production means that the opportunity cost of investment in cattle has been low – as the preponderant historical share of total private investment going into cattle bears witness (see Chapter 9).

Absence of the peripheral features of the economy would not only raise cattle keeping costs but also provide competitive outlets for investible funds, thereby further limiting net accumulation by the individual cattle owner.

On the basis of the discussion above, the determinants of net accumulation by the individual cattle owner can be summed up as follows:

Net accumulation (individual): trend

$$= f \left(\frac{\text{Investible funds}}{\substack{\text{Drought-viable herd size, cash-viable herd size, Return to} \\ \text{alternative investments}}} \right)$$

Link 3

43

where 'Drought viable herd size' is a constant and changes in 'cash viable herd size'

$$= f \left(\frac{\text{Cattle price index}}{\text{Cash costs price index}} \right)$$

where technical coefficients of cattle production are constant.

Moving away from the determinants of net accumulation by the individual cattle owner to those of aggregate net accumulation, and taking a longer-term view, reveals the crucial role of the aggregate supply of investible funds in determining net accumulation. The explanation is as follows. In Link 3 'cash viable herd size' is fairly stable over the long term because the trends of change in cattle prices and cash costs of cattle keeping are likely to be in the same direction. On the other hand, the supply of investible funds and the return to alternative investments have increased considerably, through the rapid expansion of income post-Independence and the increased demand for goods and services in the growing urban centres (particularly from the early 1970s). But the impact of the improved return to alternative investments on net accumulation has probably been slight. Firstly, historically the returns to cattle production have been so superior to alternatives that there has been a substantial gap to close before investment would respond to marginal changes in profitability (see p.55). Secondly, there are barriers against entry into manufacturing and trade. Markets are small and trade licences are rationed; only a minority of even the larger cattle owners are in a position (in terms of education and experience) to invest directly in other sectors, while indirect (portfolio) investment is severely limited by the absence of a money market; urban property (an ideal alternative investment – given its high profitability and minimal demands on the investor's time and business skills) continues to be dominated by foreigners and institutional housing schemes which limit possibilities for absentee ownership (notably the Self-Help Housing Scheme).

In short, investment to date in trade, services and manufacturing has been carried out with funds drawn largely from sectors other than the cattle sector, particularly foreign sources. Moreover, part of the incomes generated in these urban-based sectors is reinvested in cattle (particularly savings from salaries and wages). Thus even in the early 1980s the trend in the domestic supply of investible funds continued to be the overriding determinant of the trend in net accumulation of cattle. Therefore we can write:

Net accumulation (aggregate): trend
$$= f \text{ (Investible funds)}$$

Link 4

The argument is now in place that a low elasticity of substitution of investment in cattle for investment in alternatives to cattle, reflecting the peripheral nature of Botswana's land resource and economy historically, is at the root of aggregate net accumulation, the issue will be left until Chapter 10 where further implications are considered.

It remains only to note that no matter how explicable continuous accumulation is in terms of the material benefit accruing to the individual herder therefrom, additional explanation is required if private accumulation takes place at social expense by overgrazing i.e. if 'it would pay the community to control cattle numbers through collective agreement' (Livingstone 1977:217). Under these circumstances society is at less than a Pareto optimum i.e. the gain to the community from controlling grazing could be used to more than compensate individuals for private benefit lost.

Putting aside the untrue assertion that pastoralists cannot manage communal grazing – Hardin's (1968) 'tragedy of the commons' thesis[5], disproved by the instances of regulation of grazing in past and present pastoral societies, including Botswana (Schapera 1943:Ch.XII) – there remain three possible reasons (not necessarily mutually exclusive) why society might remain at this sub-optimal position. Firstly, social organization might have broken down; secondly, society may have a particularly high rate of time preference (Livingstone ibid.) while range degradation is a long-term process; thirdly, society may not perceive that range degradation is taking place. Given its long-term nature, range degradation is not readily visible below the seasonal and drought-cyclical changes in the veld. In the absence of meticulous scientific observation of changes in plant species over long time periods only the most obvious symptoms (gullying, total sheet erosion) are indisputable.

Where the number of cattle kept on a given stretch of range has increased secularly and their output not obviously decreased, as in Botswana, it is not clear to herders (nor is there consensus among scientists) that private accumulation has been at future social cost in range degradation[6].

To sum up this section on the source of aggregate net accumulation: Ideological explanations of cattle accumulation behaviour are unsound. As regards material explanations, evidence from Botswana supports strongly net accumulation of cattle as a strategy to maximize the individual herder's micro-economic benefit; a structural explanation is offered of how this has occurred.

(iii) *Offtake: experience in Botswana*

Historical statistics of aggregate offtake percentage in Botswana probably provide an inaccurate record of actual performance – even over the period 1953–83 for which a consistent run of figures is available. The problem lies both in the estimation of domestic slaughter, based partly on hides exports and partly on guesswork, and in the estimation of the national herd size.

Table A1 indicates an average offtake of 8% to 10% per annum. There is no clear trend towards increase or decrease, and even much earlier estimates are of similar magnitude[7]. More definite is the observation of increases in offtake rates in the first year of a major drought and in single drought years (1959, 1965, 1973, 1979, 1982) – much of which is probably 'pre-emptive offtake' in anticipation of mortality (plus some slaughter to provide for higher cash needs in the face of failed crops).

Besides the statistical difficulties there are also conceptual problems which hinder assessment of Botswana's offtake experience. Firstly, there is a definition problem: offtake numbers are commonly measured either including or excluding herd mortality. Botswana's figures (Table A1) exclude mortality and this is the measure which will be adhered to throughout this study, not because mortality is insignificant but because the emphasis is on producers' decisions regarding offtake. Secondly, there are interpretation problems. Offtake is often assumed to be synonymous with herd productivity – extremely misleading where the herd is kept for milk, draught and savings purpose as much as for meat. A more crucial issue for the present study is that offtake numbers and offtake rate (offtake numbers/cattle population) do not necessarily move in the same direction, since offtake rate depends additionally on factors determining cattle population. Since the internal dynamics of the cattle population under the impact of major disasters are important in explaining variations in Botswana's cattle numbers (p.36), offtake rates are likely to have varied partly for reasons independent of herders' motivation to hold or dispose of cattle. This is a major stumbling block in the way of efforts to explain offtake rate behaviour in Botswana in terms of herders' motivation (following Low, Kemp and Doran 1980)[8]. In sum, problems of data quality and interpretation render any hypotheses concerning offtake only speculative.

Historical changes in offtake numbers to be explained include both long-run changes (the historical trend) and short-run changes (fluctuations from the historical trend).

Regarding the long-run trend in offtake numbers the hypothesis advanced here is that it is governed by the historic trend in cattle population in a more or less proportional relation i.e.

Offtake numbers: trend
=f (Cattle population: trend)

Link 5

This is justified by:

(i) the apparently relatively stable long-term offtake rate (Table A1);
(ii) the reasoning that expansion of cattle production with an unchanged management system and productivity should result in offtake supply (oxen, old cows and bulls) increasing roughly in line with cattle population[9];
(iii) the observation that market demand (both export and domestic) has over the long term become increasingly less of a restriction on sale of cattle i.e. thus allowing cattle supplies increasingly to determine the trend of cattle sales (offtake).

Regarding short-term fluctuations in offtake from the long-term trend, two explanatory hypotheses are suggested. Firstly, during the colonial period fluctuations in export demand determined fluctuations in offtake numbers i.e. when export demand rose offtake numbers quickly rose to meet it[10], and fell with falling export demand. Underlying this hypothesis is the assumption that severe marketing imperfections (restricted availability of export markets, buyers and transport) were the primary constraint on sale of cattle. Thus:

Fluctuation from trend in offtake numbers in colonial period
=f (Import demand in regional markets)

Link 6

Secondly, in the post-colonial period supply side factors increasingly become the major determinant of offtake numbers[11], as marketing imperfections diminish and export markets expand. Furthermore, as large herds form an increasingly major proportion of the cattle population fluctuations in offtake supply will tend to reflect investment rather than subsistence strategies of herders. Combined with market availability, this indicates that risk of loss (through drought mainly, but also through possible future market closure or fall in price) is the crucial determinant of short-term changes in offtake:

Fluctuations from trend in offtake numbers
= f (Risk of loss: by mortality, threatened market closure,
threatened price fall)

Link 7

implying that the higher the risk of loss, the higher the level of offtake above its trend, and vice versa.

The impact of the mid-1930s, mid-1960s and mid-1980s droughts on the cattle population indicates that major deviations of rainfall below average are a major element in risk of loss. But no general relation between rainfall levels and offtake exists for present data. Thus correlating offtake rate estimates (the only figures available) for 1953–77 with rainfall data (lagged one year) and with Sandford's 'range condition index' (Sandford 1977: Appendix B) yields only weakly negative relations (r = −0.41 and −0.49 respectively). But given the estimated nature of the data this does not necessarily mean that offtake is not sensitive to smaller rainfall deviations.

Evidence supporting Link 6 is abundant not only in the numerous restrictions placed upon BP exports by beef importing countries in the region but also in the nature of the export marketing system in the Protectorate, within which the main actors were cattle traders whose shipments for export were regulated by quotas imposed by the BP administration (to accommodate the quota restrictions imposed by the importing countries). Their finance for cattle buying was drawn largely from South African and Northern Rhodesian livestock auctioneers and butchers and therefore limited by the demand for beef in these markets. They owed their prominent role in the marketing system to the severe marketing imperfections in transport, communications and knowledge which made direct sale of cattle on the Johannesburg or Copperbelt markets impossible for almost all Tswana herders.

Chapters 5 and 6 provide more detailed evidence on how export offtake was determined by import demand in regional markets during the colonial period. Link 6 depends heavily on the assumption that fluctuations in export offtake reflect fluctuations in overall offtake; with so small a domestic market and limited home slaughter this assumption seems plausible.

The evidence supporting Link 7 is as follows:

(i)   In the post-colonial period marketing constraints (unavailability of export opportunities, road and rail transport, trek routes, handling facilities, co-operatives) have been reduced substantially in all but the remotest areas. Slaughter quotas at the Botswana Meat Commission Lobatse have probably become the main constraint in this period, particularly in the drought of the 1980s. This constraint is being reduced by the new Maun abattoir and will be further reduced by the planned Francistown abattoir. In short, removal of the most obstructive marketing imperfections during the post-colonial period ended the applicability of Link 6, meaning that demand for cattle was no longer the main constraint on offtake numbers, thus leaving their determination increasingly up to supply factors.

(ii) Although most cattle owners have small herds most cattle are owned by larger herders, so that aggregate offtake supply depends mainly upon the offtake strategies of larger herders. The Rural Income Distribution Survey (1976:111) found 51% of all cattle owned by 5% of rural households. Households with more than 40 head were found to own 64% of all cattle. Recent Agricultural Surveys of the Ministry of Agriculture indicate even higher proportions of total cattle numbers in larger herds: 70% of cattle in herds of over 40 head and 58% in herds of over 60 head, (averages for years 1980–83).

(iii) With total income directly correlated with cattle ownership (Colclough & Fallon 1980:27) estimates of subsistence level incomes convert to ownership of some 40 to 60 head of cattle, above which one would expect consumption considerations to play a decreasingly important role in offtake strategy and investment considerations (including investment in 'human capital' through payment of school fees) an increasingly prominent role. How prominent is not yet clear owing to scant empirical evidence on offtake motivation.[12]

(iv) Income from crop production is a minor proportion of total income both for poor households and particularly for those with more cattle (Rural Income Distribution Survey 1976: 97–100). Therefore fluctuations in crop yields from year to year are unlikely to affect aggregate offtake numbers greatly.

Links 4 and 5 go against the stream of present thought on the subject of determination of annual fluctuations in offtake: Roe's argument (1980: 9, 31) concerning the high correlations of BP cattle exports with grain prices (+) and with cattle exports/grain prices (−) in the colonial period; and the increasingly influential[13] Low, Kemp and Doran (1980) 'cash needs/supply of subsistence' model fitted by multiple linear regression to Swaziland. Both of these suggest that annual variations in offtake can be explained from the supply side in terms of the balance between herders' subsistence needs and their supply from sources other than cattle sale or slaughter, namely subsistence cropping and migrant labour. If the rains fail, subsistence crops are inadequate and the need for cash (to buy food) is the greater. The cash can be got either by migrant labour or sale of cattle. The higher migrant real earnings are the more easily can the cash shortfall be met and therefore fewer cattle need be sold.[14]

The clear evidence of the diversified economic strategy of Tswana households and of the 'savings' role of cattle makes the 'cash needs/supply' hypothesis of very likely applicability to the offtake behaviour of smaller herders. But, owing particularly to the importance of demand factors (market imperfections) in the colonial period and the dominance of larger herders in the post-colonial period, it seems to have been of relatively minor importance in *aggregate* offtake determination. Moreover, there are problems with existing formulations of the 'cash needs/supply' model.

Roe's high positive correlation of cattle exports with current sorghum prices 1918–59 reflects above all the positive correlation of each with time, since both exhibit a strong upward time trend. There is no significant correlation (r=0.18) between detrended sorghum prices and cattle exports. Similarly, the high negative correlation of cattle exports with the ratio of cattle/grain prices seems to illustrate less the offering of more cattle for sale in response to an increasingly cattle-expensive grain import bill than coincidence of two very long-term trends.

This is suggested by examination of the cattle export time series (Table A1) in which the major increases in export numbers correspond to increased market opportunities (notably 1918, 1926, 1942, 1949, 1958). Moreover, the trend in both cattle prices/grain prices and cattle exports since 1960 is strongly upwards (Tables 9.2 and A1) i.e. they have been positively correlated since 1960[15].

The 'cash needs/supply' model which Low, Kemp and Doran (1980) argue explains most of the variation in Swazi offtake 1949–77, is based on the following equation:

$$\frac{\text{Offtake numbers}}{\text{Herd size}} = a_0 = \frac{\text{Slaughter for consumption and ceremony}}{\text{Herd size}}$$

$$+ a_1 = \frac{\text{Human population}}{\text{Real cattle price. Herd size}}$$

$$+ a_2 = \frac{\text{Rainfall deficiency}}{\text{Real cattle price. Herd size}}$$

$$+ a_3 = \frac{\text{Mine worker earnings}}{\text{Real cattle price. Herd size}}$$

in which a_0 is assumed to be a constant proportion, a_1 represents 'basic cash need' which is assumed proportional to human population, while a_2 and a_3 indicate to what extent the basic cash need can be satisfied from sources other than cattle sale: a_2 determining the size of the subsistence grain crop and a_3 the cash earning opportunities through migrant labour; a_1, a_2 and a_3 are all per unit value animal of the national herd.

A number of pitfalls await the researcher trying to fit this model to Botswana:

(i)   Data for population, migrants' earnings and offtake rates are too poor for annual variations in them to carry much weight.

(ii) The dependent variable is offtake percentage but this has been argued to exhibit substantial variation *independent of offtake numbers* owing to changes in its denominator (herd size) under the impact of drought (p.36).

(iii) Rainfall deficiency in period $t-1$ is a dummy variable intended to indicate the adequacy of the staple maize crop and thereby how much of basic food needs must be purchased in period t by sale of additional labour or cattle.

But drought in t−1 can provoke increased cattle sales and slaughter in t in order to pre-empt mortality (Link 7), which is independent of subsistence cash needs.

(iv) No account is taken of perceived subsistence needs rising at a faster rate than population – which has probably happened; the more so if, as is possible, cattle ownership (and therefore aggregate offtake) was at the same time becoming increasingly concentrated in the hands of larger herders with their higher perceived subsistence needs. Indeed, one of Low, Kemp and Doran's most crucial conclusions (that 'the inverse price/supply relationship is . . . shown to hold for both the long- and the short-term situations . . . because . . . the secular increase in real cattle prices has caused the basic need variable

$$\frac{\text{Human population}}{\text{Real cattle prices. Herd size}}$$

to decline over the analysis period' 1980:231) is dependent on the unlikely assumption that aggregate 'basic needs' of the herders who provide the offtake rise no faster than the rate of increase in population.

(v) The model is designed to explain an observed downward trend in offtake rate from the Swazi herd. In Botswana, by contrast, the trend offtake rate has apparently remained constant (Table A1).

Before ending this discussion of offtake experience in Botswana the question of the impact of changes in cattle prices upon offtake should be considered.

In terms of Link 7 changes in real cattle prices are one factor among others (the major one being drought) determining the level of risk of loss, and of rather more importance (given the rapid price increases of recent years) in setting the availability of investible funds. Thus no specific and necessary relation is postulated between cattle prices and offtake. Only if a real cattle price increase is expected to be permanent might it, *ceteris paribus,* cause a negative fluctuation from the upward trend in offtake numbers. But with cattle prices bearing upon offtake only indirectly (through risk and availability of investible funds), and being only one of several determinants of either, any statistical relation between the two is likely to be weak and indefinably lagged. Indeed the correlation coefficient between percentage fluctuations of export numbers and real cattle prices from their trends is totally insignificant over the period 1953–80 ($r=0.06$).

This conclusion runs counter to that of Ndzinge, Marsh and Greer (1982:15) who, applying a multiple linear regression model to Botswana over the period 1966–80, found that 'price is a major determinant of number of cattle slaughtered in a given year' with increases in price eliciting increased slaughter. Their result is very likely biased by: the mid-1960s drought (bringing exceptionally low offtake in its wake); the rapid price rises of 1972–75 coinciding with a return to pre-drought offtake level; the coincidence of falling real price levels in the mid-1970s with the offtake limitations resulting from the Foot and Mouth disease outbreaks; the real price increase of 1979–80 coinciding with the lifting of Foot and Mouth disease restrictions on cattle movement and a record BMC throughput.

To sum up the conclusions of this discussion of offtake experience in Botswana:

1. Understanding of herders' offtake strategies from historical data on offtake in Botswana is made hazardous by the multiple uses of cattle, poorness of data, and the internal dynamics of the cattle population under the impact of major droughts.
2. The upward long-term trend in offtake numbers reflects a similar trend in cattle population.
3. Short-term fluctuations from the offtake trend have been mainly determined by export market demand in the colonial period and by the risk of loss during the post-colonial period. There is little empirical evidence for or against the latter conclusion but it appears to provide a better explanation than does a 'cash needs/supply' model.

(iv) *Investment*
The other principal elements besides cattle numbers and offtake in the development of the means of cattle production are investment and innovation.

Not only has investment in Botswana been concentrated historically in the beef industry (until the beginning of the mining boom of the late 1960s) but within cattle production it has been concentrated in water point creation and herd accumulation, reflecting the return to cattle compared to alternative accessible investments and the lack of water as the main constraint on expansion of cattle production.

Long-term historical data on investment are non-existent. But national accounts data in the post-colonial period (Table 9.1) show the increase in value of cattle inventories as making up some 90% of gross capital formation in Agriculture, Forestry and Fishing and a third to a half of gross capital formation in those sectors to which cattle owners potentially have investment access as an alternative to cattle accumulation.

Waterpoint creation, much of it for stock watering, was a major focus of public investment in the 1930s to 1950s (Roe 1980:22), as the Administration strove to expand its virtually sole export industry and (with migrant labour remittances) main source of tax revenue (Table 9.3). In the post-colonial period water point construction for stock watering has become increasingly a matter of private investment, which has been substantial.

According to the record of the Geological Survey Department, 4 285 boreholes were drilled in the period 1966–81, of which 57% were privately drilled, the vast bulk of these being for stock watering. Very few government boreholes have been drilled for stock watering purposes,[16] being practically all for village and town water supplies.

From a theoretical standpoint, the historical emphasis on investment in waterpoints can be understood in terms of relative resource scarcity. Capital (the means of creating boreholes and dams) has been the constraining factor and grazing land the plentiful and privately costless one, therefore consumed heavily in rapid geographical expansion of production. Production has not been labour intensive and this, together with the low cost of family and semi-vassal labour, has ensured that labour availability has not constrained expansion of production.

To compare properly the returns to cattle investment with those on alternative investments accessible to cattle owners it is necessary to take into account the 'hidden' return on cattle as an activity supplementary to wage or salary employment – the principal means in the post-colonial period of maximising the household's security. Investment in, for example, a manufacturing activity instead of cattle would compete for the employable labour time of the household. Similarly, the 'in kind' benefits of cattle keeping (draught power, milk and capital growth through natural increase) must be included. Given the strong 'revealed preference' for investment in cattle rather than crops it is clear that existing sample studies have severely underestimated the relative superiority of returns to cattle investments[17] – despite the recent increases in the ratio of crop/ cattle producer prices[18].

On the basis of the discussion above, two factors stand out as determinants of the amount of investment in cattle production historically: the supply of investible funds (both public and private) and the superior returns to cattle investment. But the hypothesis is put forward here that the returns to cattle keeping historically have been so superior to the limited alternatives available that alteration of the marginal relative profitability of cattle production has not affected the amount of investment. In short, the profitability gap between cattle and alternative investments (including bank deposits) has been so great that investment volume has not been affected by historical widenings or narrowings of the gap. Under this assumption, the quantity of investible funds available becomes the only determinant of investment flows into cattle production. Furthermore, since net accumulation is by definition part of investment in cattle (being the change in herd inventory), we can write:

$$I = f \text{ (Investible funds)}$$
$$+ \text{Net accumulation of cattle}$$

Link 8

Prominently absent from Link 8 are cattle prices relative to those of alternative agricultural investments (e.g. grains or sheep). Owing to the low elasticity of substitution of investment in cattle (defined at p.57 below) the prices of cattle relative to those of other agricultural products (e.g. grains or mutton or wool) do not determine fluctuations in cattle investment.

Support for Link 8 comes from the observed historical pattern in waterpoint creation: in the colonial period even large cattle owners had little access to investible funds, so that public investment figured prominently, but starting only when Colonial Development and Welfare funds became available in the 1930s and expanding in the 1940s and 1950s according to funds granted (Roe 1980:22). In the post-colonial period savings from increasing profits on cattle production, from expanded salary and wage employment and from greater access to loan funds made for much increased private investment in water points.

Link 8 neglects investments in fencing and consumable investment goods (medicines, feed etc.). The assumption made is that these have been very small compared to investment in net accumulation and water point creation.[19]

(v) *Innovation*
With the clear exception of boreholes, the historical picture of cattle management in Botswana is characterized more by continuity than change, even in its phase of rapid expansion since the 1950s. As with theories of offtake motivation, explanations of this continuity range from the ideological (resistance to change) to the economic and institutional (communal land tenure). The ideological argument of resistance to change was fuelled in the past by over-estimates of the return to managerial innovations and of the facility with which they could be implemented. Such over-estimates were at the root of the failure of the CDC northern ranching operation in the 1950s and the Ncojane ranches (part of the First Livestock Development Project) in the 1970s.

The view taken here is that economic constraints, specifically the scarcity of investible funds and (later) the high opportunity cost of skilled (i.e. salary or wage employable) labour time, have been the major factors shaping the historical pattern of innovation in cattle production.

Besides boreholes (the essential precondition for expansion of production into areas where water is at levels too deep for a well) innovations have been limited to those demonstrating the highest, surest and quickest returns to small and irregular inputs of capital and skilled labour.

Thus disease control (free and subsidized vaccinations) and mineral supplementation (bonemeal and salt) have been adopted eagerly. But managerial innovations which require much capital and continual input of skilled labour and yield only long-term returns (such as paddocking, grazing management, breeding season, early weaning etc.) have been adopted only by many of the largest freehold farmers, whose savings from rising real cattle prices in the post-colonial period have enabled them to develop their ranches fully for the first time.[20]

By contrast, the ranches allocated in the 'Commercial Areas' under the Tribal Grazing Land Policy are mostly run on an absentee-ownership basis and few have yet adopted managerial innovations (Odell 1981:39).
Thus:

$$\text{Innovations} = f\left(\text{Investible funds}, \frac{\text{Return to employable labour}}{\substack{\text{Opportunity cost of} \\ \text{employable labour}}}\right)$$

Link 9

In Link 9 investible funds determine the access to innovations, while the return of the innovation to employable labour relative to opportunity cost of employable labour determines the selection of innovations. The observed pattern of highly selective and skewed innovation can be interpreted in terms of Link 9 as follows: *selection* of innovations by herders of different sizes has been fairly similar, but herders' *access* to innovations has been unequal, thus the effective adoption of innovations (boreholes in particular) has been skewed towards larger herders. An implication of Link 9 is that involvement of cattle owners from rich to small peasant in the salary and wage economy has raised the opportunity cost of employable labour and discouraged managerial innovations generally, while providing investible funds for purchase of medicines, mineral supplements, water and breeding stock.

(vi)   *Summary of links in the development of the means of cattle production in Botswana*

The nine links discussed above as critical in the historical development of the means of cattle production in Botswana are brought together below:

Definitions:

Aggregate net accumulation:

Additions to cattle>Subtractions from cattle

(Births+Imports)>(Deaths+Sales+Home slaughter)

Offtake numbers = Sales+Home slaughter

Drought-viable herd size: Minimum individual herd size necessary to sustain the breeding core through a major drought. Estimated at some 20 head.

Cash-viable herd size: Herd size above which the herd yields a positive net cash flow. Estimated at 30 to 40 head.

Employable labour: Labour which can obtain salary or wage employment outside farming. The opportunity cost of using 'employable labour' in farming is thus the wage or salary forgone.

Elasticity of substitution of investment in cattle for investment in alternatives to cattle:

$$= \frac{\dfrac{\triangle \text{ Investment in cattle}}{\triangle \text{ Investment in alternatives}}}{\dfrac{\triangle \text{ Price of cattle}}{\triangle \text{ Price of alternatives}}}$$

Links

CATTLE POPULATION

Cattle numbers: short term changes
=f (Major deviations of rainfall from average)

Link 1

Cattle numbers: long term trend
=f (Waterpoints, Medication)

Link 2

NET ACCUMULATION OF CATTLE

Net accumulation (individual): trend

$$=f \left(\frac{\text{Investible funds}}{\begin{array}{c}\text{Drought-viable herd size, cash-viable herd size,}\\ \text{Return to alternative investments}\end{array}} \right)$$

Link 3

Since (i) the lack of attractive alternative uses for the land and labour used in cattle production has kept the cash cost of cattle production down;

(ii) drought-viable and cash-viable herd sizes tend to be constant;

(iii) the return to alternative uses for investible funds has not greatly restricted the aggregate long-term availability of investible funds to cattle production, even in recent times, owing to difficulties in switching investment out of cattle;

(iv) part of savings from income generated in other sectors is reinvested in cattle production.

Therefore Net accumulation (aggregate): trend
=f (Investible funds: trend)

Link 4

OFFTAKE

Since expansion of cattle production has occurred in general by geographical extension of a largely unchanged management system:

Offtake numbers: trend
=f (Actual cattle numbers: trend)

Link 5

Since during most of the colonial period marketing imperfections were so great, and demand usually less than potential available supply:

Therefore *Colonial period*
Offtake numbers: proportionate fluctuations from trend
= f (Import demand in regional markets)

Link 6

Since marketing imperfections have been substantially reduced and the offtake of larger herders (motivated more by investment considerations than cash needs for consumption) is increasingly dominant in aggregate offtake; and given net accumulation:

Therefore *Post-colonial period*
Fluctuations from trend in offtake numbers
= f (Risk of loss: by mortality, threatened market closure, threatened price fall)

Link 7

INVESTMENT
Applying the same arguments used to justify Link 4, and since the amount of net accumulation in any period (i.e. the inventory change) is part of investment:

Therefore Investment in cattle production
= f (Investible funds) + Net accumulation

Link 8

INNOVATION
Innovations adopted are determined by the availability of investible funds and by the criterion used to choose between types of innovation.

Since recent household strategy has been to maximize off-farm employment of its employable labour, the major criterion for selection of innovations is the return of the innovation to employable labour relative to the cost of the innovation in terms of inputs of employable labour. Thus:

$$\text{Innovations} = f\left(\text{Investible funds}, \frac{\text{Return to employable labour}}{\begin{array}{c}\text{Opportunity cost of}\\ \text{employable labour}\end{array}}\right)$$

Link 9

59

Considered together these links indicate that investible funds are the key exogenous factor in the historical dynamic of the means of cattle production in Botswana: on the basis of the trend to aggregate net accumulation availability of investible funds has dictated public and private investment in cattle (principally water points investment if cattle inventory changes are ignored) which in turn has increased cattle population.

Thus the main axis of the model can be summed up as:

Net accumulation (aggregate): trend
$\equiv \triangle$ Cattle numbers: trend
$= f$ (Investible funds)

The availability of investible funds historically has depended upon the state of beef export markets, migrant workers' remittances, colonial policy and domestic economic growth. Two long historical periods stand out, which are approximately the same as those identified in Chapter 2, as the two developmental phases in the world beef trade. Firstly, in the period up to the end of the Second World War investible funds are in short supply and expansion of the forces of production is limited. Secondly, there is rapid expansion thereafter owing to rising international beef demand, a more favourable colonial investment policy and domestic economic growth resulting particularly from mining developments.

(b)   Relations of Production

In the first phase (i.e. to 1950) specific changes in the social relations of cattle production are difficult to identify, more so because they were limited since the type of external changes occurring (regional demand for cattle imports, cattle prices) did not alter the condition of capital starvation in the industry which prevented its expansion. Cliffe and Moorsom (1980) go so far as to argue that the blocking of the industry's development in the 1920s to 1950s, plus the restriction of commercial opportunities mainly to white settlers, stalled the process of accumulation by the Tswana aristocracy which had begun with the rise of the cattle export industry. Parson's analysis (1979) is similar, stressing the importance of this phase as one of establishment and consolidation of the colonial presence in the creation of a 'labour reserve' economy – characterized by large-scale migration of a semi-proletarianized 'peasantariat'. Colclough and McCarthy (1980) emphasize that this period did see accumulation by the aristocracy, hence increasing social differentiation, owing particularly to the 10% commission received by chiefs on collection of taxes on behalf of the administration (see also Hermans 1974:96).

What is clear is that during this phase when 16% to 18% of the entire population in the south and east of Botswana were absent as migrant workers at any time (Massey 1980:110) the economic relations among people came to be mediated increasingly through imports and exports via the network of trading stations, under pressure of tax payments and rising consumption needs. It is thought to have placed stress on cattle production relations within families, through all responsibility shifting to those members at home (Kooijman 1979:225), to have encouraged cattle smuggling and to have worsened cattle management (according to much discussion in the Advisory councils in the 1940s, and Schapera 1947:164). But the extent of this impact is unclear, and even if very extensive seems not to have constrained subsequent expansion of cattle production at all, especially since real wages in cattle production did not rise but remained at the most basic subsistence level.[21] The adverse impact of migrant labour on arable agricultural production through withdrawal of labour is more plausible (Massey 1980:116, Roe 1980, B.P. Agricultural Division 1947).

The picture of the state of social relations of cattle production is rather clearer in the succeeding expansionary phase. It is useful first to disaggregate the totality of cattle owners. Three recent sociological studies of households' economic strategies in contemporary Botswana provide guidelines for disaggregation and analysis (Kerven 1977, Cooper 1980 and Gulbrandsen 1980). The broad thrust of their conclusions is similar and runs approximately as below, following Cooper's analysis in simplified form:

1. Urban salary and wage earners are closely involved with cattle and crop production via their nuclear and extended households;
2. A positive relation tends to exist between their position in any one of these activities and in the other two;
3. Thresholds or breakpoints exist above which the households' options increase markedly: in cattle and crops these are at about 40 head (sufficient to provide for drought and regular

offtake needs and to provide a breeding core to survive a drought) and about 15 bags of grain (enough to cover staple food needs) per annum.

On this basis he suggests the following class groupings (simplified):

Class category	Estimated % of H.H.s	Jobs	Lands	Cattle
Rich and very rich peasantry	15	Skilled and educated	15 to hundreds of bags. Surplus. Hire labour.	40 plus Hired herding
Middle and poor peasantry	50–60	Semi and unskilled	15 bags minus. Household labour	1–40 Mainly 'relatives' herding
'Lumpen' peasantry and proletariat	25–30	Domestics, shop assistants. Petty self-employed and unemployed	Seldom have lands	No cattle

Source: Cooper 1980:137

Figure 3.4   *Social classes in Botswana, defined in terms of employment, lands and cattle (following Cooper)*

A further category should be added to Cooper's disaggregation for the present purpose: the very large cattle holders and ranchers, the 5% of rural households who alone own some 50% of the national herd according to the Rural Income Distribution Survey (1976:113).

For the 'Middle and Poor Peasantry' the consequence of their sub-breakpoint position in cattle and at the lands is that they are crucially reliant on urban wages, and '. . . the majority of these workers are keeping up their lands and cattle linkages out of necessity, but their cash inputs seldom enable them to reach . . . self-sufficiency in food, nor to reach into the "rich peasant" (40 plus head) level in cattle' (Cooper 1980:139). These observations concerning the small, even negative, cash returns from small cattle herds receive further support from other recent studies (Carl Bro 1981:4.131, Bailey 1981: Table 5.19).

The increasingly difficult situation of small herders is emphasised by Gulbrandsen for the Bangwaketse: on the one hand rapid population growth and the splitting of large herds on the death of the owner are creating increasing numbers of household units with unviable herds trying to establish themselves, while on the other hand earning opportunities through migrant mine employment are diminishing and, together with pressure on communal land resources, are making the chances of building viable herds more remote (1980:182–5).

Looking at the top end of the cattle distribution there is the probability of substantially increased accumulation, particularly post-Independence. Large cattle owners and ranchers were best placed to sustain their breeding herds through the mid-1960s drought and therefore to generate savings during the rapid rise in cattle prices 1970–74, to invest in additional water sources and stock. Although statistical evidence is lacking it is likely that a disproportionate amount of total investment in cattle production in the period was undertaken by the largest cattle owners and ranchers, thereby increasing their relative control of land and proportionate ownership of the national herd.

Although the outline model of development of cattle production regarded neither land nor labour as a constraint on aggregate historical accumulation of cattle it is clear that the expansion of cattle production has now begun to alter the social relations in land particularly, as water point owners attempt to establish permanent rights to land (the TGLP can be seen in this light) and to exclude prior users (notably hunter-gatherers) therefrom (see Chapter 9). Similarly in the lands areas, the growing movement to establish drift fences and define grazing and arable zones results from the growth of both cattle numbers and fields.

III Summary

The purpose of this chapter has been to identify the principal historical relations between cattle production and beef exports. With the availability of investible funds being the key exogenous factor in the dynamic of cattle production, beef exports (directly and indirectly a major source of private and public investible funds) have played an essentially similar role as other major sources of investible funds, namely migrant labour and (most recently) mining.

The expansion of extensive cattle production has been accompanied by far-reaching changes in the social relations of cattle production with increasing concentration of cattle ownership, increasing numbers of small unviable (or marginally viable) herds and increasing pressure by large cattle owners for privatisation of grazing lands as the 'frontier' of cattle expansion ends.

Part II – History

Part I was concerned with stating the hypotheses of the study and providing background on the international beef trade and cattle production in Botswana necessary for understanding the causes and effects of developments within Botswana's cattle and beef export sector.

The long-term growth pattern in both the world beef trade and cattle production in Botswana was found to be similar: a period of growth to the 1920s, collapse in the 1930s and growth re-established in the 1950s. Briefly, two long 'waves' separated by the Second World War.

Part II examines the affairs of the cattle and beef export sector in both of these 'waves'. In the first (c.1900–1949), the export sector is characterized as a reserve industry on the South African periphery (Part II A, Chapters 4, 5, 6); in the second (post 1950) as a growth industry within a still peripheral economy (Part II B, Chapters 7, 8, 9).

Part II A: Reserve Industry on the South African Periphery

Chapter 4
Establishment of a Reserve Industry
c. 1900–1923

During the first two decades of this century, beef cattle became the chief export of the Bechuanaland Protectorate. This occurred as a result of colonial consolidation (levying taxes, establishing 'native reserves' and 'European' freehold farming blocks and trading stores) and of the growth of the Johannesburg market on the one hand, and as a result of the decline of earlier exports (hunting products and gold) on the other. In short, during this period the Protectorate became 'locked in' to a role within Southern African accumulation as both a labour reserve and a supplier of cheap meat.

The beef cattle export industry so established was a 'reserve industry' – its product exported in its crudest form, its fortunes wholly vulnerable to the vagaries of external events and to manipulation by opposing interest groups in the South African meat industry, its own interests unprotected by an effective political power, its formal status 'outside' the state to which it was effectively subject.

Section I discusses the reasons for the rise of the trade and Section II the nature of the crisis it faced in the slump following the First World War, which led to South African protectionism and the entry of the Imperial Cold Storage and Supply Co. (ICS) into the Protectorate – the two dominant features of the next period in the industry's history, which culminated in its collapse in the mid-1930s. Section III concludes.

I. The reasons for the rise of the trade

Cattle supplies were the reason for the earliest European interest in the territory of the Tswana.[1] But until the late nineteenth century they were only one of a number of traded goods and less important than hunting products.[2] It was the establishment and rapid expansion of mining in South Africa from the 1870s, with its urban concentrations of mining and industrial workers at Kimberley and on the Witwatersrand, which created a demand for cheap sources of protein – with meat being a most convenient form given its abundance, acceptability and ease of transport on the hoof.

The trade from north of the Molopo before 1900 was probably small, intermittent and confined to breeding and draught stock for farming areas in the Cape and Transvaal. These lay closer than the still small mines and towns.[3] Moreover the Rinderpest epidemic of 1896 and Boer War of 1899–1902 must have been severe disruptions; they also resulted in substantial imports of meat from Australia and South America to South Africa.

A number of factors underlie the rise of cattle exports from the Bechuanaland Protectorate during the first twenty years of the new century. Firstly, the expansion of the mines; secondly the location of South Africa's cattle production; thirdly the nature of the meat demanded for the labour compounds; fourthly colonial consolidation in the Protectorate.

The main concentrations of cattle in South Africa were situated remotely from the expanding Witwatersrand behind the eastern escarpment in Zululand, Natal and the Transkei.[4] They were also more prone to tropical cattle diseases (particularly East Coast fever) than cattle on the highveld. By comparison, Southern Rhodesia and Bechuanaland Protectorate were well situated to supply the Witwatersrand. The nature of the market favoured drawing supplies of cattle from 'native reserves' (of which the Protectorate largely consisted); the mine and industrial compounds demanded cheap meat above all and the reserves (owing to their numerous cattle,[5] lack of alternative markets and absence of land rent) were the cheapest source.

With meat supplies being drawn from increasing distances to the

Witwatersrand, specialized intermediaries (dealers and speculators) emerged to organize the buying of livestock, linking to commission agents at the main markets. These commission agents saw to the transactions with buyers, and provided the dealers and speculators with finance for livestock buying.[6] Cold storage facilities at the main centres became an important link in the marketing chain. Owing mainly perhaps to the economies of scale in cold storage it was here that the largest agglomeration of capital in the meat industry was centred. Briefly, by 1905 the Imperial Cold Storage and Supply Company had emerged as the dominant force in South African meat wholesaling; it was formed through a merger of De Beers Cold Storage and Combrinck and Co., which had held the meat import supply contracts for the British troops during the Boer War.[7]

While the burgeoning export market would no doubt have given rise to African entrepreneurship in the Protectorate's cattle trade[8] it occurred at the same time as the consolidation of colonial administration in the territory, which favoured the formation of a predominantly white-owned trading system. The concession of white farming 'blocks' in the early 1900s brought settlers. Best asserts that they 'were ranchers first and traders second, but they quickly realized the close relationship of the two pursuits. They built up their herds with African livestock exchanged for clothing, hardware and other general merchandise' (1970: 600–601). Whatever the settler's priority may have been, a network of mainly European-owned trading stores arose which linked in easily with the highveld cattle buying chain, drawing finance from agents and dealers on the Witwatersrand. White traders also enjoyed the favour of the Government in excluding both Asians and Africans from commerce.[9] In the reserves traders were allocated or were rented, grazing rights by the chiefs and trekked cattle out – either directly for export (by rail or on the hoof) or first to the white farming 'blocks' for holding or growing out. Cattle trading and holding became and remained for the next half century, the basic operation of these 'blocks' (henceforth referred to as the freehold farms as they are commonly known, although Ghanzi was leasehold until the late 1950s).[10] 'The life of the Native does, it is true, still offer little scope for European enterprise apart from the operations of traders' remarked Pim (1933: 17). Imposition from 1899 of the 'Native taxes' (payable in cash), to pay the costs of colonial administration, provided an important incentive to cattle owners to sell.

Two major geographical components of the cattle trade in the Protectorate began to emerge. Firstly, the bulk of the trade emanated from the Ngwato reserve – the largest reserve, containing the most people, some two-thirds of the cattle population and the largest herds – forming the hub of the export trade to the south, with the cattle exported directly or held in the Tati, Tuli and Gaberones blocks. Secondly, a trade from Ngamiland to the Katanga mines began from 1914 owing to a disastrous epidemic of bovine pleuro-pneumonia in Barotseland from where the mines' meat supplies had previously been drawn (Van Horn 1977: 156; Pim 1933: 126).

Though uneven and intermittent (see Appendix Table A1) this trade to the Copperbelt was to remain the main market for Ngamiland cattle until 1967. The third component centred on the Ghanzi farms in the western Kgalagadi, buying immature stock from Ngamiland and the surrounding Kgalagadi villages and trekking them south.[11]

The rise of the cattle export trade coincided with the gradual decline of other commodity exports, principally hunting products and gold from the Tati.[12] Although in a good rainfall year grain exports could be substantial (e.g. £21,000 in 1909)[13] they were intermittent and increasingly less frequent.

Cattle exports escalated unevenly. Between 1905 and 1910 they were fairly stagnant (averaging about 3,000 head per annum according to official figures, though unrecorded exports might have been much higher). Superficially, this reflected the appearance of bovine pleuro-pneumonia ('lung sickness') in the Protectorate with resulting South African import restrictions. But Pim noted that an earlier outbreak of East Coast fever '. . . not in the Protectorate itself but in the adjacent areas of Rhodesia and the Transvaal, had already led to the imposition of restrictions on exports to the Cape Colony, then the best market, and the appearance of lung sickness (in 1905) led to these restrictions being intensified. Following on the Act of Union in 1909 the restrictions were extended to the other three provinces' (Pim 1933: 14). Coincidentally, the 1905–10 period seems to have been one of slack demand and domestic oversupply of meat in South Africa.[14] Thus this episode may be the first instance of what was to become a recurring pattern of veterinary restrictions against imports being imposed or tightened by South Africa whenever domestic prices weakened.

Exports were boosted after 1910 both by the recovered South

African market and by the opening of the Johannesburg municipal abattoirs in 1910 with their adjoining quarantine markets.[15] This '. . . enabled, for the first time, farmers from the buffer and quarantine areas, and the surrounding countries of Rhodesia, Bechuanaland, Swaziland and South West Africa, to forward their stock in sealed trucks for sale on the Johannesburg markets, which were otherwise closed to them'.[16] The Johannesburg quarantine market was to provide the main official outlet for Bechuanaland cattle sales until mid-century. Cattle sent to the quarantine market had to be sold and slaughtered immediately, with the meat passing directly to the consumers i.e. it was forbidden from entering the retail trade. Whatever veterinary grounds may have motivated these restrictions they caused quarantine market meat to be sold at a discount below the open market price by preventing the 'quarantine cattle' from being held over when prices were low and by limiting buyers to those wholesalers who could dispose of it quickly and directly to consumers; in effect, this meant the few wholesalers holding supply contracts for mine, industrial and other institutional compounds.

Export volume from Bechuanaland increased substantially to over 12,000 head per annum and the Protectorate government noted in 1914 that cattle exports to Johannesburg had become 'by far the principal export of the country' (Colonial Annual Report for Bechuanaland Protectorate 1913: 14: 6).

The rise of the export trade had brought with it the need for regulation of veterinary conditions, stock theft and fraud. The Veterinary Services Department was started in 1905, cattle brands were registered and penalties fixed for stock theft (Proclamation 7 of 1907). Buyers of cattle for export were obliged to take out expensive licences (£100 deposit), since '. . . it was felt that the natives required protection against possibly unscrupulous or fraudulent dealing on the part of some of them, who were merely birds of passage with no stake or interests in the country, and who in the event of proceedings being instituted against them would probably disappear as suddenly as they had come'[17] (Proclamation 39: 1911). This measure also had the effect, intentional or not, of confining cattle exporting to larger dealers.

The Bechuanaland Protectorate government also moved, rather belatedly, to extract revenue directly from the increasingly valuable cattle export trade – through a cattle export tax (Proc. 12 of 1916), the proceeds of which were meant to cover expenditure by the

Veterinary Services Department.[18] Cattle exports already contributed substantially to government revenue in an indirect manner through being the major source (at this time) of cash income for payment of the 'Native taxes'.[19]

The greatest boost to cattle imports into South Africa during this period came with the First World War, during which imports of cattle for other than immediate slaughter were permitted for the first time (and only time – since they were cut off again in 1923, never to be reinstated) since 1905. South African government sources cited veterinary improvements as the reason in the case of the Protectorate: in 1917 '. . . the Union government recognizing that the Southern Protectorate was a clean cattle district, decided to allow the introduction therefore of breeding animals as well as slaughter cattle, and subsequently extended this concession to animals from Ngamiland'. Quarantine camps were established at Ramatlabama and Sikwane on the southern border, 'the conditions of export being that the animals should serve a fourteen days quarantine in a fenced camp . . .'[20] Exports to South Africa then escalated rapidly – to 19,000 head in 1916–17 and 31,000 in 1920–21, by which stage 94% of Bechuanaland's cattle exports went to South Africa.[21]

But the actual reason for South Africa permitting the unrestricted import of cattle into the open markets was the shortage of meat during war-time – not any sudden attainment of new standards of veterinary hygiene in Bechuanaland, Southern Rhodesia and Swaziland! 'On the outbreak of war in 1914 South Africa became an exporting country practically overnight . . .'[22] supplying its generally low grade meat[23] (not otherwise in demand in the world beef trade at the time – see Chapter 2) to the warring armies. Exports of beef increased from 1 million lbs in 1910–14 to 143 million lbs in 1915–19.[24] From 1917 to 1919 slaughter stock prices in South Africa rose almost 70%[25] (in line with prices of most other agricultural commodities). Ready sources of meat were needed to cover the deficit created by exports and to satisfy the expanding urban demand during the war-time boom, for which investment in domestic manufacturing production (moving into the gap left by reduced imports) was partly responsible.

The war also proved extremely profitable for the Imperial Cold Storage and Supply Co. (ICS). After surviving liquidation proceedings in 1911 it entered a period of prosperity and expansion (into fruit, dairy and fish storage and meat export), achieving its greatest successes through its near monopoly of war-time meat exports (secured through controlling all the major coastal meat plants, except for the Union Fresh Meat Company at Durban).[26]

II. The Post First World War Crisis

As dramatic as the onset of war-time boom conditions which accelerated the Protectorate's entry into South Africa's markets was the post-war collapse after 1920 (summarized in Table 4.1) which heralded her re-exclusion. By 1924 slaughter stock prices had fallen to half of their 1920 level, export volumes had dwindled and export prices had crashed.

The post-war slump ushered in a period of instability culminating in the depression of the early 1930s. Since the strategies adopted by South African farmers, meat traders and government in the early 1920s to try to restore profitability were to have an enormous impact on the Protectorate during the next twenty years, it is necessary to dwell on them briefly.

Table 4.1: *The Post-war slump of the South African beef industry: a statistical picture*

	Cattle slaughtered in South African abattoirs	
1918–19		350,000
1922–23		381,000
1923–24		445,000

	South African beef exports, export prices and values		
		Prices	
	Volume (lb)	*(pence per lb)*	*Value (£)*
1919	46,363,000	5.89	1,138,000
1922	1,741,000	4.81	35,000
1924	9,601,000	2.57	119,000

	South African meat prices (pence per lb)		
	Beef	*Mutton*	*Pork*
1920	6.80	10.68	11.54
1924	3.91	7.68	7.48

Sources: Union Office of Census and Statistics:
"Official Yearbook of the Union of South Africa", No. 8 p.1058.
"Union Statistics for 50 years", Table H9.

Firstly, the dominant feature of the South African meat industry during the market collapse of the early 1920s was the sharp conflict which arose between farmers and meat packing and wholesaling interests – predominantly the ICS. The conflict was no doubt provoked by ICS's relatively monopolistic position in meat wholesaling and retailing at a time of steeply falling prices. Within ICS itself J. G. van der Horst (architect of the company's post-1911 reconstruction) was ousted as managing director by Sir David Graaff in 1921 – an associate of Jan Smuts and a man with the ambitions of Rhodes. Graaff resumed control of the company at a time when its popularity was as low as its market control was high. Such unpopularity, argued the Board of Trade and Industries in 1925, '. . . may in general be attributed to the chequered career and, at times, singular methods of cold storage enterprise. In the trade there have been too many commercial adventures, too many combines, overcapitalization, too many reconstructions, too many attempts at market control, and too great use of political influence' (1925:10). Secondly, the different strategies adopted by the white farmers' organizations, ICS and the state reflected this conflict.

Farmers' Reactions: South African white cattle farmers' reactions to the crisis were threefold.

(a) Agitation for embargo of cattle imports, from Southern Rhodesia and Bechuanaland Protectorate, was the most concerted response of farmers' associations from 1922 to 1924.[27]

(b) Agitation for regulation of monopolistic activities of middlemen (specifically the ICS), alleged to be manipulating the trade to the disadvantage of farmers.[28]

(c) Initiation of cooperative marketing agencies designed to secure a better return to the farmer. The Meat Producers' Exchange was formed in Johannesburg in 1921 with the object of stabilizing prices and eliminating unnecessary middlemen from the meat trade.[29] The Farmers Cooperative Meat Industries Ltd. (FCMI), formed at about the same time, had similar ambitions for Natal.

Of these three reactions to the crisis by white beef farmers the first was to achieve the most immediate success – especially after dissatisfied white farmers and industrial workers (following the 'Rand revolt' of 1922) had replaced the South African Party government of J. C. Smuts with the Nationalist–Labour coalition under J. B. M. Hertzog in 1924. Smuts' party was seen as representing 'big business', and one political charge made was that Smuts had made special concessions to favour the ICS.[30] The new government moved quickly to raise the rather token import restrictions imposed by its predecessor and initiated a period of severe agricultural protectionism which was to endure until the Second World War. At the same time (October 1924) the new government ordered a full commission of enquiry[31] by the Board of Trade and Industries into the affairs of the ICS and meat marketing in South Africa. The recommendations of the commission (unified cooperative societies controlling cold storage facilities in all major urban areas, under a statutory board of control) foreshadowed events of the mid-1930s, but were not immediately acted upon.

The third reaction by farmers (attempting to form independent marketing cooperatives) was a total failure – owing to mismanagement and intervention by the ICS.

ICS' reactions: The reaction of ICS and its associated companies to the market collapse was also threefold.

(a) *Export expansion:* In 1923 the Smuts government passed a Beef Export Bounties Act, paying one quarter penny per lb of beef exported as a subsidy, with the object of relieving the market of excess cattle.

Finding foreign markets was a problem, South Africa being unable to compete with the cost efficiency of South American countries on the British market. But in 1924 the first shipments of beef to Italy took place, Mussolini having embarked on a policy of importing frozen beef to keep urban living costs down. South Africa had managed to secure a quota in Italy by subsidising the Italian shipping lines (Van Biljon 1938: Ch. VIII).

The Beef Bounties Act was heavily geared to the benefit of ICS. Section 3 limited firms and societies to whom the bounty was payable to those which furnished the Minister within one month with 'a written undertaking that it would also act as agent for producers of slaughter cattle for the slaughtering, preparing and disposal at the producers' risk overseas of any beef . . . .'.[32] Only ICS and the FCMI (by then an ICS subsidiary) and the independent (but defunct by 1925) Union Fresh Meat Works, supplied the undertaking. 'When authority was given to the three firms to draw the bounty, nothing was done to lower their charges to the producer. Nor did the bounty go to the producer in the shape of a higher price for his export quality beef, it was actually lower than what he realised for the same article in the local market . . . It seems to be the general view that any benefits to the producer under this Act will be indirect.'[33]

(b) *Controlling the cheapest sources of beef:* Although the general stagnation of world beef markets limited the initial operation of the Beef Export Bounties Act (from £72,000 budgeted for bounties in 1923–24 only £1,225 was paid out), the opening of the new market for low-grade frozen beef in Italy, [34] together with the availability of export bounties from neighbouring countries[35] clearly encouraged ICS in the pursuit of its second strategy against the slump – a strategy which suited Graaff's business style. This was to secure monopoly control over large supplies of cheap beef, by entering into investment contracts with the administrations of South West Africa (under South African mandatory control), Southern Rhodesia and Bechuanaland Protectorate, for the setting up of meat works in return for a monopoly on meat exports from the territories. In South West Africa, the very favourable terms granted by the Smuts government to the ICS were a major focus of Nationalist-Labour criticism of ICS. They included a fifteen-year monopoly of exports overseas and 500,000 morgen of land for a nominal rental.[36] The ICS presence was to become the dominant issue in the beef industries of these territories during the later 1920s and 1930s.

(c) *Co-opting the cooperatives:* The third ICS strategy also related to controlling cheap sources of meat. The cooperative Meat Producers' Exchange set up in 1921 represented potentially powerful competition in the making – reinforced by what Graaff saw as '. . . the moral support of the whole government of the day and the sympathy and goodwill of the mining people . . .'.[37] In 1921 Prime Minister Smuts suggested to Graaff that the crisis in the meat trade owing to the price collapse might be countered by ICS teaming-up with the meat producers' exchange to handle the marketing of its members' meat. He made similar overtures to the Exchange itself and to the Farmers' Cooperative Meat Industries Ltd. (FCMI).

Reluctant negotiations followed, and, as a result of pressure from Rand Mines, an agreement was reached whereby Rand Cold Storage Ltd. (an ICS subsidiary) would distribute all Exchange meat.

Complaints of a meat combine followed,[38] farmer support for the Exchange fell away, and in the first year of its operations it imported twice as many cattle (from Southern Rhodesia, Bechuanaland Protectorate and South West Africa) as it obtained domestically – leading to further calls in Parliament for import restrictions.[39] Owing to mismanagement and alienation of members, the Exchange collapsed in 1923 when Rand Cold Storage gave notice to terminate its distribution agreement.

Concerning the FCMI, the negotiations with ICS resulted in the effective incorporation of the cooperative by 1925, through its receiving financial assistance from ICS repaid in shares sufficient to give ICS a controlling interest.[40]

In sum, state reaction in South Africa to pressures from both farmers and meat wholesalers was protectionist: import restrictions to appease the farmers and export subsidies, primarily for the relief of the meat trading interests concentrated in ICS.

The first import restriction was the ending in February 1923 of unrestricted entry of cattle from Southern Rhodesia and Bechuanaland. The Ramatlabama and Sikwane quarantine camps were shut down, and cattle imports were once more confined to the Johannesburg quarantine market.

The build-up of protectionist forces in South Africa was watched with dismay in the Protectorate. The bleak outlook for the people of the Protectorate in mid-1923 was poignantly summed up by Isang Pilane, Chief of the Bakgatla in an appeal to British Royalty (reminiscent of Khama, Bathoen and Sebele's appeal to Queen Victoria in the 1890s):

'The Union of South Africa has stopped cattle from crossing the border, with the exception of cattle that are railed direct to the Johannesburg quarantine market, for immediate slaughter. Today a certain section of the inhabitants of the Union is agitating for a complete embargo on all cattle from Rhodesia and the territories under His Gracious Majesty's Protection. If this becomes law, we see no hope for ourselves as a Nation and we humbly pray that Your Royal Highness should avert the threatened evil.

We are all South Africans, and can recognise no such artificial barriers as legally or morally right. The labour of our hands has assisted to build up the diamond and gold industries in the Union, and is still doing so. When drought and disease have visited our neighbours in the Union, we have sold them breeding stock freely and with goodwill, to enable them to replenish their herds, and we cannot understand what fault we have committed that such harsh measures should be proposed against us.

We see that the Great War has left poverty and distress behind it, and that our country has not escaped, but this is no reason why members of the same household should propose to destroy each other: Rather should we unite and endeavour to devise some common means to help each other to survive the evil times'.[41]

III. Conclusion

By the early 1920s the Protectorate had become established as a reserve area of the South African economy, mainly through colonial consolidation. The cattle export industry, growing with the Johannesburg market, was established within this formation as a reserve industry. But with the end of the War the expansionary phase ended and the full costs of being a reserve industry were threatening to be loaded upon it: namely to bear the cost of efforts by power groups within the South African industry to recover their profitability, without any recompense.

With the market collapse and looming South African protectionism the Bechuanaland Protectorate colonial government found itself in a three-sided crisis. Firstly, the major source of purchasing power for imports for the population of Bechuanaland Protectorate was under threat – also the major domestic source of government revenue.

Secondly, Bechuanaland Protectorate was falling victim to the protectionist policy of a state with which she was effectively integrated in almost all but name. South Africa was virtually the only market for exports and source of imports; customs receipts from the agreement of 1910 were the second most important source of government revenue; plans for full political integration with South Africa stood on the South African statute book (South Africa Act 1909). Alternative markets for Bechuanaland Protectorate beef did not exist, the export trade to the Copperbelt being only nascent at this time and confined to Ngamiland.

Thirdly, the post First World War collapse of commodity markets (which occurred in all western countries) ushered in an era of protectionist commodity trading in which governments, through international bargaining, were cast in as important a role as were the commodity producers and traders themselves. In the case of meat exporting, in which national veterinary standards are so important a component of product acceptability internationally, the government role became particularly crucial. The Bechuanaland Protectorate colonial government, lacking any independent resources, or a sizeable domestic market to use as a bargaining counter, was most ill-equipped to defend her major export trade, as the subsequent historical period was to prove.

Chapter 5
Consequences of Marginality I:
Collapse in the Depression 1923–39

The first two decades of the century had seen the establishment of beef cattle exports from Bechuanaland Protectorate as a 'reserve industry' on the South African periphery. In the next two decades the industry is caught up powerlessly in the maelstrom of industrial and national conflict in the region precipitated by falling local and world markets.

On the one hand exports of its cattle to South Africa are restricted to protect South African farmers; on the other hand the Imperial Cold Storage and Supply Co. (ICS) enters the Protectorate to try to profit from the restrictions. It sets up an abattoir which proves economically inoperable as a result of the imperial government's complicity with South Africa in imposing a 'voluntary' embargo on Bechuanaland Protectorate beef exports to South Africa.

Between the conflicting regional forces stands the Protectorate's government (i.e. the local colonial administration) trying on the one hand to defend the single gain the territory has reaped from the depression (an export abattoir), and on the other to find alternative markets and to build up dairy exports as an alternative to beef cattle sales to South Africa. With an indifferent imperial government and few resources of its own, it is outmanoeuvred by Southern Rhodesia for the Copperbelt market and has no redress against South Africa's increasingly tight import and transit restrictions, culminating in the total embargo from 1933–35.

Moving beneath the surface struggle for markets is the current of economic forces. The recovery of the South African market after 1933 coincides with the great drought of the mid-1930s. The 'smuggling' trade into South Africa, and the drought, reduce the cattle population by half sweeping away the government's vain attempt to establish beef exports overseas. The abattoir is finally abandoned and all attention turned to stemming the outflow of cattle, but without the resources to do so.

The dominant theme of the period is the manner in which an industry, despite enjoying a comparative advantage, is broken by the lack of an effective national government with the resources to protect its interests against foreign machinations and protectionism. It is in the nature of a 'reserve industry' that it is forced to bear the costs of falling markets.

I.   ICS and The South African Weight Restrictions

(a)   The Cattle Conference of 1923: Britain Concedes a Principle

After the exclusion of imported cattle from the open markets of South Africa (February 1923) pressure from white farmers for a total embargo continued to mount and by August the South African Ministry of Agriculture assured a farmers' conference that: 'The government will approach the administrations of the neighbouring states and territories with a view to devising some effective means whereby undue flooding of Union markets with animals of inferior quality may be obviated'.[1] To this end, Southern Rhodesia and Bechuanaland Protectorate (the principal cattle exporters) were invited to a conference at Pretoria in October 1923, together with Basutoland and Swaziland.

For the High Commission Territories a crucial question of principle was on the table at this conference; whether South Africa would be permitted by the British government unilaterally to infringe the terms of the 1910 customs union agreement with the High Commission Territories which specifically provided for the free flow of goods and services among the signatories. Britain's view was made clear in the High Commissioner's instructions to the Resident Commissioner (BP) before the conference, advising him: '. . . to be very cautious in any reference to the Customs Agreement . . . It is more important than ever that nothing should be said or done at this stage . . . to affect maintenance of the Customs Agreement'.[2] The customs union agreement provided for a fixed proportion (1.3% approximately) of the customs and excise duty revenues of the common customs area to be paid to the governments of the High Commission Territories. It was an important (and costless, for the British Treasury) source of revenue for administering the territories; the imperial government was clearly concerned that it should not be threatened.

The outcome of the conference (specifically the 800lb minimum liveweight limit on oxen imported) was short-sightedly regarded by the High Commission Territories and Southern Rhodesia as a victory when compared to the alternative of a total embargo – especially since the 800lb. limit was a low one imposed largely to appease public opinion in South Africa rather than exclude imports.[3] It had hardly any impact on Bechuanaland Protectorate's cattle exports. But, as Resident Commissioner (BP) Rey was to complain in 1934: 'The vital importance of the question of principle does not appear to have been realized'.[4] The door was thus opened for South Africa to tighten import restrictions at will on the same grounds on which these initial weight restrictions had been conceded.

Despite the obvious historical importance of the Cattle Conference of 1923 its proceedings were largely a formality because informal negotiations had been underway for some time, including the possibility of ICS establishing export abattoirs in Southern Rhodesia and Bechuanaland Protectorate. The enthusiasm of the BP administration for the ICS proposals clearly made them more willing to compromise the principle of free trade. Thus the Resident Commissioner's (BP) comment after the conference that '. . . if the Cold Storage scheme, which is under preliminary discussion, comes into being . . . the cattle industry of the Protectorate may be regarded as assured for many years to come'.[5]

ICS had initiated the negotiations with Southern Rhodesia and the Bechuanaland Protectorate in order to turn to its advantage whatever import restrictions might be imposed and export subsidies awarded. This was to offer to set up export abattoirs in return for a monopoly of their beef exports, on the model of the agreement reached with the South West Africa administration in 1922.[6]

In the event, the specific form of import restrictions agreed to at the conference (weight restrictions) seems to have been tailored to ICS's requirements, which were to obtain cheap supplies of low grade cattle for its overseas frozen beef contracts (mainly Italy) and its Johannesburg mining compound supply contracts.[7] There may also have been a racial motive behind the weight restrictions as Ettinger (1972:22, 23) suggests. There were many Afrikaner farmers in Swaziland, Bechuanaland Protectorate and Southern Rhodesia whose livelihood depended mainly on buying immatures in the 'native reserves' and growing them out; weight restrictions would both assure their access to immatures and affect their export market relatively little.

South African import restrictions combined with overseas export bounties (the other product of the 1923 Conference) meant cheaper and more profitably exploitable cattle surpluses in Southern Rhodesia and the Bechuanaland Protectorate. This point was not lost on other interested meat exporting firms. By early 1924 overtures had been made by Tati Company interests and Liebigs extract of meat company. The Tati Company offered a 'boiling down plant' in return for '. . . the right to purchase all the cattle which the natives have for sale over a certain period of years . . . and it is quite understood that if the business matures the natives may rely upon at all times being treated fairly and squarely'.[8] Liebigs intended to set up at Messina in the Northern Transvaal (near the junction of the BP and Southern Rhodesian borders) to '. . . absorb the poorer quality cattle which are unfit for, or are debarred from going to, the Union meat markets'.[9]

Seeing its interests threatened by Liebigs, ICS immediately announced its own intention of setting up at Messina '. . . in order to relieve the congestion caused by the surplus of scrub . . . cattle in the Northern Transvaal as well as in Southern Rhodesia'.[10] But the Messina plans failed to materialize and BP negotiations with Graaff (ICS) were already sufficiently advanced as to exclude the Tati proposal.

By April 1924 a draft agreement had been set out in terms of which ICS undertook to erect within 18 months a 'modern well-equipped' abattoir capable of handling at least 100 head per day, and to purchase at least 10000 head of cattle per annum in Bechuanaland Protectorate. In return they would receive exclusive cold storage and meat export rights for 10 years and a free grant of 250 000 morgen of Crown Land along the Molopo river. Lobatse was to be the location of the abattoir.[11]

The entire project was then almost aborted by the Secretary of State's refusal to permit the further alienation of Crown Land[12] and his unhappiness with the monopoly rights to be granted to ICS which was under '. . . public investigation from standpoint of national interest' by the new Nationalist-Labour government in South Africa.[13] Resident Commissioner (BP) Ellenberger sprang to the defence of ICS, arguing that: 'Enquiry into meat industry is . . . being instituted in order to discredit previous Government by showing if possible that contracts prejudicial to real interests of country were negotiated between Smuts and ICS . . . Commercial morality of Graaff's firm does not appear involved . . .'[14]

Through the raising of the South African weight restrictions by the newly elected Nationalist-Labour pact government under Hertzog in 1925 the BP administration finally convinced the Secretary of State to yield, on the grounds of the urgency of establishing an alternative market. The only concession that the BP could secure had been a year's delay in implementing the raised weight levels – short of Britain agreeing to transfer of the Protectorate to South Africa. Southern Rhodesia, to whom the new restrictions were applied immediately, had as an anticipatory measure, already concluded its cold storage agreement with ICS (September 1924).[15]

The final agreement with ICS (June 1925) contained only a rent-free lease of the Molopo land for 25 years, not a cession as in the Rhodesian case. The BP administration and High Commissioner congratulated themselves on securing an agreement which they considered more favourable than Southern Rhodesia had obtained. Sir David Graaff even requested that it be kept secret '. . . lest its publication . . . should expose him to the criticism that he had granted better terms to Natives than he was prepared to offer to a white population with responsible government'.[16] In fact there was little to choose between the two agreements, the main difference being that in the Rhodesian case a guaranteed producer price was stipulated, in return for which the government guaranteed ICS profits of at least 10%.

The entry of ICS was not universally welcomed within Bechuanaland Protectorate. Traders expressed their anxiety that the ICS might enter into the cattle trade itself, buying cattle directly from African herders instead of through them.[17] The Barolong people occupying parts of the Molopo land ceded to ICS protested against the order that they must be prepared to move if required to do so[18] while the Bangwaketse participated most reluctantly in the demarcation of the border between their reserve and the ICS land.[19]

But ICS made no attempt to fence the Molopo land let alone occupy it. They concentrated their initial efforts on buying into trading businesses in order to obtain cattle supplies readily, being most active in the Ngwato reserve where the largest numbers were available, and invoking Tshekedi Khama's displeasure thereby.[20] The cattle purchased were railed to Durban for slaughter at the FCMI works[21] and exported to Italy. Traders' fears were allayed by large purchases of cattle made from them. By contrast the construction of the Lobatse works went ahead only slowly and behind schedule. ICS's interests at this time were clearly in obtaining immediate cattle supplies for their Italian contract and in making use of their surplus manufacturing capacity in South Africa to process them.

(b)   Undermining the abattoir: the 'Voluntary Embargo' of Bechuanaland's beef exports

When the ICS Lobatse works were nearing completion at the end of 1927 (a full year later than the contract specified) the High Commission took the unnecessary diplomatic step of assuring the Union government that in accordance with South African Government Notice No. 40 of 1926 no meat from animals below the minimum import weights would be slaughtered at Lobatse for export to South Africa. The South African response to this gratuitous assurance was to state that it was considering the embargo of BP beef altogether, on the grounds that BP could not be exempted 'from the prohibition which at present operates against the import of beef from Rhodesia'.[22] The Southern Rhodesian ban had been imposed in 1925. The High Commission's assurance had raised the matter anew in South African government offices.

The High Commissioner replied merely that he appreciated South Africa's current agricultural difficulties and would not therefore press the matter of acceptance of Lobatse beef 'until circumstances are more propitious'.[23] He added that Southern Rhodesia had been given compensation for the ban of their beef. South Africa then undertook to 'consider sympathetically any proposals on the part of the Protectorate which, whilst not adversely affecting the interest of the Union, might provide some *solatium* to the Protectorate for the potential loss of trade involved'.[24] Inexplicably, the matter was taken no further by the High Commission. The obvious *solatium* was a reduction on South African railway rates as enjoyed by Southern Rhodesia.[25] The matter of entry of Lobatse beef was not raised again until after the Second World War, despite the absence of any formal exclusion thereof by South Africa.

South Africa's stance indicated a concern to restrict the machinations of ICS on the South African beef markets and to provide another sop to white farming opinion, rather than to decrease the volume of beef imported. Exports to South Africa would not be affected overall since cattle exceeding the embargo weight could still be exported live instead of being slaughtered at Lobatse, as the BP administration pointed out in frustration. ICS's unpopularity with the South African government had increased further since the commission of enquiry of 1925[26] and accusations of ICS manipulation of meat markets were a major factor leading to the legislation of 1932 and 1934 setting up the Livestock and Meat Industries Control Board to regulate the sale of meat in South African urban areas.

ICS reacted strongly to the prohibition, declaring that the company would suffer 'severe financial loss' and must limit the operation of the works as a result, since 'it was always intended that the preparation of meat for the fulfilment of mining contracts held by the company in Johannesburg, as well as export, should be undertaken from Lobatsi'.[27]

The question then arose of the fulfilment of the terms of the 1925 agreement. When by late 1928 the BP Cold Storage Limited had not begun operations, the High Commissioner reminded ICS of its obligations, arguing (incongruously, in view of the content of his correspondence with the Union government over the meat ban) that: 'There was never any suggestion that the output of the works should be sold in Johannesburg, and the argument that the Company had been gravely handicapped by the action of the Union government . . . had no bearing on the Company's obligation to commence slaughtering at Lobatsi'.[28]

ICS in turn complained that 'it is difficult to understand why the Administration itself was a consenting party to the closing of a natural outlet for its principal industry. Altogether we cannot but feel that our interests have not been safeguarded . . .'[29]. They were unprepared now to operate the works which had become uneconomic both because of the ban on beef to South Africa and because South African railway rates on meat had not been reduced as anticipated at the time of the agreement, making live railage of cattle more worthwhile than that of meat.

The BP administration and the High Commission found themselves now with no means of demanding the operation of the works. Funds certainly would not be forthcoming from the British government for a state take-over and no other meat firm was now expressing interest. No profit would derive from simply cancelling the agreement under these circumstances. All they could do was to castigate ICS verbally that they were 'unable to accept any of the Company's excuses as set out in their letters . . . either in regard to the failure to commence slaughtering or the purchase of stock'[30] (ICS had not purchased the contracted 10000 head per annum in each year since the agreement).

In summary, with the downturn of markets after 1920 the Protectorate's beef cattle export industry required a firm defence of its interests by the colonial power if it was not to be saddled with a disproportionate share of the burden of the slump. Instead Britain conceded South Africa's breach of the customs union agreement and then threw away the one gain (the Lobatse abattoir) reaped by the Protectorate from the South African restrictions by imposing the 'voluntary embargo' of Bechuanaland beef exports to South Africa. The abattoir thereby became a stillborn investment. For the ICS the situation was not without gain despite the non-viability of the abattoir. The South African weight restrictions had created an otherwise officially unsaleable surplus of lean cattle which ICS drew on for its overseas contracts, railing them out and processing them at Durban.

II. The Dog in the Manger: ICS and the Protectorate's Beef 1929–31

In 1928 and 1929 ICS and Bechuanaland cattle owners reaped the benefit of a brief upturn in both prices (export and South African) and export volume. But thereafter prices slipped to their lowest level of the century, reaching their nadir in 1933. ICS found itself in a financial crisis and the international conflict within the region over markets was extended to shares of the overseas export contracts, bringing further losses for the Protectorate.

(a)   ICS's financial crisis and speculative strategies in the
       Protectorate

ICS's objective in entering into the agreement to set up the Lobatse
abattoir was to gain control of BP's cheap cattle resources in order
to use them for fulfilling overseas and South African supply contracts. However, another objective became apparent in the late
1920s.

   This was a purely speculative one: to secure whatever assets and
concessions might either be useful for future exploitation if and
when market conditions improved enough to make it worthwhile,
or (and this was more to the point at the time) might be used to
advantage by competitors. This speculative motive became primary
during succeeding events as the company entered a financial crisis
and world market prices collapsed.

   ICS's speculative objective was first apparent with regard to land.
In late 1928, in the same breath as they defended their unprepared-
ness to operate the Lobatse abattoir, ICS offered to set up a meat
extract plant in BP 'in order to further assist in the removal of scrub
cattle from the Territory' and as 'part of the suggested arrangement
in regard to us leasing one million acres of land'.[31] Government, by
now most chary in its dealings with ICS, replied that its attitude on
the land question would depend on the outcome of the negotiations
for the meat extract plant.[32]

   The pattern of the negotiations foreshadowed the more dramatic
events which were to follow in 1931. When in early 1929 the
administration demanded a rent of £1 000 per annum for the one
million acres, negotiations for the meat extract plant broke down.
The administration's bargaining hand was then fortuitously (and
temporarily) strengthened by a new offer from Liebigs of a
meat extract works, either at Lobatse or just over the border in the
Cape Province of South Africa. ICS responded by delivering the
machinery for a meat extract plant to the Protectorate. When no
concrete offer emerged from Liebigs the ICS machinery was
removed.[33]

   By 1930, it was clear that ICS was in a critical position financially:
overcapitalized and rift by conflict within its directorate. Sir David
Graaff was forced to retire.[34] This crisis was blamed on 'the large
number of unprofitable subsidiary enterprises embarked upon during recent years'.[35] The Lobatse works stood idle and the Bulawayo
and Walvis Bay plants were under threat of closure.

Circa late 1930, ICS made a bid to rescue its Southern Rhodesian operation. This sparked off an inter-firm conflict over beef supplies and markets in which the South African and Southern Rhodesian governments, as well as BP, became embroiled. The episode is related in some detail since it illustrates well the position occupied by the Protectorate in this period with regard to the interests and power of foreign meat firms and governments.

(b)   The Southern African 'Beef War' of 1931

ICS bought a small cold store in the Congo with the object, it seems, of obtaining meat supply contracts for fulfilment from Bulawayo.[36] ICS's move into the Congo disturbed the balance of power between ICS and the only other major meat supply conglomerate of the region, the Southern Rhodesia based Congo Rhodesian Ranching Company of Mr Barnett ('Bongola') Smith. Bongola Smith's companies [37] held all the major meat supply contracts[38] in the Congo, fulfilling them with live cattle railed from Southern Rhodesia. Smith, through his company connections in Belgium, enjoyed close relations with the Belgian government. [39]

At about the same time that ICS was breaking into Smith's 'home territory', Smith bought up the only non-ICS associated coastal meat works in South Africa, the Union Cold Storage Company in Durban.[40] This move was made in order to enter the overseas export trade and (according to Smith) in retaliation for ICS entering his preserve. By tendering rock bottom prices,[41] Union Cold Storage secured substantial shares of the 1931 continental supply contracts in competition with ICS. ICS previously had been unchallenged for this market.

The involvement of the Bechuanaland Protectorate in the struggle between Smith and ICS resulted from the outbreak of Foot and Mouth disease in Southern Rhodesia in March 1931. In response to this outbreak Northern Rhodesia embargoed the transit of live cattle from Southern Rhodesia thus preventing Smith from supplying his Congo contracts.

South Africa, taking the opportunity to cast further her protectionist net, embargoed the transit of both beef and live cattle, thereby leaving ICS's Bulawayo works without access to the overseas market. The Congo also embargoed the entry of both live and dead meat from Southern Rhodesia – the latter apparently at the instigation of Smith, to head off any attempt by ICS to move into the gap left in the Congo. In the meantime, Smith filled that gap with supplies of deboned beef railed from his Durban works.

Through the stalemate between the two firms – one (ICS) monopolizing Rhodesian meat exports and the other (Smith's) monopolizing the Congo's meat import contracts – Southern Rhodesia was cut off from the only remaining market for her cattle. The Southern Rhodesian Government therefore intervened in its own interest to arrange a settlement between the two.

Not wanting to turn the government down flatly, ICS reluctantly entered into negotiations for sale of the Bulawayo plant to Smith, but asking so high a price (£140 000 against Smith's valuation of £35 000)[42] that sale was out of the question. Smith then offered to hire the works on the condition that ICS undertook to keep out of the Congo market, which was unacceptable.[43]

At this point (August 1931), Smith approached Bechuanaland Protectorate Resident Commissioner Rey with an offer to slaughter cattle in the Protectorate for export to the Congo, either at the ICS's idle Lobatse works (if the Administration could induce ICS to sell), or at a new abattoir to be built in Francistown.

By all accounts, 1931 had been a most severe year for the Bechuanaland Protectorate. With produce prices at their lowest levels of the century the rains failed, marking the onset of the great drought of the early 1930s. Compounding the hardship, South Africa had seized the chance provided by the Southern Rhodesian Foot and Mouth outbreak to embargo completely the import and transit of Bechuanaland Protectorate cattle. After vigorous Bechuanaland Protectorate appeals and the erection of a 700-mile long police cordon along the border with Southern Rhodesia to prevent cattle movement, South Africa relented partially to permit entry from the relatively cattle-poor south[44] of the country. Nevertheless, the principal area of supply of Bechuanaland's principal export had been cut off from its only market.[45]

Resident Commissioner Rey grasped eagerly at Smith's offer which represented a three-fold opportunity for relief: to provide a market for the embargoed northern cattle; to break out of the sterile monopoly agreement with ICS,[46] and, by establishing a new market, to escape from exclusive dependence on South Africa.

A verbal agreement was quickly thrashed out with Smith whereby he would erect a 100 head per day abattoir at Francistown, the administration lending him £5 000 towards the £25 000 capital costs. Rey's strategy was that once a firm contract with Smith was concluded, the ICS agreement should either be terminated (on the basis of the firm's several infringements thereof), or ICS should be forced, under threat of termination, to accept an agreement whereby Smith would operate in the embargoed north of the territory. At worst, it would still be worthwhile to buy ICS out and use the Lobatse cold storage for dairy products (as ICS were already doing).

The High Commissioner responded enthusiastically, cabling the Secretary of State for immediate authorisation to lend £5 000 for the Francistown abattoir, and pressing for '. . . this exceptional opportunity of gaining a foothold in the Congo market to be taken...'. Strenuous resistance from ICS was anticipated against '. . . so formidable a rival'. 'The Government is, however, in a strong position and I do not despair of reaching an agreement'.[47]

But forces more powerful than ICS were at work to block the agreement with Smith. The delayed reply from London was lukewarm, suggesting instead a joint conference of Bechuanaland Protectorate, Southern Rhodesia and Northern Rhodesia in order to negotiate transit of embargoed Southern Rhodesia and Bechuanaland Protectorate cattle. The opinion of the Dominions Office was also voiced that bringing Smith into the Bechuanaland Protectorate would amount to 'taking sides' in his dispute with ICS and encourage monopolistic tendencies. Southern Rhodesian lobbying in London was clearly in evidence.

Resident Commissioner Rey replied angrily:

> 'Proposal appears calculated to sacrifice our interests in vain attempt to help Southern Rhodesia' by linking 'our cattle which are clean with Southern Rhodesia cattle which are diseased'.[48]

With further pressure from Rey and the High Commissioner permission was finally (mid October) forthcoming from London to negotiate the Francistown abattoir agreement. But a crucial rider was attached to Rey's instructions: the first step must be that the High Commission obtain from ICS a firm undertaking that they would not carry out their contractual obligations. The Imperial Secretary was despatched from Pretoria to Cape Town specifically for this purpose. In the meantime Smith was to be told nothing.

ICS had much to lose in the affair – far more was at stake than their idle Lobatse works. If Smith ousted them from their cold storage contracts in Southern Rhodesia and the Protectorate he would increase his control of resources in cheap cattle significantly and further undercut ICS in bids for future continental contracts. Furthermore, in their parlous financial state ICS had pledged their assets to their bankers, including the concessions in Bechuanaland Protectorate and Southern Rhodesia, the loss of which could therefore be fatal.[49]

ICS now seized this opportunity (which by design of London or bungling of the High Commissioner had been put into their laps) to take the initiative in the matter out of Smith's and Rey's hands. They played their role well. Arguing that they held 50% of the Congo market they pleaded that their negotiations with the Congo for entry of beef from Bulawayo were about to be finalized. If successful then Bechuanaland Protectorate would receive a share of the Southern Rhodesian quota to the Congo. If unsuccessful the ICS would themselves set up an abattoir at Francistown! The High Commissioner agreed to hold the matter until the ICS directors' meeting of 14th October – a meeting which was then delayed until the 23rd, and yielded only the request for a further ten days grace in which to conclude the Congo negotiations. The only compensation demanded by the High Commissioner in return for these delays was that ICS purchase 600 head of embargo zone cattle – an undertaking which remained unfulfilled.[50]

Rey was furious at this turn of events:

'Needless to say the contentions advanced by the Imperial Cold Storage are mostly rubbish and inaccurate . . . (T)heir whole object was, of course, quite clearly to prevent . . . our negotiations with Smith for the establishment of a factory at Francistown'.[51]

Abundant evidence was available that ICS were not established in the Congo market and that Southern Rhodesia most certainly would not share with Bechuanaland Protectorate any Congo quota it obtained. The suggestion was ludicrous that ICS would erect a second abattoir in the Protectorate when their first was standing idle!

As far as ICS's Congo negotiations were concerned, far from promising a favourable outcome they had in fact been halted. While ICS had found London on their side against Smith's interest in Bechuanaland Protectorate, they were now blocked by the imperial factor in the Congo. The local administration had finally acceded to Southern Rhodesian and ICS appeals for entry of Bulawayo beef only to meet with stubborn refusal from Brussels to admit beef until such time as live cattle could also be admitted – ostensibly as an absolute veterinary safeguard! Clearly, Bongola had not been idle in exercising his Belgian connections.

By late October it was clear to Rey that ICS's blocking tactics and Smith's being kept in the dark had lost the Francistown abattoir for Bechuanaland Protectorate. Smith had been motivated to make the offer partly in order to supply his Congo contracts and (most importantly) in order to enrol the support of the British government in his efforts (i) to wrest control of Bechuanaland Protectorate cattle supplies from ICS and (ii) to obtain from South Africa transit permission for Bechuanaland Protectorate cattle and beef to enable him to fulfil his continental contracts. What he had not bargained for (but which was now becoming clear) was that London would sacrifice Bechuanaland Protectorate's economic interests whenever they were in conflict with those of Southern Rhodesia and (as was shortly to be brought home to him) South Africa.[52]

In early November, Smith withdrew his Francistown abattoir offer with the excuse that his losses on the 1931 contracts were too great and the 'exchange situation' too uncertain to permit the investment. But clearly the substantive grounds lay elsewhere.[53]

Smith's concern now was to complete his 1931 continental contracts, for which he required urgent permission from South Africa for the transit of 1 000 Bechuanaland Protectorate embargo-zone cattle to his Durban works. He was most keen not to lose any leverage which the British government might be prepared to exert on South Africa for this purpose. In appeasement for the withdrawal of the abattoir offer he therefore intimated that South Africa had, at his insistence, given him a secret assurance that he would be permitted to fulfil at least 25% of his future continental contracts with Protectorate cattle, on the grounds that these were essential for winning the contracts.[54]

However, with regard to the immediate consignment of 1 000 head the Union Secretary for Agriculture had refused. At first he had cited veterinary difficulties regarding off-loading *en route* as the reason. But when Smith offered to avoid off-loading *en route* within South Africa altogether he cabled back: 'Merely mentioned off-loading difficulties *en route* but as you are aware this not only reason why restrictions imposed on cattle northern Protectorate' and

'Minister moreover of opinion that cattle procurable in Union'.[55]

South Africa's motives in imposing the embargo on the disease-free northern Protectorate were thus revealed clearly: not only to keep Bechuanaland Protectorate cattle out of the South African market but also to force the filling of the continental beef export contracts with South African cattle.

But if Bongola Smith had thought that such evidence of flagrant abuse by South Africa of veterinary regulations at Bechuanaland's expense would sting the British High Commission to do something about it, he was quickly to be disillusioned. The only appeal to South Africa came from the Bechuanaland Protectorate Resident Commissioner himself, and this was confined to the transit of 1 000 head – lest mention of more fundamental issues indicate knowledge of South Africa's private arrangement with Smith and thereby jeopardise the 'guarantee' to allow 25% of future contracts to be fulfilled in Bechuanaland Protectorate! Predictably, the appeal failed. 'They now know that they have got us cold' commented Rey.[56]

This was the last card that Bongola Smith played in the Protectorate. He excused himself from a verbal offer made to purchase 10 000 head per year in return for grazing rights. The effectiveness of Smith's business style in this period of protectionism and counter protectionism lay in operating from states in which he could in the 'national cause' obtain government support for his dealings. In Bechuanaland Protectorate the colonial power had shown clearly that there was to be no defence of 'national interests' against foreign machinations and protectionism. It was therefore no place in which to tie up money in an export-oriented investment.

By the end of 1931 the winnings and losses were clear, the scoreboard reading roughly as follows:

ICS: Defeated Smith in Bechuanaland Protectorate (with substantial help from Southern Rhodesia and the Dominions Office). Failed completely to break into the Congo market. The victory in Bechuanaland Protectorate was more substantial than the mere blocking of Bongola Smith suggests: ICS had demonstrated that it could flout the terms of its agreement with Bechuanaland Protectorate and get away with it.

'Our position now', commented Rey, 'is, of course, infinitely worse than when we started negotiating with Smith . . . They know that our only remedy is to cancel the contracts, which won't help us in the least now that Bongola is out of the running'.[57] ICS's counter-offers evaporated and they under-fulfilled by half their cattle purchasing obligation with impunity. The High Commissioner washed his hands of the matter.[58]

Bongola Smith: Won in the Congo and lost in the Protectorate. The latter was no substantial defeat since he suffered no financial loss and gained the knowledge that Bechuanaland Protectorate was an unsafe investment proposition. His victory in the Congo was substantial and marked the success of his overall challenge to ICS: entry into ICS's continental export market and exclusion of ICS from his own Copperbelt market. In 1932 he edged ICS out of the Italian contract altogether, and in 1934 sold the Union Cold Storage to them. In the Congo, despite the cut-back in copper production in 1932, his company ELAKAT prospered, remaining dominant until the 1960s.

Southern Rhodesia: Failed to secure an immediate market for its embargoed beef. Succeeded in preventing a permanent loss of the Congo market to Bechuanaland Protectorate by blocking Smith's investment plans in the Protectorate.

South Africa: Succeeded in manipulating veterinary regulations to its own advantage with impunity. No losses.

Bechuanaland Protectorate: For all parties there was some gain to set against any losses – except Bechuanaland Protectorate which lost right across the board: Congo market, Francistown abattoir and South African market and transit rights.

III.   Switching Products: Defeat in Dairying

The problematic attempts by the Protectorate government to get foreign meat companies to locate in the territory have been the focus of discussion so far. The government's other major strategy in the late 1920s and early 1930s to reduce the impact on incomes of falling markets and South African import restrictions met with no greater success. This was the campaign to promote dairy production for export. In terms of export revenues in the 1920s, hides and smallstock sales were the principal sources after cattle sales, followed by sales of cream to South Africa and Southern Rhodesia.

In the mid-1920s the BP administration embarked on a dairy promotion campaign, encouraging cattle owners to cream their milk as a source of cash, retaining the skimmed milk for domestic consumption. A dairy expert was appointed[59] and a Dairy Department established.

The reason for the relatively greater interest in dairy promotion, by comparison with hides and small stock, seemed to be that the Administration believed that dairy export could be developed quickly and effectively using relatively few resources: with whole milk already available at cattle posts and farms it was only a matter of applying a simple hand-operated separator to obtain cream, the relatively slow deterioration of which (by comparison with fresh milk), allowed time for marketing to a creamery to produce butter, cheese or ghee.

The campaign was at first strikingly successful, coinciding as it did with a time when outlets for other livestock products were urgently needed. White creamers' objections to Africans being allowed to participate 'on the grounds of cleanliness and the possibility of communication of disease'[60] were rendered groundless by inspection, and the value of dairy products exported had risen to almost £9000 by 1931[61], with most originating from the Tati zone and Lobatse block.

ICS took advantage of the increasing dairy traffic to make use of their idle abattoir and cold store at Lobatse for butter churning and storage. Tati cream was exported to Southern Rhodesia. In late 1931, at the height of the abortive northern abattoir negotiations, the Rhodesia Cooperative Creameries Ltd. agreed to set up a butter factory at Francistown. Despite ICS objections (on the grounds that the Lobatse creamery would lose business thereby and that they should in any case have been given the first option on a Francistown creamery), the RCC creamery materialised – just before the series of Foot and Mouth disease outbreaks beginning in January 1933 which were to result in the embargo of virtually all the Protectorate's export produce (see p.99). Through the existence of their processing and storage facilities the Lobatse and Francistown creameries enabled both the earlier lifting of the dairy embargo (November 1933, together with hides and skins) and the continued production of cream for stockpiling of butter during the embargo.[62] The cattle embargo was lifted only in mid-1935.

The successes in the dairy industry in the early 1930s led commentators to overglorify its potential. The Pim report (1933:133) went so far as to raise the question of whether cattle owners in BP should concentrate on producing meat or cream. The Union Superintendent of Dairying (E. Hardy) commented on his 1933 visit:

> 'The possibilities of the Protectorate from a dairy point of view are so enormous that one feels justified in raising the question as to what the position will be in regard to finding a market for the large quantities of dairy produce which are likely to be produced once the schemes of (water) development and cattle improvement at present in operation and contemplated are producing results'.[63]

But for once, export marketing provided relatively few problems. With the establishment of the South African Dairy Industries Control Board in 1930[64] Bechuanaland Protectorate was brought under its jurisdiction and, theoretically at least, received equal treatment with South African producers.[65] The main obstacle lay rather at the point of production. Although dairy output increased rapidly to the early 1930s it then reached a ceiling of some half a million pounds of butterfat per annum, worth less usually than the erratic small stock and hides sales and confined to the white farming blocks and African cattle posts most accessible to road and rail. Decline set in during the mid-1930s. This was in large part due to the general disruption of the cattle industry by drought and 'smuggling' (halving the cattle population), poverty, and the consequent abandonment of farms in the Tuli Block and Tati.[66] But the decline was based upon the smallness of the surplus of milk that could be obtained without supplementary feeding together with the dependence of both calves and children on the limited full-cream milk supply.

Poverty, and the recovery of beef prices, drew opposition to the dairy promotion campaign. In 1935 Chief Bathoen complained that inspectors from the Dairy department came often 'to urge the Bangwaketse to cream all the milk produced by their cattle and that they (should) live on skim milk. Lectures on the usefulness of cream have been given here in the last ten years and each time the tribe unanimously replied that they cannot do without milk, it being a necessary article of diet'.[67] The Medical Department of the Administration was most outspoken, questioning the advisability of pursuing the development of the dairy export industry at a time of increasing TB and deteriorating physique among Batswana:[68]

'The establishment of Native dairies and the collection of cream from cattleposts has been strenuously developed in the Native reserves, with the object of bringing revenue into the country. It is questionable if the small additional revenue will in any way compensate for the reduction of the much needed milk and cream in their diet' (Annual Medical and Sanitary Report BP 1934).

In the resulting conflict with the Dairy Department (and the Resident Commissioner), the Medical Department found an ally in the Veterinary Services Department, concerned with calf mortality:

'I consider that commercial dairying cannot be reconciled with the true welfare of the cattle industry, except where special conditions for additional feeding are present. The country is an arid one and does not (except immediately after the rains and in exceptional animals) permit the cow to secrete more milk than can be beneficially used by the calf'.
(Chief Veterinary Officer Hay 1940).[69]

By the late 1930s the Medical Officer in Ngwato reported favourably upon the improved health of children which he associated with the decline in creaming.[70] When the Union Superintendent of Dairying revisited BP in 1942 he found the Lobatse creamery no longer operating and the cream collection network from cattleposts considerably reduced.[71] Creaming remained at most a declining sideline. The Francistown creamery closed ca. 1960. Even with a doubled cattle population, by 1970 commercial sales of butterfat were only half a million pounds compared to over three quarters of a million pounds in 1931.

To sum up, already by the early 1930s when dairy exports were at their peak it should have been clear that the ambitious plans for expansion of the industry were misfounded and that it would in no way substitute for cattle and beef exports as a source of revenue. But the great drought and cattle selling were major disruptive factors.

IV. Anatomy of the Collapse

In the 1933–37 period occurred the great drought and cattle selling which cut the cattle population back to its early 1920s size and resulted in the final abandonment of ICS's Lobatse abattoir. Not until the early 1950s did the cattle population recover to its 1933 level. A 1939 government report reviewed the experience as follows:

'In 1933/34 over 1 000 000 head of cattle were inoculated against Foot and Mouth disease in the Protectorate and the total cattle population can be estimated conservatively at 1 250 000 head. Today the cattle population of the Territory is known, as the result of an accurate census, to be 650 000 head. After making generous allowances for losses through disease and drought a reasonable estimate of the number of cattle smuggled from the Protectorate into the Union during the four years 1935–38 is between 350 000 and 400 000 head. The price of cattle in the Protectorate has risen steadily since 1935 until it has reached its present level of approximately 9s. per 100 lbs liveweight which may be termed 'smuggling parity' i.e. Union prices less smuggling expenses.'[72]

The causes of the collapse are complex, involving the coincidence of a rising market for cattle in South Africa on the one hand, and on the other drought, South African import restrictions and failure of the Bechuanaland Protectorate government's bid to export beef overseas from Lobatse. These two groups of causes are categorized below as the 'forces of demand' and the 'forces of supply' respectively.

(a)   The forces of demand: the rising market for cattle in South Africa in the mid-1930s

The South African government reacted strongly to the collapse of agricultural prices after 1929 by stepping up hugely its agricultural subsidization (including subsidies for stock purchase) and export promotion (Export Subsidy Act of 1931). It also took every opportunity to block imports: in the case of beef this meant invoking veterinary grounds for embargo at the least excuse. A marketing board (The SA Livestock and Meat Industries Control Board) was set up in 1932 to regulate the marketing of meat to the major urban centres.

But it was the rapid expansion of gold production after 1932 which provided the public resources for the subsidization programme and was itself the main force reviving the South African demand for meat. When Britain devalued the pound sterling in September 1931 the South African government at first refused to follow, but then did so in 1932. This created a bonanza of revenue for the mining houses and the state. Between 1933 and 1934 South African government revenue increased by almost one third (£29 million to £38 million) through the more than trebling of its gold mining tax revenue (£3.5 million to £14.5 million).[73] Gold mining became much more profitable overnight; its rapid expansion was based upon drawing in increasing amounts of migrant labour through vigorous recruiting campaigns in the reserves. In Bechuanaland labour recruiting and drought raised the proportion of the population away in South Africa on migrant labour from 6% in 1936 to 10% in 1940 (Massey 1981: Fig. 3.1).

With the growth in labour recruitment and incomes came the increased demand for meat. Prices of South African slaughter stock bottomed out in 1933 and then rose by 44% to 1935.[74] With Protectorate cattle exports to South Africa having been totally embargoed for over two years (1933–35) the result was to increase greatly the gap between cattle prices in South Africa and the Protectorate.[75] This in turn increased the attractiveness for South African border farmers of buying cattle from Bechuanaland Protectorate both for replenishing their drought-ravaged draught and breeding stock and for 'growing out' for the Johannesburg market.

(b)   The forces of supply: the rising need of Batswana cattle owners to sell

(i)   *Drought and SA import restrictions*
Ever since the South African weight restrictions had been raised to an effective level in 1926 the BP cattle price had been depressed relative to that in South Africa, making sale across the border more attractive. Ironically, within the customs union area it was this 'free trade' which was declared 'illegal' and not the illegal trade restrictions which forbade it. At first South Africa had reacted sharply to the 'smuggling' trade, demanding that BP take preventive measures – particularly against Isang Pilane of the Bakgatla whom they regarded as a major culprit.[76] But the small size of the trade

rendered it a minor irritation to which, until the early 1930s, the South African veterinary authorities largely turned a blind eye.

However, the severe drought of the mid-1930s created poverty and a desperation to dispose of stock before they too died. Moreover, after the Foot and Mouth disease outbreak of 1933 South Africa embargoed virtually all Protectorate produce under the cloak of veterinary protection: grains, dairy products, hides, karosses, handicrafts and fruit.[77] The colonial annual report for Bechuanaland for 1933 commented that 'from a trade point of view, the year is one of the darkest on record . . . and the purchasing power of the country was reduced to such an extent as to constitute a state of penury for its inhabitants'. Finally, when the South African market re-opened in April 1935 it was for an annual quota of 10 000 head, still subject to weight restrictions (BP's exportable surplus was some 30 000 to 50 000 head).

The result of the increasing demand in South Africa and the rising need to sell in the Protectorate was that 'smuggling' was trans- formed from a 'profitable hobby' into a vigorous trade, initiated and financed by South African cattle speculators and farmers (and so humorously depicted by the South African writer H. C. Bosman, in his stories about South Africa's Marico district, flanking the Protec- torate's southern boundary).[78]

The South African government demanded of the High Commis- sioner that the flood of cattle be stopped, even making the limited reopening of the market in April 1935 conditional thereon. But the additional police patrols which the BP government was obliged to deploy for this purpose failed to stem the tide and in 1937 South Africa set up its own police cordon along the border. This was apparently more effective, but with the increasing relative price of cattle in the Protectorate the 'smuggling' trade was self-stabilizing in any case.

(ii) *The failed attempt to secure an overseas export trade for the Lobatse abattoir*

An additional factor increasing the need of Batswana cattle owners to dispose of their stock through the 'smuggling' trade was the failure of the BP government's major policy initiative for the indus- try in the mid 1930s. This was to build up an overseas beef export trade for the Lobatse abattoir. Some background is necessary.

After the Bechuanaland Protectorate government's defeat in the 'meat war' of 1931 it found itself in a clearly defensive position with respect to getting ICS to fulfil its contractual obligations. This situation was worsened by ICS's failure to win any of the 1932 Italian contract in competition with Union Cold Storage, as well as the continuing South African embargo on the north of the country (because of the Foot and Mouth disease in Southern Rhodesia), even for transit.

The administration had attempted in late 1931 to relieve the plight of the embargoed white Tati farmers by organizing a new trek route from Francistown to Kazangula to enable embargoed cattle to reach the Copperbelt market. However, the first consignment of 1 000 head provoked so much protest from Ngamiland traders[79] and the Northern Rhodesian veterinary authorities (allegedly at the traders' instigation)[80] on the grounds of an oversupplied Copperbelt market, that the administration undertook to send no more.

From the point of view of export volume, some relief came to BP with the mid-1932 lifting by South Africa of the embargo on the northern Protectorate and Union Cold Storage's purchasing of some 8 000 head for the Italian contract (aided by a special rebate on railage costs and a 'high subsidy').[81]

But the major event of 1932 was the outcome of the Ottawa Commonwealth Conference, at which the Commonwealth countries (i.e. the dominions Australia, New Zealand, Canada, South Africa and Southern Rhodesia) had pleaded for a larger and more secure share of the British import market. The non-Commonwealth quota (mainly from Argentina, Uruguay and Brazil) of chilled beef in the British market was to be held at its 1931 level. Therefore future increases in the market would be left to be fulfilled from Commonwealth sources – including those (like South Africa and Southern Rhodesia) which had been unable to secure a firm foothold in that market owing to South American competition. Preferences were granted across a wide range of agricultural commodities.

A new spirit of cooperation blew from South Africa. An invitation was extended to attend a conference to discuss policy on chilled beef exports in the light of Ottawa. ICS, anticipating the South African government's stance, warned BP immediately:

'There is at present a demand in Great Britain for a class of beef which in the past was not classed as high grade, but which is found to be nutritious. It is this class of beef which Brazil and Uruguay chiefly export, and I am satisfied that this country can produce large quantities. Don't tie yourself to

grades – let the British butchers decide . . . I would strongly
advise you not to commit yourself to any standard laid down
by the Union Department of Agriculture . . .'[82]

Indeed, from the South African point of view the benefits of Ottawa
to BP were to be only indirect:

'If the best of the South African cattle were selected for
export (to the UK) this would open to a greater extent the
Johannesburg market for less good cattle and would enable
the still lower qualities to go out . . . for the French or Italian
requirements'.[83]

Furthermore, it was clear that South Africa's conciliatory and cooperative attitude was a matter of need rather than choice: they
might well have to depend on neighbouring territories' cattle to fill
British quotas, and had also been told in Ottawa that the concession
was for southern Africa as a whole.[84]

Under these circumstances, the outcome of the conference was
not as unfavourable for BP as might have been expected. After first
suggesting stringent minimum quality standards,[85] South Africa
relented in the face of Southern Rhodesian and BP opposition,
insisting only that the cattle for chilled export should be less than
five years of age.

But the co-operative 'spirit of Ottawa' in southern Africa was
thereafter quickly snuffed out by the continuing decline of British
beef prices, leading the Dominions Office to respond to the conference by noting that '. . . it would be most unfortunate if South
African producers were led to believe that there was an actual or
prospective gap in the chilled beef supply which they might fill with
advantage.'[86]

Confronted with a restricted market rather than an open door,
plans for a joint southern African marketing effort for chilled beef
evaporated as Southern Rhodesia and South Africa scrambled for
individual chilled beef quotas. Southern Rhodesia, having finally
obtained transit permission for her embargoed beef from South
Africa in September 1932, began a vigorous (and subsidized)
chilled export trade to Britain. Bechuanaland was now faced not
only with an over-supplied British market but also with lack of any
independent status under the Ottawa agreement (having been par-
celled with South Africa for the purpose), as well as competition
with Southern Rhodesia and South Africa.

BP's hopes of quickly emulating Southern Rhodesia were in any case dashed by the outbreak of Foot and Mouth disease in January 1933 which resulted in the embargo (import and transit) by the Union, of all Protectorate produce. But the South African embargo and the fading away of the Copperbelt market (owing to cut-backs in copper production), together with the need to dispose of drought-stricken stock, made the securing of an overseas export market urgent.

In order to export to Britain at this time the Lobatse abattoir was practically essential, the only alternative being to move cattle live to the ICS abattoir at Walvis Bay – since South West Africa, unlike South Africa,[87] did not embargo the transit of BP cattle.

The government tried for both these options and began the preliminary organization of a chilled beef export trade. Discussions between the government, ICS and white traders and ranchers in November 1933 produced a plan of action similar to that already put into operation in Southern Rhodesia. A stock owners' association (modelled on the Rhodesian Stockowners' Association) was to be set up to co-ordinate production of chillers (i.e. cattle young and fat enough to be suitable for the chilled market). ICS undertook to adapt the Lobatse works for chilling and begin slaughter for export as soon as possible there and/or at Walvis Bay. Recognizing that feed rather than breed was the crucial factor in raising chillers, enquiries were to be made into getting cheap Southern Rhodesian maize and into raising public funds for an export bounty on chilled beef to make feeding worthwhile. A levy to be imposed on live exports to Johannesburg (once that market reopened) was suggested towards this purpose.

But the plan failed to get off the ground. Firstly, it ran into immediate opposition from London, the Dominions Office discouraging both the proposed investment in the Walvis Bay stock route and a proposal to renew Liebig's interest in the territory (which the BP administration had put forward as a hedge against the vagaries of ICS). They were also most reluctant to award any UK chilled beef quota at all to BP at this stage. Secondly, no concrete moves were made to organize the production of chillers. Although a BP Stockowners Association was constituted (February 1934) by EAC members (limiting its membership to whites) it did nothing and was reported dead within the year. Thirdly, ICS were back-tracking once more, arguing that too few cattle in prime condition were available to start a chilled export trade.

While Resident Commissioner Rey was busy remonstrating with London about their unwillingness to yield a chilled beef quota to BP (arguing that the erection of trade barriers by the UK against one of its own protectorates legitimized and encouraged similar barriers by South Africa),[89] the Federated South African Meat Industries (FSAMI, an ICS subsidiary) opened the Lobatse abattoir for slaughter in September 1934. The immediate purpose was to slaughter and freeze 600 head for the newly-won 1935 Italian army contract on which the South African government (contrary to its stated post-Ottawa policy of promoting quality beef export) was paying export bounties.[90] FSAMI made use of the accumulation of cattle in the Protectorate since 1931 to acquire supplies at the very low price of 5s. per 100lb. CDW., to the displeasure of both farmers and traders, who accused the company of opportunism.[91] FSAMI then refused to keep the abattoir open beyond the 600 head unless given a subsidy in order to offer prices competitive with the 'smuggling' trade; otherwise it could not get enough cattle, the world price of frozen beef being below 'smuggling parity'.

With the opening of the abattoir and with the chilled beef export proposals having become obviously unviable, the BP government turned its efforts to keeping the abattoir open for frozen exports by trying to raise funds to subsidise FSAMI, to secure additional markets and to halt the 'smuggling' trade.

The government therefore co-operated readily with South African demands for increased policing of the border to prevent 'smuggling'. By pleading the predicament of the embargoed Protectorate Rey finally managed to extract from London a small UK frozen beef quota (2 500 head) and an operating grant (£500 per month) to the end of the first quarter 1935. With the subsequent extension of the UK quota and operating subsidy for a further two quarters, over 13 000 head were slaughtered between December 1934 and October 1935.

But therewith the beneficence of the British Treasury ended. Although allowing the UK quota of 7 500 cwt. per quarter to continue, the Treasury was adamant that no further British funds should be used to subsidize Lobatse's operation since the Johannesburg market had re-opened (April 1935), albeit still subject to the weight restrictions and limited to 10 000 head per annum. Anxiety regarding overt British association with Lobatse's exports to Mussolini's army in Eritrea in the face of League of Nations' sanctions may have been a further reason.[92] If a subsidy were essential then it should be raised domestically by increasing the newly-imposed cattle export levy (discussed below) from 10s. to 15s. or 20s.

Throwing the Protectorate government back on its own meagre financial resources (and fund-raising potential) for beef export subsidy, brought it into immediate conflict with white cattle farmers.

Already in early 1935 the government had introduced a 10s. per head levy[93] on exports to the partially reopening South African market (Proclamation 33 of 1935) in order to supplement the British Treasury subsidy to FSAMI. When discussed at the EAC (March 1935) members had demanded that the levy funds '. . . be placed to the credit of the producer and . . . in no way be used for any other purpose than for subsidising of the export of prime beef overseas'.

Given the perceived urgency of keeping Lobatse functioning, Resident Commissioner (BP) Rey was in no mood to entertain the attempts of white farmers to co-opt the levy funds for their few prime animals, as they had succeeded in doing in South Africa and Southern Rhodesia:

> 'The proposed restriction of the levy to prime beef exports is an effort to benefit the European producer at the expense of the native, inasmuch as European farmers produce mainly prime cattle,[94] whereas natives produce the major portion of the poorer quality cattle. And as the levy is paid as to 80% or 90% by the native producer (for, of course, it is passed on to him by the trader, who buys his cattle) it is only fair that he should benefit by it'.[95]

With the ending of the British Treasury subsidy the government faced outright confrontation with the EAC in its efforts to raise the levy further and use its proceeds for keeping the abattoir open. At the February 1936 EAC meeting the majority opinion denounced any levy at all and insisted that supplying the abattoir was 'out of the question for European producers within the Protectorate unless the Imperial Government will provide a subsidy'.[96] The meeting closed with a protest and suggestion that 'it is time the Council ceased to exist' since its advice was never heeded. A hint of 'organized opposition' to the levy was also made.[97]

The Government was prepared to push ahead and raise the levy. But at this point the High Commissioner intervened to scotch further support plans for Lobatse: only the existing accumulated funds from the levy were to be so used, thereafter no more, thus providing for only another three months of subsidized operation.[98]

The High Commissioner's motive was not made clear. But following after London's suggestion of domestic financing for the abattoir from levy funds it seems likely that he felt Rey was putting the government too far out on a limb in alienating white opinion so drastically; perhaps the more so coming in the wake of the recent alienation of black opinion through the measures limiting the power of the chiefs.[99] Whatever the reason, it signalled the end of the Lobatse abattoir since effective competition with the 'smuggling' trade was now out of the question.

When the abattoir re-opened in March 1936 to slaughter and freeze cattle for the Italian army in Ethiopia it managed to process only 6 000 head and closed down for lack of cattle supplies. Plans to re-open in early 1937 were abandoned owing to a limited outbreak of Foot and Mouth disease causing suspension of transit rights through South Africa. After operating briefly later in the year on a special assignment to slaughter the 2 200 head aphthized[100] during the Foot and Mouth outbreak the abattoir closed for the last time. An ICS offer (provoked by nationalization of their Bulawayo plant) to re-open on the basis of a guaranteed return in the British market and guaranteed cattle supplies was once more turned down by London. Ironically, at the same time that Lobatse was being wound up, BP was awarded an ample three-year quota of 45 000 cwt. (approximately 12 000 head) per annum of frozen beef in the recovered British market.[101]

During its two and a half seasons of operation (1935–37) the abattoir had processed 21 000 head. During the same period, with the South African beef price rising, and the lack of markets alternative to Lobatse, the 'smuggling' flow became a flood of some 50 000 to 100 000 head per annum.[102] The period of ICS domination of BP's beef export trade was now closing. From being the centrepiece of policy concern in the 1920s and '30s ICS had become irrelevant in the face of the large scale 'smuggling'. The perceived urgency now was to staunch the outflow of cattle.

In Southern Rhodesia and South West Africa ICS was also on the way out. Southern Rhodesia took advantage of the lapsing of the ICS monopoly agreement in 1937 to set up the parastatal Cold Storage Commission and gear up her chilled beef export trade with Britain.[103] In South West Africa the Walvis Bay abattoir closed for the last time under ICS control at the end of the 1936 season (having completed its slaughterings for the Italian contract), not to be re-opened until 1942 as a government war measure.[104] In the Protectorate, ICS's swansong was to take out its anger over being nationalized in Southern Rhodesia by protesting vigorously over the proposed live exports to the Cold Storage Commission in 1939, threatening to claim compensation for not having been given first option on processing the cattle. No claim was forthcoming and the dormant agreement was finally terminated mutually in 1946.

V. Conclusion

With an indifferent imperial power and skeleton local colonial government the Protectorate's chief export industry had been at the mercy of monopolistic firms, foreign governments and drought during the harshest economic period of the century, and collapsed accordingly. The result was a drastically reduced cattle population and elimination of any immediate possibility of establishing a meat processing industry.

Even for states with substantial economic and political resources the 1920s and '30s were a time of great waste of productive capacity. For a 'reserve' territory with practically no developed resources and hardly any effective government the damage was magnified. This was most evident in the Protectorate's inability to sustain the one 'development gain' which the struggle to regain profitability between ICS and South African farmers threw its way, the Lobatse abattoir. Neither the economics of the 'reserve industry', nor the condition of the world beef trade, favoured the location of an export abattoir in the Protectorate in competition with the live export trade, particularly in the face of the exclusion of Lobatse beef from South Africa.[105] Therefore to reap the benefits of sustaining an export abattoir (the ability to reach overseas markets and become more independent of South African protectionism) a real cost had to be borne. The Protectorate government had neither the resources to sink into export subsidization (as both South Africa and Southern Rhodesia had done) nor the political muscle to displace the cost onto the live trade and thereby sacrifice the short-term individual interest of farmers for their long-term collective gain. Paying the cost of establishing a viable beef export industry was to re-emerge as a major issue in the 1950s with the setting up of a new Lobatse abattoir.

Chapter 6
Consequences of Marginality II: Regulation in Vain 1939–49

The period which forms the subject of this chapter is an intermediate one between the collapse of the Lobatse abattoir in the late 1930s and its reconstruction in the early 1950s. The principal features are the BP government's fruitless preoccupation with regulation of the industry in a period of rapid recovery of export markets in the region. The experience underlines the degree to which the fate of the industry depended upon external market changes and also emphasises the inability of the government (already clear from the 1930s) to impose any autonomous changes on internal cattle marketing in the face of opposition from cattle traders. The post-war change in British colonial policy and the consequent arrival of the Colonial Development Corporation ended this phase by 1949, and was to result in sharpened conflict with cattle trading interests during the subsequent run-up phase to the re-establishment of the abattoir.

I. Background to Intervention

The world experience of the 1940s as a period of rapid increases in production and demand entered Bechuanaland through the rapid growth, industrialization and urbanization taking place in South Africa and, to a lesser extent, Southern Rhodesia. Both of these countries faced quickly growing domestic demand for food and both became beef deficit zones for the first time.[1] SA slaughter stock prices (nominal) doubled between 1939 and 1949.[2] Bechuanaland's cattle were in strong demand, and exports rose steadily (Table A1). BP cattle prices (nominal) increased 60% while veterinary regulations suddenly became only a minor obstacle to exports, even though Foot and Mouth disease outbreaks were no less common during the 1940s than the 1930s.[3] Traders reported increasing turnover and the value of merchandise imports doubled between 1942 and 1946.[4] Ordinary revenue of the government almost trebled during the period (mainly through increased income tax, customs revenue and 'Native tax' receipts), by comparison with an increase of only one third during the previous decade (1929 to 1939). Similarly government expenditure was up two and a half times, with much of it accounted for by water point development in an effort both to increase the cattle population and distribute it more widely in order to diminish overgrazing in the settled areas.[5]

If policy towards cattle production was designed to repair through water development damage done by the drought and smuggling of the 1930s, policy towards internal and external marketing of cattle was geared even more to the objective of preventing a recurrence of such losses. The means selected to implement this marketing policy (state regulation of cattle buying, cattle movement and exports) reflected a trend in many countries (e.g. Britain, its dominions, Argentina) towards greater state intervention in agricultural marketing. This trend resulted from the severely depressed commodity markets and farm incomes in the 1930s, followed by war-time shortages and stringency.

In South Africa the formation of the Livestock and Meat Industries Control Board in 1934 and the increasing relative importance of the urban domestic market resulted in growing regulation of supplies to the main cities and abandonment of the former policy of export promotion. With the outbreak of war concern with maintaining floor prices quickly turned to efforts to contain price increases. But failure of these efforts resulted in the imposition of full price control (on British lines) in the main consuming areas.[6]

In Southern Rhodesia meat rationing was introduced. While no meat marketing board had been formed in Southern Rhodesia the Cold Storage Commission (formed in 1938 to take over the ICS assets) fulfilled a similar function, and as in Northern Rhodesia (where a marketing board was set up and the meat demand of the copper mines was rising quickly) regulation of cattle marketing was introduced in order to increase the domestic supply of beef. In Southern Rhodesia the Cold Storage Commission and Liebigs were given preferential buying rights at cattle sales in the African reserves and compulsory culling of cattle was introduced in the reserves – both moves which displaced the cost of the beef shortage onto African farmers.[7]

In Bechuanaland the government had good reason after the experience of the 1930s to feel the need to control the exploitation of its principal agricultural resource and followed, somewhat belatedly, the trend among others toward using legislation to try to achieve this purpose.

II. Futile Legislation

In 1939 three new overseas marketing opportunities arose which together encouraged the government to issue a Control of Livestock Industry Proclamation (Proc. 1 of 1940, with subsequent amendments) in order to make a renewed attempt at a policy of taxing exports to South Africa to provide funds for subsidizing overseas exports. The previous attempt had been defeated by massive cattle smuggling into South Africa, so the new legislation contained elaborate restrictions on cattle purchase and cattle movement in order to prevent smuggling.[8] There were other considerations too in the motive to restrict smuggling:

'(T)he Administration in its own interest will have to take active steps to prevent a resumption of smuggling . . . Stocktheft and illicit traffic in arms, ammunition and liquor are on the increase; the Natives are being corrupted; disregard, if not contempt, of the law is being engendered in the minds of the people. Such a state of affairs cannot be allowed to continue indefinitely'.[9]

By 1939 the government felt that the 'evil results' of cattle smuggling had become clear to all except 'the less responsible elements who have prospered from the trade'. South Africa was pressing for stricter measures.[10] The time had come for the industry 'to put its house in order'.[11] Since the prevailing assumption was that South Africa was basically a beef surplus economy, the increasing South African beef shortage since 1936 could not be bargained on as the beginning of the long-term trend it actually was. Rather the need was felt to become established in the British market, regarded as the only really stable market,[12] and therefore to grasp the new opportunities in this direction which now presented themselves.

The first new overseas marketing opportunity came from the Cold Storage Commission of Southern Rhodesia (CSC) which, experiencing a shortage locally of stock suitable for its chilled beef export trade to Britain, offered to take all stock over 800 lbs that BP could offer.[13] R. C. Arden-Clarke, unlike his predecessor Rey, was prepared to raise the levy on cattle exports to Johannesburg in order to provide funds to subsidise this selective export trade (which would mainly benefit white ranchers),[14] and he received the backing of the European Advisory Council (November 1939) for the venture.

Secondly, the outbreak of war produced an immediate call from Britain to South Africa for all the beef she could export. With no surplus immediately available from South Africa or Southern Rhodesia the appeal reached BP and arrangements were provisionally made for BP cattle to be slaughtered at Kimberley, Durban or Bulawayo for export to the UK by ICS.

The third opportunity was the possibility that Bovril might be interested in setting up a meat extract works in BP, for which purpose a representative of theirs (H. S. Walker) was despatched to BP.[15]

Walker's report (the Walker–Hobday report)[16] reflected the interventionist mood of the time in extreme form. It argued that until the cattle population of BP had been substantially built up once more (at least to its pre 1935 level) there would be no basis for establishing a viable export abattoir; strict regulations should be enacted in order to rebuild the cattle population; moreover, since British prices were lower than those in southern Africa, an export subsidy fund would have to be accumulated to pay the difference.[17] The report's principal recommendations formed the basis of the Control of Livestock Industry proclamation (No. 1 of 1940), the two main components of which were: (i) both cattle buyers and cattle exporters would have to be licensed and submit regular returns to Government on their transactions; (ii) the cattle export levy was to be re-introduced at 5/– per head and proceeds used 'solely for subsidizing the export of beef to the UK or other overseas market' (para. 21).

The Control of Livestock Industry legislation met with circumspection from the African Advisory Council (AAC) and hostility from the European Advisory Council (EAC). The AAC welcomed the provisions to curb stocktheft (compulsory rebranding within 72 hours of purchase, defined places of legal sale, outlawing of touts) but doubted the Administration's capacity to enforce even the pre-existing cattle removal permit regulations.[18]

Hostility of white farmers and traders was total. One reason was that the new overseas export opportunities of 1939 and the re-establishment of an abattoir, had become remote even by the time the legislation was published in January 1940. Firstly, the war caused the chilled beef trade to the UK to fall away completely as all meat shipments were now frozen (as in the First World War), so that white farmers' hopes of subsidized export of 'chillers' via Southern Rhodesia were dashed. Secondly, Bovril had decided definitely against setting up in BP.[19] Thirdly, the South African Meat Board had warned that should BP exports overseas result in reduced supplies to Johannesburg 'they would view the matter very seriously, and there was little doubt that this action might affect future arrangements and relations'.[20]

Other reasons were the threat the legislation posed to the livelihoods of Lobatse and Gaberones block farmers and cattle traders who depended on cattle smuggling,[21] its racial discrimination (Africans, not thought to be the main actors in smuggling operations, were excluded entirely from the licensing provisions), and its probable total ineffectiveness through unenforceability: 'What looks well in a statute book may not look so well out on the veld on a dark night'.[22]

Successive amendment through the early 1940s failed to make the legislation any more effective, acceptable to cattle traders, or appropriate to the rapidly improving market conditions, for the opposite of which it had been designed. A comparison of export marketing in 1940 and 1942 is illustrative:

(i)   Exports to Johannesburg rose from 19 600 to 33 700. Moreover the minimum weight restrictions on cattle imports were lifted in 1941, in response to a white farmers' delegation from BP to Pretoria appealing against the hardship inflicted by the new BP legislation.[23]

(ii) The next best market, Northern Rhodesia, absorbed over 10000 head in 1942 by comparison with 7000 in 1940.

(iii) Demand in Southern Rhodesia could not be satisfied; only 820 head supplied in 1942 against some 7000 in 1940.

(iv) Demand from the Congo could not be met at all, since all Ngamiland cattle were being sent to Northern Rhodesia for British war purposes.

The 34000 head exported in 1940 was itself a record official export level. The 45000 sold in 1942 produced fears that herds were being run down once more and insufficient oxen would be available for draught power requirements. Thus in response to South Africa lifting the weight restrictions on imports (1050 lbs for oxen) the Administration promptly imposed its own export weight restriction of 900 lbs in order to prevent the loss of immatures.[24] The Foot and Mouth disease outbreak of 1944 which halted exports briefly was regarded as a welcome relief by the Administration.[25] Under these circumstances a major legislative initiative to establish alternative markets could make no headway. Moreover, the other principal objective, to prevent 'smuggling', was itself achieved by the growing regional market providing adequate official sales outlets at the best prices available, thus rendering the regulatory measures of the Proclamation superfluous.

Finally, the legislative package itself was shown to be contradictory, as emerged after renewed anxiety in 1945 over the possibility of post-war beef surpluses in South Africa[26] precipitated planning of frozen beef exports to Britain through the Cold Storage Commission of Southern Rhodesia, using a doubled export levy to provide the necessary subsidy (British prices still being below those in South Africa).[27] It was pointed out that use of the levy for this purpose could backfire and actually *increase* smuggling, by imposing an additional cost on the legal exporter and thereby reduce the official price relative to the smugglers' price.[28] Alternatively, the increased levy would be passed on to African cattle owners (from whom some 90% of cattle eventually exported originated) and thereby decrease African tax receipts. In addition to these problems, the EAC predictably once more opposed the use of levy funds for subsidy of export of 'unimproved' stock. The Administration was spared the task of trying to resolve this legislative conundrum by the continuing high demand in the late 1940s from South Africa, Northern and Southern Rhodesia and the Congo.[29]

At the end of the decade the policy was effectively abandoned by substantive amendment of its two principal components:

(i)   the purpose for which levy funds were to be used was changed from 'solely for subsidising the export of beef to the United Kingdom or other overseas market . . .' to '. . . for the general benefit of the livestock industry in the territory' (Proc. 21 of 1950);[30]

(ii)   compulsory returns to the Veterinary Department of cattle purchase and export transactions were suspended indefinitely (High Commissioner's Notice 126 of 1953).

This reversal was not a surrender to the continuing EAC demands for repeal of the legislation, nor a newly found faith in the reliability of the South African market; rather it was a recognition by the Administration of the realities of a situation over which it manifestly had no control. Such recognition was made easier by the arrival on the scene in 1949 of the Colonial Development Corporation, a new force which had the resources to make a material impact.

III.   Conclusions

The experience of the 1940s served to re-emphasize the poverty of the BP government and the grip which the regional market, the South African government, and the 'reserve trading system' had upon the industry. In the 1920s and 1930s the tide of the regional market and South African policy had turned against Bechuanaland's cattle export trade, leading to its subsequent collapse. In the 1940s the regional tide turned in favour of the trade and undermined BP government policy once more. From the short-term point of view this undermining could be regarded as a fortunate upturn in the market which rendered unnecessary a plan for marketing further afield. But from the long-term standpoint it represented a further failure to break away from total dependence on the regional market and subordination to South African policy.

The experience also illustrated in extreme form the policy incoherence of a government representing and responsible to no one but a largely uninterested colonial power. Had the regional markets *not* improved (with official access to South Africa therefore remaining low, a consequent widening of the BP–SA cattle price differential and hence increased 'smuggling') the Protectorate government would have been no more able to control the situation than it was in 1935–38, despite the elaborate set of marketing laws enacted. In short, given the government's severe administrative limitations the policy was inappropriate, whatever the regional market conditions. Two more contradictions within the policy further illustrate this point: firstly, the export levy itself tended to encourage 'smuggling'; secondly, a vigorous live export trade (as took place in the 1940s) meant sacrificing the possibility of an export abattoir – thus Bovril's unwillingness to enter the territory. With the government's stated policy goal being to promote re-establishment of an export abattoir the obvious priority was to secure admission to South Africa and the Copperbelt for BP-slaughtered beef. But no move was made in this direction either by the government or the High Commission. The issue was taken up only in 1949, and then by the Colonial Development Corporation, responding to the post-war change in imperial colonial policy.

Also at the level of export policy in the period there is a marked contrast between the futility of the Protectorate administration's interventions and the effectiveness with which Southern Rhodesia set up a much more complex regulated marketing system at the same time. Besides the Southern Rhodesian government's far greater financial and manpower resources the control of the state by locally based interests (white settlers in this case), pursuing their own economic objectives, made for coherent, if oppressive, interventions by the state. By comparison, BP policies were full of prevarication, as the history of the Cattle Export Levy illustrates.[31] Northern Rhodesian intervention in cattle marketing (in the form of price control by the Cattle Marketing and Control Board, set up in 1937)[32] was also notably more successful than the Protectorate's. Here the factor of possessing a substantial and geographically concentrated domestic market (the copper mines) facilitated control.

Part II B: Growth Industry within a still Peripheral Economy

Chapter 7
Transition: Controlled by the CDC 1949–1960

This period marks the transition in the industry's history from 'reserve industry' to potential 'growth industry' (as defined in Chapter 1 p.8). The transition resulted from: (i) the thrust by the imperial government (through the newly formed Colonial Development Corporation) to set up a viable export abattoir in the territory, originally as part of its efforts to increase commodity supplies in the sterling area; (ii) the preparations for decolonization in the late 1950s which began to put cattle owners in control of both government and the industry; (iii) the new, expansionary trend in the world beef trade and the changing demand in favour of lean, boneless beef.

Reflecting its transitional nature, this period was characterized by the most overt conflict in the industry's history. The forceful but clumsy entry by the capital-rich CDC provided a direct challenge to the 'reserve trading system' which controlled the live export trade, since the viability of an export abattoir in the territory required (as the experience of the 1930s and 40s amply demonstrated) diversion of live exports to the abattoir. Given the unfavourable economics of locating meat manufacturing in a peripheral area, the abattoir provided returns to cattle suppliers inferior to those from the live trade – as long as regional markets (effectively the only markets accessible to live exports) were strong.

The strong regional demand of the early 1950s cut both ways for the CDC. On the one hand it enabled CDC and the government (its junior partner effectively) to force the hands of South Africa and Northern Rhodesia to agree to accept beef in place of live cattle. On the other hand, the strong regional demand made for a buoyant live export trade, so that diversion of the cattle to the newly completed abattoir in 1955 created a substantial opportunity cost for cattle suppliers (from the north specifically), who consequently waged a vigorous campaign against the opening of the abattoir. The CDC's bungling methods and vast discretionary power provided additional targets in the campaign.

But when the regional markets turned sharply downwards from the mid-1950s and new opportunities opened coincidentally in the British market, the viability of the abattoir was no longer in question. The focus of conflict shifted to CDC's control of the abattoir, its undisclosed profits therefrom, the profits of the South African entrepreneur engaged by CDC to market its beef overseas and the demands of northern cattle suppliers for a northern abattoir independent of CDC control.

With the move towards decolonization the role of the Tswana aristocracy – at once the principal cattle owners and the politically most powerful individuals – came to the fore in resolving the conflict over control of the export industry. The realization grew in government that given the inevitability of a beef export monopoly in the hands of the abattoir company and the overwhelming importance of the industry economically and politically, control of the company would have to be in the hands of the cattle producers themselves through a statutory corporation. With the formation of the BP Abattoir Company in 1960 the first step towards nationalization was achieved.

At root, the transition from 'reserve industry' to potential 'growth industry' was effected by means of the CDC's capital resources and discretionary power, and in spite of the CDC's managerial ineptitude and lack of clear direction. Owing to the unfavourable economics of the CDC's holding grounds and to the prevailing marketing imperfections from remote areas, a continuing though increasingly subsidiary role for cattle traders and speculators remained.

Section I deals with the major world and regional factors affecting the industry during the period. Section II analyses the conflict which developed around the CDC abattoir. Section III concludes.

I. Background

Changes in the world and regional beef economy and in British colonial policy are the major external factors shaping the course of the industry in this period.

(a) World and regional beef economy

Regional marketing opportunities for BP beef continued their buoyant 1940s trend until 1956 and then declined sharply. From 1957 the British market, lower priced than southern Africa, offered openings for the first time to marginal Commonwealth beef producers. Together these changes called for a sharp alteration in marketing strategy and produced declining returns from exports in the later 1950s.

The general economic slowdown of the later 1950s reduced copper production in Northern Rhodesia and the Congo and with it their demand for meat; mine meat rations were also abandoned in 1956. Efforts to increase domestic beef production and 'decontrol' of beef prices in Britain in the mid-1950s reduced import demand.[1] In South Africa beef prices were also 'decontrolled' (1956), and thereafter the quota given to Bechuanaland Protectorate was not increased (in this period). The monopoly control of beef imports into the Federation of Northern and Southern Rhodesia and Nyasaland given to the S. Rhodesian Cold Storage Commission (CSC) by the Federal government in 1957 cut BP almost entirely out of the N. Rhodesian market in favour of supplies from S. Rhodesia, which was now reverting to its pre-war surplus position.

The alteration of the world beef trade in the late 1950s which created new openings in the British market resulted from the increasing US beef deficit, causing New Zealand and Australia (the only exporters of refrigerated beef veterinarily acceptable in the US) to switch their supplies from the UK to the more attractive US market. The gap in the British frozen beef market which was thereby opened[2] favoured peripheral Commonwealth suppliers in particular, since Commonwealth preferences were available in the

Table 7.1: *UK: Domestic production and imports of beef and veal*

Year	Domestic production	Imports	Total (000's of tons)
1934–38 (av.)	49%	51%	1 184,7
1956	62%	38%	1 242,5
1961	64%	36%	1 178,7

Source: As for Table 7.2 below.

Table 7.2: *UK: Per cent of beef and veal supplied by source*

Year	New Zealand	Australia	Argentina	Irish Republic	Yugoslavia	Other
1934–8	4,0	8,1	30,1	3,1	–	5,9
1956	6,4	8,1	20,0	3,2	–	0,3
1961	1,0	2,7	13,0	8,7	1,4	3,5

Source: 'Report of a Committee of Inquiry into Fatstock & Carcase Meat Marketing & Distribution' HMSO Cmnd. 2282 1964, Table 24.

form of exemption from the heavy tariff on imports of boneless and canned beef.[3] Furthermore, boneless beef, consisting mainly at the time of cheaper, leaner frozen cuts for manufacturing and the catering trade, was the type of beef they were best able to supply, and the market for it was expanding, being a product 'more compact, lighter and more easily handled than the equivalent amount of meat in carcase form'.[4]

In short, changes in the world and regional beef trade during the 1950s divided the period into two from the standpoint of BP's beef export industry: (i) the years to 1956 during which the strong regional demand persisted, absorbing all BP's surplus at prices above those obtainable on external markets;[5] (ii) the later 1950s when volume restrictions on BP exports in regional markets tightened (although regional prices remained steady, above the falling world price) while preferential opportunities opened up on the lower priced British market.

(b)   British Colonial Policy

The most concrete manifestation of Britain's new post-war colonial policy of investment in colonial production was the CDC. As the Secretary of State for the Colonies cabled to colonial governments in launching the CDC in 1947:

> 'The functions of the CDC which will be responsible to me will be to initiate, finance and operate projects for agricultural or other development in the Colonial Empire. . . . Need for such expansion (of colonial production) is of course very much in public mind at this moment owing to prospect of continuing shortages of certain commodities and increasing difficulty in obtaining adequate supplies of dollars for purchases of food and raw materials from America . . . (T)he colonies are almost uniformly in need of further capital investment just as much as the UK and the world at large is in need of increased production of main colonial commodities. Each side therefore stands to gain equally from these proposals'.[6]

CDC's sister in the effort 'to strengthen the resources of the sterling group as a whole'[7] was the short-lived Overseas Food Corporation (responsible for the disastrous Tanganyikan Groundnuts Scheme). Both were constituted under the Overseas Resources Development Act of 1948.

The House of Commons debate on the bill, focussing on the ambiguous answerability of the corporations, was prophetic of one source of the conflict over CDC's Lobatse abattoir. Briefly: '. . . the existence of these corporations gives rise to new constitutional problems which will require time and the evolution of new procedural precedents to solve. On the one hand there is the need to preserve the rights of Parliament to be kept informed . . . On the other hand the Corporations are commercial organizations which should not be exposed to meticulous political interference'.[8]

The ambiguity regarding CDC's statutory accountability extended also to its project selection criteria. 'Commercial soundness of the scheme' was to be a 'vital consideration' after the primary criteria of the colony's and sterling group's need for the scheme, distribution of schemes among colonies and yield/dollar-input ratio 'have been carefully studied'.[9] However, CDC projects were not to make a loss.[10] From the point of view of the individual colony's government CDC projects were to be regarded like any other commercial operation, being subject to taxes, rates etc. But the Corporation would not be debarred 'from taking advantage of utilities, capital equipment or general public facilities or services financed from the (Colonial) Vote . . .'.[11]

Furthermore no guidelines were set at the start regarding future ownership and control of projects initiated by CDC. In the case of the Lobatse abattoir there was only vague reference to 'future participation' by non-CDC interests. Inevitably, disputes over the ambiguous accountability and performance criteria of CDC projects would turn to questions of ownership and control. While disputes were unlikely over small projects (individual factories, estates, farms) they were unavoidable in the case of the Lobatse abattoir which involved a CDC export monopoly over the territory's only industry of any significance, in which every major political figure in the country had strong personal interest. Thus the ambiguous constitutional nature of CDC was one root cause of the escalating conflict through the 1950s between CDC, cattle traders, breeders and government.

The expansionary finance which characterized the new colonial policy also put increased funds directly into the hands of the BP government. A Colonial Development and Welfare grant of £400000 was made available specifically for new boreholes, and drilling went ahead on an unprecedented scale,[12] contributing (together with the lack of any serious drought in the 1950s) to the 34% increase in the cattle population 1949 to 1959. Veterinary expenditure was expanded considerably following the restitution in 1955 of the UK grants-in-aid to balance the colony's budget.

II.   CDC in Bechuanaland: Control and Conflict

(a)   1949–56

(i)   *Beginnings: 'Bold and Imaginative' Failures*
'Appreciating . . . the immense benefits that this efficient and disinterested body can confer, I assured Lord Trefgarne (CDC chairman) that we would give him every assistance in our power to encourage the Corporation to invest in this Protectorate'. RC (BP) Sillery 1949.[13]

The giddy enthusiasm with which the prospect of CDC investment in BP was greeted by local officials in the late 1940s reflected the acute capital starvation of the territory. Officers received the unprecedented instruction to prepare projects 'on bold and imaginative lines'.[14] 'Meat and maize' were the first choice, to consist of an export abattoir (70000 head per annum), holding grounds for the abattoir and a ranching and farming scheme in the northern state lands on the grandest scale. Initial plans for the northern operation were to build up a herd of 356000 head over twenty years, with an annual offtake of 70000; arable activities were designed to enable BP to become a substantial net exporter of grains; the holding covered 11000 square miles and was to employ 3000 people![15]

Lobatse was selected as the abattoir site in preference to Mahalapye or Francistown owing to the cheap availability of the old ICS abattoir buildings and the appearance of a better water supply.[16] CDC also took over on a 99-year lease the 600000 acres of holding grounds along the Molopo river previously assigned to the ICS but never used.[17]

Opposition to the CDC abattoir plan arose as early as 1948–49 when the project was first mooted, and emanated mainly from established cattle traders. It focussed on CDC's monopoly export demand, on the anxiety that CDC would by-pass 'established channels' of sales (i.e. traders and speculators) by buying cattle directly in the tribal areas, and on the concern that the cattle buying finance provided to traders and speculators by Johannesburg livestock agents would be lost if the live export trade were stopped.

In order to allay these fears and make the abattoir attractive to the established cattle trade CDC had undertaken in 1950:

(i)   to be 'bound to purchase all cattle offered at Lobatse abattoir subject to our option of deciding to slaughter immediately or to hold'.[18]

(ii)   to purchase only from licensed suppliers (the previous export licence to be adapted accordingly);

(iii)   to pay a price equivalent to that received at Johannesburg for live sale of cattle (net of transport, abattoir and other incidental costs incurred in exporting cattle live); this price to be known as 'Johannesburg parity'.[19]

At this stage CDC clearly believed that provided it secured a monopoly of beef and live cattle export, and access for BP beef to regional markets, it could operate the abattoir efficiently enough in order to guarantee payments to cattle suppliers equal to Johannesburg prices f.o.r. Lobatse (at that time reportedly higher than British prices f.o.r. Lobatse). If this 'Johannesburg parity' could be maintained, along with the promise to buy all cattle offered, then the cooperation of cattle suppliers could be relied on and the risk of defeat by 'smuggling' thereby be averted. This policy represented a clear break with the earlier futile efforts of government in the 1930s and 1940s to make beef exports viable by subsidizing them with funds raised by taxing live exports.

Although CDC had succeeded in securing a commitment to cooperation from cattle suppliers and agreement from South Africa and Northern Rhodesia to accept beef in place of live cattle,[20] its early operations were nothing short of disastrous. The northern state lands operation, started in 1950, with heavy outlays on machinery and fencing, had lost so heavily by 1954 through crop failures, stock diseases, predators, floods and bad management that it was cut down to a fraction of the original size by hiving off the Bushman Pits ranch to the Ngamiland Cattle Exporters Association,[21] abandoning arable farming and maintaining a herd of only 9 000 head on the remaining Nata and Pandamatenga ranches. Thereafter it continued to die a slow death, confining itself to fattening and middleman operations (exporting Ngamiland cattle on the hoof to Northern and Southern Rhodesia through Pandamatenga) by making use of CDC's cattle and beef export monopoly.[22] It was abandoned in 1963.

The Molopo holding grounds also accumulated losses, amounting to £45 000 in 1953 alone, blamed on delays in the abattoir opening, amid government accusations that CDC mismanagement was causing heavy overgrazing along the river. Together with its retreat in the north CDC announced in 1954 its intention to cut down the Molopo operation and abandon the holding grounds scheme altogether:

> 'Whatever may have been the original idea of the holding ranch, our experience proved beyond a peradventure that Molopo cannot purchase cattle in poor condition or at near-slaughter weight and hope to grow them out without loss. Nor can it hope to maintain cattle in condition to provide a reservoir on which the abattoir can draw during the slack season – because the slack season is also the dry season when cattle lose condition'.[23]

The reaction of government and cattle breeders was consternation.[24] The issue was that somebody had to bear the cost of holding the cattle in condition into the dry season if the abattoir was to operate on a year round basis *and* slaughter cattle in good condition. CDC's undertaking to assume this cost had been one of the major local benefits envisaged for the scheme,[25] which had induced local agreement to the CDC export monopoly. Furthermore, with the holding ground abandoned CDC was no longer in a position to fulfil its promise to buy all cattle offered to it.

As regards the Lobatse abattoir itself, opening was delayed two years (to September 1954) owing to delays in delivery of machinery, condemnation of the new building and ensuing litigation against the design consultants.[26] The District Commissioner, Lobatse, wrote in June 1954:

'The apparently reckless approach to all three schemes
(Molopo ranch, Northern ranches, Lobatse abattoir) by local
employees of the corporation and the lavish and what would
appear to be wasteful expenditure followed by drastic
retrenchments in the case of the two ranching projects, and
the pulling down of the newly-built but structurally unsound
abattoir, has been watched with growing anxiety by a public
whose whole cattle economy is about to pass into the hands
of that organization'.[27]

In this climate of gathering anxiety the government and EAC sought to check whether CDC would in fact be able to fulfil its final and most crucial undertaking, namely to pay 'Johannesburg parity'. To their dismay the calculations indicated that, owing to higher railage costs for beef than for live cattle and to higher processing costs at Lobatse than at Johannesburg, the abattoir would not be able to sustain 'Johannesburg parity' without subsidization.[28]

The result of these disastrous beginnings was a vigorous campaign in mid-1954 to prevent the opening of the abattoir, led by cattle trading interests but with wide support from breeding interests and government.[29] Accusations that the country had lost faith in the CDC, that the abattoir could not possibly operate profitably, and that the existing favourable regional export markets for live cattle could not be recovered after the inevitable collapse of the abattoir were broadcast through press and public meetings, and a boycott of the abattoir was threatened.[30]

Only by an intensive last-minute public relations campaign in BP by the CDC chief executive himself underwriting CDC's promise to pay 'Johannesburg parity' for cattle and undertaking to write down by half the £900 000 capital outlay on the scheme (to bring the book value in line with the actual valuation of the installations and thereby to reduce the burden of debt servicing costs) was co-operation regained – and this only for a single year's trial operation.[31]

But during its first (and second) year of operation the Lobatse abattoir reportedly made substantial profits (undisclosed to the public or government) and appeared superficially to have confounded its critics. However, 'a core of opposition to the project remained' (Ryan 1958:51), specifically in the North-east of the country (Serowe, Francistown), since the abattoir's profits were in fact achieved at the expense of a net revenue loss to northern cattle sellers. To understand how this came about it is necessary to review briefly the impact of the abattoir's establishment upon cattle marketing from the north and eastern areas. The BP cattle trade as it emerged from the 1940s was two directional: some half of the 70 000 head exported were sent north and east to the Copperbelt of Northern Rhodesia and the Congo, and to Southern Rhodesia (to make up the deficit of cheaper beef there). The other half went South to Johannesburg. Severe shortages of meat on the Copperbelt in the early 1950s led N. Rhodesia to pay a premium price for BP cattle, in order to obtain them in competition with the strong South African demand. Additionally, the railage from the senders' station in BP was paid by the purchasers (the Northern Cattle Export Pool). The purchasers for the Congo (ELAKAT) also gave transport cost concessions.[32]

With the exception of the five to ten thousand head exported on the hoof from Ngamiland via Kazangula and Pandamatenga, all exports to the north and east were railed, making the railage concession an important overall saving. Moreover practically all the cattle railed to the Congo, N. Rhodesia and S. Rhodesia were sent from the north and east of the country (Francistown, Serowe, Mahalapye area) which contained the largest concentrations of cattle in the territory.

The advent of the Lobatse abattoir and CDC's export monopoly meant immediately that all cattle (except from Ngamiland) had to be sent south to Lobatse for processing. Prices to the cattle seller were f.o.r. Lobatse (i.e. the cattle seller paid railage to Lobatse) while CDC now reaped the benefit of the transport concessions to the north by receiving f.o.r. Lobatse prices (i.e. buyers paid railage) for the beef railed to N. Rhodesia and the Congo as well as the higher northern prices, while standardizing producer prices throughout the country to 'Johannesburg parity'.

In short, the substantial profits (rumoured to be between £50 000 and £150 000) made by the abattoir during its first two 'boom' years of operation were distinctly *private* profits masking a short-term *social* trading loss (i.e. excluding increased employment and other indirect income benefits resulting from the establishment of the abattoir) by comparison with the alternative of live export. Firstly, the source of the abattoir's profits was the losses carried by northern and eastern suppliers: (i) the premium beef prices f.o.r. Lobatse which N. Rhodesia and the Congo continued to pay above 'Johannesburg parity' between 1954 and 1956; (ii) the 'notional' deductions from cattle purchase price (equal to marketing costs of live cattle to Johannesburg) which CDC was permitted to make as part of 'Johannesburg parity' (see p. 124) but which she did not actually incur on sales to N. Rhodesia and the Congo since the beef prices were f.o.r. Secondly, the higher processing costs at Lobatse than at Johannesburg and the inward railage of cattle from the north to Lobatse were deadweight losses socially.[33]

Straightforwardly what this meant was that the abattoir's profits were derived from the lucrative sales to the north while losses were made on sales to Johannesburg as long as 'Johannesburg parity' was paid to cattle suppliers. Thus, for CDC, a fortunate difference between prices in the northern and southern markets had enabled it to effect what the government in the 1930s had failed to achieve: namely to force cattle suppliers to subsidize the operation of the abattoir at the expense of their profits from the live trade. Luck was on CDC's side in that the subsidy burden fell on northern suppliers, who had no readily available 'smuggling' market and were therefore forced to pay the cost themselves while continuing to sell their cattle to CDC.

CDC's capacity to honour its promise to pay 'Johannesburg parity' had turned out to be based on the successful outcome of one (or both) of two gambles: (i) that processing and marketing costs from the abattoir would be lower than costs on live exports to Johannesburg; (ii) that Lobatse beef and by-products (the '5th quarter') could be sold at prices higher than those ruling in Johannesburg. With the reality being higher processing costs at Lobatse than

Johannesburg, continued payment of 'Johannesburg parity' relied by 1956 upon the higher northern beef prices paid f.o.r. Lobatse and was bound to be threatened by a decline of that market.

(ii)   *Overview to 1956*

The difficult beginnings of the CDC Lobatse abattoir had by 1956 created three problem issues which sooner or later would have to be resolved.

Firstly there was the severe regional disparity of distribution of the abattoir's benefits and costs creating a north-south split in allegiance to the project.

For southern traders and speculators particularly, events had turned out much better than could have been expected. Their cattle supplies had in any case been sold south to Johannesburg, not to the higher priced northern markets, and so were unaffected by the standardization of all producer prices to 'Johannesburg parity'. The feared competition from CDC in cattle buying had fallen away along with the Molopo holding grounds, leaving largely intact for the time being the marketing problems of limited quotas and market accessibility among smaller cattle breeders, which assured the position of traders and speculators in the marketing chain. For the larger cattle breeders in the south there were clear benefits in that the market for their cattle had expanded at no cost to them, since the abattoir was marketing to the north as well as to South Africa, while direct marketing had become simpler – as evidenced by the increasing number of breeders registering as licensed suppliers to the abattoir.[34]

For northern traders, speculators and breeders of all sizes the immediate impact was negative: prices were lower than previously[35] and they now had to pay cattle railage costs. The request by northern interests for railage cost equalization for all suppliers had split the EAC (November 1954) along north-south lines (with the latter in the majority) and had been turned down by government. Further enflaming the issue was the fact that 55% of the beef exported from the abattoir was railed to the northern markets, thereby underlining the costly location of the abattoir given prevailing marketing patterns. Finally, shortage of slaughter capacity at Lobatse during the flush season meant that quotas had to be cut 'when the N. Rhodesian butchers would have been ready and eager to take their live exports' which 'made the monopoly appear irksome and unnecessary to them' (Ryan 1958:52).

129

Secondly, Northern and Southern Rhodesia had accepted Lobatse beef in place of live imports of cattle reluctantly and only because of their urgent need for additional beef at the time. The Northern Rhodesian meat marketing system in particular was based on an extensive network of private holding grounds in the hands of a consortium of Copperbelt butchers, with only a minimum of cold storage space. Beef imports instead of live cattle meant loss of value added on additional growing out, loss of the '5th quarter' (i.e. hides, offal and other by-products) and increased investment in cold stores. A 1954 commission of inquiry into the beef industry of the newly formed Federation of the Rhodesias and Nyasaland noted these costs of the changeover to beef imports and remarked that '. . . it appears that the changeover cannot but result in an increase in the price of beef to the consumer. . . . The question has also been raised as to whether the continuance of the supply on the hoof cannot be insisted upon . . .'[36]. Thus retaliation from within the Federation in order to regain live supplies was a clear possibility once their bargaining position strengthened. Ironically, BP's victory over the N. Rhodesian butchers in getting them to accept beef instead of live cattle was to aid the ascendancy within the Federation of the Southern Rhodesian Cold Storage Commission, from whom the retaliation would come.

Thirdly, the guarantee of 'Johannesburg parity' as the pricing standard, used to 'sell' the abattoir to the BP public, had turned out in practice to be a source of short-term profit for CDC but an acute public relations risk in that it was a guarantee from which CDC would clearly have to retreat if the northern market declined.

(b)   1956–60

(i)   *The mid-1950s marketing crisis*
The sudden decline in regional demand for her beef with which BP was faced at the end of 1956 resulted from events in the Federation and South Africa.

In the Federation a reduced beef deficit and the gaining of control over Federal imports by the S. Rhodesian Cold Storage Commission (CSC) were the reasons. The advent of Federation in 1953, with its purpose of lowering trade barriers among its member parties, had offered diametrically opposed possibilities of benefit for the two dominant interest groups in the Federal beef industry: CSC and the N. Rhodesian butchers' cartel. For the CSC it meant a ready market on the Copperbelt for the surplus of high-grade meat which its exploitative policies[37] (dictated by white ranching interests) produced. For the N. Rhodesian cartel it meant the possibility of buying cheap, low-grade and immature cattle at S. Rhodesian auction sales. The ensuing struggle '. . . for markets; for export and import rights; for trading rights and the right to buy cattle . . .'[38] (including a CSC campaign to discredit the quality and hygiene standards of BP beef sold on the Copperbelt)[39] was won by the CSC, through gaining exclusive Federal import rights, through preventing the butchers from obtaining live cattle in S. Rhodesia and finally, in 1959–60 (now constituted as a Federal body), through buying out the installations (including the Livingstone abattoir) of the largest N. Rhodesian butchery group and assuming full control of N. Rhodesian meat marketing.

External events had aided the CSC victory. Firstly, the N. Rhodesian acceptance of BP beef in place of cattle '. . . was a first step in weakening the power of the larger butchers in N. Rhodesia'.[40] Secondly, the falling copper market (reducing employment) and the abandonment of rations in favour of a full cash wage for miners, both further reduced the power of the butchery cartel.

In South Africa beef prices were 'decontrolled' in early 1956,[41] fixed prices being replaced in the major urban areas by carcase auction 'on the hook'. Removal of the price ceiling reportedly increased SA domestic supplies[42] and BP's 'flush season' quota was cut to 500 carcases per week. Exports to South Africa had remained steady at 30–35 000 head since the mid-1940s while over the same period total BP exports had increased from some 45 000 to 70 000 head per annum on the strength of the increased demand from the Copperbelt. When CSC indicated that Federal imports, some 25 000 carcases in 1956, would be less than 10 000 in 1957, the export volume of 70 000 head could only be sustained if South Africa increased the BP quota; but this did not materialize. Increasing South African imports from Namibia (SA's main external source of beef supplies) may have been one reason; complaints regarding the destabilizing effect of Lobatse supplies on Johannesburg auction prices may have been another.[43] The Congo, also suffering from the copper slump, was not prepared to take more than its contracted amount of some 12 000 head.[44]

The effect of the reduced Federal demand and cut 'flush season' quota to South Africa was increased queuing for slaughter quotas at Lobatse – since the CDC had no holding grounds and storage capacity for only one week's kill. The rapidly increasing cattle population exacerbated the problem.[45] Demands from northern cattle owners for export on the hoof or alternatively a northern abattoir itensified. The abattoir's profitability was immediately reduced by the severely decreased Federal sales and lower returns on its South African sales, resulting from auctioning its chilled beef against SA freshly killed beef.[46] It was clear that CDC, with no alternative markets, would have to compromise with CSC and northern interests in order to export more and retreat from 'Johannesburg parity'. An outbreak of Foot and Mouth disease in mid-1957, closing the South African market for 10 months, precipitated the issue.

(ii)   *End of 'Johannesburg Parity': CDC forced to compromise*

As recently as 1955 CDC and Government had thought BP's regional export market prospects so strong that she could start setting her own export price, above that of the markets in which she was selling. But in 1956 protracted negotiations with the Federation for a long-term supply contract finally came to nothing partly because of BP's insistence on carcase, not live, exports.[47] The rapid erosion of her bargaining position thereafter reiterated the vulnerability of the industry in its extreme export dependence and narrow export marketing base.

With CSC the compromise reached was to increase live exports in return for a larger import quota. During the years following to 1962 CSC was able to reduce BP exports to the Federation (to make way for increased S. Rhodesian supplies to the declining N. Rhodesian market)[48] yet receive an increasing proportion of live cattle in the quota, insist on more severe Lobatse grading standards[49] and to pay lower prices, absolutely and relative to domestic prices. The tables below summarize the situation.

By the early 1960s Southern Rhodesia had established a vigorous export trade to Britain for its better grades of beef; imports of BP's predominantly lower-grade beef arrived live to be slaughtered at Livingstone (Northern Rhodesia) and railed to the Copperbelt and S. Rhodesia (where the domestic demand was for the cheaper, lower grades) (Table 7.5). Thus CSC control in the Federation and

Table 7.3   *Federal imports and exports of cattle and beef 1956–62*

	Imports (000 lbs) (all from BP)		Net exports of beef (000 lbs.) (i.e. exports–imports) (including beef equivalent
	Beef	Cattle	of cattle imports)
1956	10 133	4	−4 425
1958	5 523	3 450	−2 934
1960	464	4 554	+16 009
1962	295	10 663	+19 571

Table 7.4   *S. Rhodesian Cold Storage Commission minimum prices compared to prices paid for imports from BP (100 lb CDW)*

	Minimum prices (average of all grades)	Prices of imports from BP (approx.)	
1950–54	70s.	1954	100s.*
1955–58	97s.		
1959–63	113s.	1962	73s.

* Estimate of price paid by Northern Cattle Export Pool f.o.r. at Francistown.

Table 7.5   *Net movement of beef from Southern to Northern Rhodesia 1962–63*

	(000 lb.)
Top four grades	3 437
Bottom three grades	−4 343
Detained and sundry	64
TOTAL	−842
Federation imports from BP	8 800 (including beef equivalent of cattle)

Source: 'Report of the Commission of Inquiry into the Beef Cattle Industry of Northern and Southern Rhodesia' (Horwood Commission), Federation of Rhodesias and Nyasaland 1963. Table IX: p.44, Appendix VI;

G. Purnell and W. Clayton 'Report . . . on the Beef Cattle and Meat Industry' 1963. Table 5.

BP's inadequate slaughter capacity and marketing problems had by the time of break-up of the Federation undone the benefits gained in the N. Rhodesian market for BP by the establishment of its own export abattoir.

To the northern trading and cattle breeding interests in BP the compromise offered was export on the hoof to the Federation and payment of all inward railage costs to the abattoir (the latter at the cost of protest from southern producers and traders, and those from Ghanzi, for whom railage was not an option).[50]

With the BP government the compromise reached was limitation of CDC's profits to 6% of the average 1958 value of the abattoir's fixed and current assets in return for abandonment of 'Johannesburg parity'.[51] However, the issue of the abattoir's prices and profits was far from settled and had become ensnarled with that of local participation in the abattoir. CDC had been anxious since 1955 to start recouping its capital from the abattoir by selling minority participation. Clearly feeling that government was prevaricating on the issue, CDC threatened to enter into partnership with the abattoir's customers (including CSC) if local participation was not forthcoming. For its part government clearly felt that CDC was acting as if it were a law unto itself in the country; CDC had backed down on all the promises on the strength of which its concessions in BP had been given. Government now refused to take the participation question further until CDC rendered full financial account of its Lobatse operations. CDC, having wanted to use its profits from the abattoir to offset CDC losses elsewhere,[52] felt that the agreement to limit its profits to 6% was already a major concession and proceeded unilaterally in 1958 to form the 'Lobatse Abattoir Co.' and '. . . at a time of maximum difficulty in marketing, pressed government to agree to transfer the Corporation's rights and duties, including the monopoly of export, to the new company'.[53]

(iii)   *Overseas marketing: resort to private management*
By 1958 BP's gathering surplus of marketable cattle above reduced regional requirements made overseas export a matter of urgency. Whether CDC was unwilling or unable to undertake overseas marketing is not clear, but in mid-1958 government and CDC took advantage of the offer of a Mafeking-based South African meat entrepreneur Cyril Hurvitz to market Lobatse beef abroad, thereby beginning a seven-year association which was both to establish

exports to the UK as a major outlet for BP beef and to provide a further focus of dispute.

In June 1958 the BP Resident Commissioner wrote enthusiastically:

'The contract with Mr Hurvitz will enable the Territory to clear its backlog of cattle, will test the availability of supplies in conditions of maximum demand, will strengthen the Territory's bargaining power with the Federation and Congo and will open up markets which are likely to be required for many years unless a canning plant is brought into operation'.[54]

CDC's sales overseas had been confined to a single small sample consignment in 1955. Indeed, as long as CDC was tied to paying 'Johannesburg parity' and regional prices were higher (net of transport and handling costs) than world prices, they also had no incentive to set up overseas marketing channels. It is a matter for speculation to what extent the limitation (March 1958) of the abattoir's after-tax profits to 6% removed the incentive, after 'Johannesburg parity' was abandoned, for CDC to expand its Lobatse management and undertake overseas exports itself.

The least of the problems in marketing overseas were the reception, storage and sale of the meat and by-products. In the UK at least these could be handled easily by London agents specializing in such operations. The critical constraint was refrigerated shipping space from South African ports, all of which (other than charters) was controlled by the SA Perishable Products Export Control Board, in association with a shipping conference. Since the Southern African 'flush' season for beef (when most cattle were marketed, being in their best condition) coincided with the SA fruit export season to Europe, there was sharp competition for space: it had to be booked well in advance and paid for at the same rate whether or not it was actually used. The alternative, of chartering a ship, involved even higher 'deadfreight' (i.e. unused booked space) risk in a business where disease outbreaks and unavailability of refrigerated trucks or cold storage space at ports could all prevent enshipment of the anticipated amount.

To minimize deadfreight risk the exporter needed access to fallback reserves of beef and cold storage space. Mr Hurvitz, a meat packer and trader ('Bull Brand' and 'Siege' meats) with a cold storage works on the Witwatersrand, canning interests in Namibia ('Damara Packers') and extensive ranches,[55] was clearly better placed than CDC to minimize export risks and, if necessary, to fill a chartered ship.

As CDC remarked in 1961, at a time of renegotiation with Hurvitz and of high Foot and Mouth disease risk:

> 'Shipping is indeed the key to the whole business. If we can find the necessary shipping there is no reason why, pending the conclusion of an agreement with Mr Hurvitz, the abattoir should not itself undertake its own overseas exports . . . (B)ut we decided reluctantly . . . in view of the danger that Foot and Mouth might spread and close down the whole of BP, that we could not run the risk of incurring the enormous penalties involved in booking shipping space which we might well be unable to fill'.[56]

Substantial as the deadfreight risks and problems of arranging cold storage and shipping to ports may have been, the CSC of Southern Rhodesia organized its own export overseas (with a London agent) of volumes not substantially greater (at the time) than BP's exports. So did the Kenya Meat Commission,[57] and, after 1966, the Botswana Meat Commission. Thus whether Hurvitz was particularly able in overseas marketing (the prevailing belief in government and CDC) or not, the eagerness with which his offer was embraced, his prolonged retention in the face of controversy, CDC's prior failure to prepare overseas marketing channels itself in the 1957–58 marketing crisis, CDC's ignorance of the marketing advantages of deboning (they dismissed it as a 'slow and laborious process')[58] – all reflected the inadequacy of CDC management in a most demanding export business.[59] Indeed CDC's main concern at this time (1958–60) appeared to be to start recouping its capital from the project.

The three Hurvitz contracts (1958–59, 1959–60 and the ECCO agreement 1961–65) were controversial because of their speculative character, being forward-purchase agreements specifying quantities (broadly) and guaranteed prices.[60] The guaranteed prices (the source of the speculative element) were also the contracts' most immediately attractive aspect: Johannesburg 'floor' price for the beef, plus a small margin (the first contract), was attractive both to cattle sellers (reminiscent as it was of the old 'Johannesburg parity', despite lacking the 5th quarter proceeds) and to CDC, since it fitted in with their pricing and payment system.

The arrangement was a gamble for Hurvitz, contingent on the relative movement of Johannesburg and world (mainly British) prices, exposing him to charges of profiteering if the gamble came off and to possible severe loss if it did not. Whether a straightforward agency contract (paying a percentage of net proceeds) was discussed at all is unknown, but would not seem to have suited Hurvitz's business style, nor CDC.

In fact Hurvitz's gamble was hedged substantially by the heavy dependence of both CDC and government upon him to dispose of an increasingly large proportion of Lobatse's total kill overseas during 1958–62 (two thirds in 1962), given the domestically over-supplied regional markets and CDC's reluctance to assume the overseas marketing burden itself. In short, they could not afford to let Hurvitz go under.

As it turned out, the Johannesburg 'floor price' (i.e. intervention price) was increased twice during 1959 and Hurvitz would have lost spectacularly on his first contract[61] had CDC and government not been prepared to alter the contract's terms (March 1959) exempting Hurvitz from paying the increased Johannesburg prices, meeting them instead from 5th quarter proceeds, therefore ultimately at the expense of producers' reserve funds. CDC (bound to its 6% profit margin and with good hide prices in 1959 raising the value of the 5th quarter) had nothing to lose in making the concession, and government wanted above all not to lose the marketing outlet. In appealing for the concession Hurvitz had stated:

'I would like to be safeguarded against a possible slump in the overseas market, in that I should have the right of appeal at all times to Government for a review of the export position'.[62]

The concession itself provided a clear reply, made without any *quid pro quo* regarding review in the event of a boom on the overseas market.

(iv)　*The Northern abattoir dispute and the establishment of BPA and ECCO*

In late 1958 the dissatisfaction of northern cattle interests with CDC and the Lobatse abattoir was focussed firmly upon the demand for a northern abattoir by the forceful bid from the Glazer brothers of Johannesburg (owners of the Tati company), consulting with Tshekedi Khama, to establish an export abattoir at Francistown.

By that time government was convinced[63] that available offtake was insufficient to justify the set-up costs of a separate abattoir complex in the north and was considering expansion at Lobatse and a cannery ancillary to the Lobatse plant as a means of solving the problems of lack of slaughter capacity and cold storage space. Southern cattle interests moreover were opposing the northern abattoir proposal strongly, and CDC, unwilling to expand their own involvement by setting up a northern abattoir itself, feared competition for throughput and increased costs at Lobatse. Furthermore, government was also by then set upon nationalizing the abattoir.[64]

Thus the urgent representations, press campaign and Francistown protest meeting of December 1958 (delivering a unanimous vote of no confidence in CDC for its poor record on quotas, prices, ploughing back of profits, marketing Ngamiland cattle and selling BP beef overseas)[65] were cold-shouldered by government. A proclamation (No. 16 of 1959) was made prohibiting the establishment of any abattoir without government licence and the Tati project memorandum was ignored. The issue ultimately came to a head in late 1960. CDC and government had finally agreed on a participation scheme and constituted Bechuanaland Protectorate Abattoirs Ltd. (BPA), on a basis which gave CDC the management contract with ownership vested equally in CDC and a Livestock Producers' Trust set up for the purpose, the contract being for ten years with the intention that the Trust should then buy out CDC entirely. At the same time CDC and government favoured a proposal originating from Hurvitz for the erection of a cannery adjacent to the Lobatse abattoir under a separate company owned 60% to 40% by BPA and Hurvitz, this company also to hold the exclusive overseas export contract for BPA and also eventually to be taken over entirely by the Livestock Producers' Trust. However the northern cattle interests had already insisted that any cannery should be located in the north.

Government organized a carefully orchestrated campaign to secure the support of the Bamangwato (producing two thirds of all cattle eventually exported) for the BPA-Hurvitz Lobatse cannery. With Tshekedi Khama having died in 1959 the advocates of the Tati abattoir had lost their most influential Ngwato ally. Seretse Khama was now the undisputed key to Ngwato support. Already an influential member of the Livestock Industry Advisory Board and the BPA board, he stood behind the BPA-Hurvitz proposal. Armed with a mandate of support from the Ngwato Tribal Council he was to be the main force at a Francistown meeting organized by government to swing the issue in the north. But the meeting backfired (the opposition having been even more carefully orchestrated) and government had to be content with pushing the proposal through the Livestock Industry Advisory Board (December 1960) on the strength of Seretse's and Bathoen's influence – their argument being that those agitating for the Francistown abattoir and cannery represented narrow sectional interests rather than the real producers (i.e. the Ngwato breeders) whose crucial concern was getting their cattle marketed not who marketed them.

Thus the organization of the cannery company at Lobatse (the Export & Canning Company, ECCO, as it was to become) went ahead in the face of trader and white farmer opposition in the north. The Tati Company application was dismissed (leading to further bitter altercation)[66] and the question unanswered as to why government was formally teaming up with Hurvitz when the grounds given for dismissal of the Tati application were nationalization of the meat industry. Feelings were further exacerbated by the secrecy surrounding the contract setting up ECCO.[67] The stage had thus been set for the major showdown of 1962–63 which would finally expedite complete nationalization.

The almost complete lack of regional markets in 1960–61[68] put Hurvitz in a strong position in the bargaining over the ECCO contract. Although CDC had disapproved of tying prices paid by Hurvitz to Johannesburg prices, on the grounds that overseas prices and Johannesburg prices move independently of each other and the producer should rather receive the real periodic proceeds of overseas sales,[69] the ECCO contract finally agreed specified ceiling prices based on Johannesburg prices, together with maximum quantities that BPA itself could sell on the regional markets, all carcasses in excess thereof to be sold to ECCO, for whom Hurvitz was the sole marketing agent. Practically all marketing expenses, including transport, were to be met by BPA. In short, the ECCO contract from Hurvitz's viewpoint was a marked improvement on his previous two agreements: it formally underwrote his risks (by removing the burden of marketing costs and paying him salary and expenses as sole marketing agent) while cutting him into the profits (10% of net profits plus 40% of dividends). Furthermore the majority of carcases for overseas export were now to be deboned, promising higher returns for the lower grades (which made up the bulk of throughput), while not raising producer prices for the lower grades.[70] ECCO profits would not necessarily mean higher prices for the producer, only reaching him by way of any bonus which BPA might declare as a result of any dividend which BPA itself might receive from ECCO by virtue of its 60% holding of ECCO – clearly too discretionary a route to satisfy producers.

III. Conclusions

By 1960 with the advent of BPA the foundations for a future 'growth industry' had been laid. The abattoir had been established in the face of hostile market forces and the export industry as a whole had been set upon the road to control by locally based interests (mainly the cattle owners themselves): future profits increasingly would be held within the country for the expansion of the industry. Having gained access to overseas markets the industry would no longer be forced to act as a 'reserve' source of supply for the regional markets – drawn on when needed, closed down when not needed – or to become the helpless victim of conflicts within neighbouring states (as happened in the 1920s and 1930s with ICS and the South African import restrictions). With control of the industry by cattle owners, plus their likely control of the future post-colonial state, the interests of the industry would be articulated forcefully and defended by the state in international negotiations to a degree that had not been possible under the colonial government.

But despite the achievements of the 1950s the transition was not yet complete in 1960: adjustments to the changes in the world and regional beef trade and British colonial policy had been slowly, incompletely and (in the case of the overseas marketing arrangements) unsatisfactorily made. The ambivalent nature of CDC itself (see Section I) and its lack of expertise in the meat business were one reason; government's lack of clear policy (until 1958) and consequent prevarication was another (most clearly in its dithering over whether to support the opening of the abattoir or not in the dispute of 1954–55). The result was that at the level of ownership and control the problems left over from the period (particularly ECCO) were to become the focus of dispute in the early 1960s during the lead-up to Independence.

Other changes wrought in the 1950s were to become permanent features of the post-colonial period. A white freehold farm settlement was created quickly and quietly on the Molopo land available after the failure of the CDC holding grounds venture. In internal cattle marketing an institutional structure was set in place that would remain with only minor changes to the present. Firstly, in order to channel the export offtake southwards to the single export abattoir (frequently short of immediately available markets or of slaughter capacity) a system of slaughter quotas and marketing agencies (private and co-operative) emerged. The major actors in the old trade (traders and speculators based on the freehold farming blocks) retained their roles (owing to the absence of holding grounds and up-country buying by the abattoir) but were increasingly joined by the larger African breeders now marketing their stock directly. In time their role would be undermined by direct marketing to the abattoir by even the smaller breeders, thus bringing about the displacement of 'traditional sources of supply' feared at the time of CDC's entry into the territory (1949). Only the best placed of traders and speculators (in terms of location of trading stores and grazing land) would then continue to prosper.

Secondly, a two-tier payment system to producers was created as a direct consequence of the almost exclusive export orientation of the abattoir. For a single year (1955) before 'decontrol' of South African prices, a single price ('Johannesburg parity' weight for grade) was paid. But with the advent of fluctuating auction-based prices there was no acceptable alternative to making an initial down-payment to producers (the 'floor price', so termed because it was equal to the SA Meat Board's support price), plus a later payment of the balance actually realized ('agterskot', first paid out monthly but later only annually after a policy of fixing 'floor' prices annually was followed). The bonus system (especially in its annual form) boosted the profitability of cattle trading activities at a time when other changes in the system were undermining it, since the published annual 'floor' prices became the up-country guide price for cattle bought by traders and speculators while they usually retained the bonus (10% to 30% of the 'floor' price, See Fig. A1) when it finally arrived.

At the level of cattle supply, expansion of both cattle population (through the drilling programme and good rains) and offtake were the main features – the latter the direct result of the new overseas exports. Extension of veterinary cordon fences and services reflected the further gearing up of the country for beef export with the prolonged veterinary isolation of Ngamiland (two years after the 1957 Foot and Mouth disease outbreaks) the main immediate social cost thereof. With no immediate prospect of a northern abattoir to enable the meat industry to continue operation in the north while isolated from the most veterinarily particular markets, Ngamiland particularly was set to become the poor relation of the country's beef export industry – most remote from Lobatse and most liable to closure owing to its more frequent Foot and Mouth disease outbreaks.

From the social point of view the most noteworthy aspect of the period was the increasing prominence of the Tswana royalty and wealthy in the affairs of the beef export industry. From a position in the late 1940s when the CDC abattoir project was little more than presented as a *fait accompli* to the African Advisory Council while vociferous white opinion was carefully negotiated with, the situation had become one in which Tshekedi and Seretse Khama were the chief figures in deciding the outcome of the northern abattoir issue in the late 1950s, and Seretse Khama was the single most influential local board member of BPA.[71] The initiatives were not yet in the hands of black leaders, but in the climate of decolonization that was upon the country their support was crucial.

Chapter 8
Post-colonial Period I: Establishment of a growth industry – Nationalization, consolidation and the EEC connection

This chapter examines the affairs of the beef export industry during the post-colonial phase to 1984. The principal events cluster loosely into two sub-periods. The first sub-period (1961–74) is dealt with in Section I. It is the time during which the colonial state is dismantled and the independent state established; within the industry it is dominated by external market growth and reorganization of interest groups in the industry around the nationalization of the Lobatse abattoir. By the mid-1970s breeding interests, through the state, are clearly dominant and the industry geared to the veterinary and product requirements of the UK market. In 1974–75 the world beef market collapses, ushering in a period of instability, and Britain joins the EEC. The 1975–84 period (Section II) is characterized by efforts to ride out the storm on volatile export markets in the face of successive outbreaks of Foot and Mouth disease, and to manoeuvre within an increasingly limiting relationship with the EEC. The role of the state in defending the industry's markets becomes crucial. Section III concludes.

I. Nationalization and the emergence of a growth industry 1961–74

(a) Export marketing no constraint

External marketing was, for the first prolonged period in the industry's history, no constraint during 1961–74 owing to market expansion and the major drought of the mid-1960s which reduced herd size and offtake substantially during 1966–69.

Both prices and volumes of beef in international trade increased markedly during the period, though revealing a strong inverse relation to each other:

Table 8.1: *Percent increase in world beef imports and prices*

	Import volume	Price
1960–65	45	28
1965–70	49	18
1970–75	21	70

Source: Table A3 and Table 2.6.

Within this overall expansionary trend Botswana's cattle exporters made price gains more rapidly than the average, and more than South African livestock producers, through having preferential access to the British market (Commonwealth preferences on boneless beef) and access by quota to the relatively high-priced South African market.

Table 8.2: *Index of Botswana, World and South African beef producer price*

	Botswana	SA	World
1960–61	100	100	100
1974	434	319	296

Source: Table A3

The Foot and Mouth disease outbreaks of 1960–61, 1966 and 1968 closed the South African market but were not a major setback since the British market (still under a liberal veterinary import regime) remained open. Only in 1961 were low prices a problem; but ECCO's losses in that year were turned into a substantial profit by

1962. Botswana even turned down in the mid-1960s ELAKAT's offer of a renewed ten-year Congo (Zaire) supply contract – the contract which had been so important in the mid-1950s marketing crisis. Foot and Mouth outbreaks recurred continually in Ngami-land during the drought of 1960–65, but the costs of these (repeated closures of Ngamiland from access for her cattle to the south and restrictions on cattle movement) were confined to Ngamiland – already in the 1950s become the poor relation within Botswana's beef industry owing to remoteness from the abattoir and high dis-ease risk. Ngamiland's intermittent exports on the hoof to Zambia were the last remains of Botswana's live export trade, and even these were halted in 1967 by the ban on further live export in order to increase the severely drought-reduced throughput of the Lobatse abattoir.

The drought itself was a further reason why export marketing was no constraint in this period: when markets were relatively tight (1967–69) cattle numbers and offtake were down (Table A1) producing difficulty even in fulfilling the SA quota (which was consequently cut in 1969). The subsequent rapid build-up in cattle numbers in the early 1970s (owing to the further heavy investment in boreholes during the 1960s and quicker herd growth after the drought, see p.36) came at a time of unprecedented price rises on world markets, therefore posing no marketing problem. Botswana was able to choose her market: thus the UK market, being the most attractive from 1968 to 1973, received most beef, but when South African prices rose sharply in 1974 65% of beef was sent there (as against 18% in 1973).

For the first time in the industry's history attention could be focussed on internal issues unfettered by major concerns about external marketing.

(b)   The nationalization debate

The issues in the debate over nationalization of the Lobatse abattoir and associated meat processing departments (deboning and canning as run by ECCO) concerned *when* nationalization should take place and with whose capital, rather than *whether* it should take place and in what corporate form.

That there was no realistic alternative to nationalization in the form of a parastatal (public utility) firm had emerged as early as 1958. Since the abattoir: (i) had been unable to compete price-wise with live exports to regional markets, and (ii) needed the bulk of the country's offtake in order to keep its processing costs down, its viability depended upon holding a monopoly of *both* live exports *and* beef exports. Handing such monopolies to a private firm, domestic or foreign, was politically unthinkable, so public ownership of a kind was inevitable. Cooperative forms were regarded as unsuitable: ownership by registered suppliers to the abattoir on the basis of purchased shares would lead to majority shareholding by the wealthiest, and a 'pure' cooperative, in which each registered supplier would have a single vote, would neither elicit sufficient subscribed capital from suppliers to buy out CDC nor provide workable managerial control.[1]

The 'semi-nationalized' Bechuanaland Protectorate Abattoirs Ltd (BPA) set up in 1960 represented both a deliberate delay by government in order to build up managerial skills and capital (in the Livestock Producers' Trust) sufficient to take over the running and ownership of the abattoir,[2] and a compromise with CDC who at this stage were not prepared to relinquish managerial control without being bought out completely.

Although BPA had been constituted with the intention of eventual conversion into a parastatal no dates were stipulated and it was generally thought feasible only within about ten years. However, BPA's overseas export marketing arrangements with Hurvitz, through ECCO, proved so controversial that the changeover was expedited. By 1962–63 there was conflict between CDC and Hurvitz, stemming from the rigid and speculative nature of the ECCO contract (see p.139). The unresolved dispute between cattle suppliers and CDC, focussing in the early 1960s on complaints of low prices and high ECCO profits, culminated in an appeal directly to the Secretary of State over the head of the High Commission.[3] Further conflict was added between government and CDC over compensation to be paid for their abandoned northern ranch holdings.[4] Two commissions of inquiry recommended a specific timetable for nationalization.[5] With the ECCO contract due to expire in 1965, the independence elections scheduled for that year and the strong possibility of securing the then general manager of the Kenya Meat Commission to run a nationalized Lobatse abattoir, government pressed CDC for immediate takeover, which was consented to after lengthy negotiation.

Nationalization and fair prices became a major election platform for Seretse Khama's government-favoured Botswana Democratic

Party. Legislation setting up BMC was passed in 1965, the ECCO contract allowed to lapse and a nine month interim overseas marketing arrangement made with another South African firm (National Cold Storage) to tide over the transition.

In summary, nationalization, planned since the 1950s, was precipitated in the mid-1960s both by the non-workability of the BPA-ECCO arrangement and, to all appearances, by the political convenience of having nationalization coincide with independence to boost the party favoured by the outgoing colonial government. With foreign interests eliminated from the export sector and government in the hands of the large cattle breeders with the blessing of the colonial power, the industry could now be expected to receive the definite political direction and priority it had always lacked.

(c)   Control of BMC

At the internal level the new state moved by the mid-1970s to place firmer control over BMC in the interests of cattle breeders generally. The circumstances leading up to this move are analyzed below.

The legislation establishing BMC was modelled on that by which the Kenya Meat Commission had been constituted in 1950 ('The Kenya Meat Commission Ordinance'). Its main feature (and principal difference from the Kenyan legislation) concerns the autonomy given the Commission from the ministerial level of government; BMC is answerable to the Minister of Agriculture only to the extent of presenting him with a statutory annual report and '. . . such other information and returns . . . as the Minister may . . . reasonably require' (BMC Act, Para. 11).[6] All control of BMC policy and actions is vested in the President, through his power to hire and fire commissioners, veto any change of policy and issue directives which BMC is statutorily obliged to carry out.

The legislation amounted to putting ultimate control of the industry into the hands of the largest cattle breeders, since the President and most Cabinet members were important breeders. Clearly, exercise of this control in their own interest would have to be, and has been, attenuated by the need to cater for other collectively powerful interests in the industry, specifically: (1) the up and coming medium-sized breeders whose rising incomes (mainly from salaries) have enabled them to invest in cattle, for which they require water, grazing land and adequate marketing facilities. (2) the much larger

147

group of very small, marginal breeders who make up a substantial proportion of the electorate.

But the structure of immediate control continued to favour the largest (mainly freehold) cattle suppliers, since they were (and remain) the most strongly represented farming group on the commission (which performs the functions of a board of directors). At one level their appointment by the Livestock Industries Advisory Committee (from which four of the ten commissioners are elected) reflects the fact that they are among the most competent and experienced cattle men in the country. At another level their period of dominance coincided with a continuation of policies which (whatever their motivation) favoured large, well-placed cattle suppliers. In part this was due to the structure that the economic limitations of the industry had imposed upon the operation of the Lobatse abattoir which favoured cattle dealers – namely that the abattoir was not viable ithout a monopoly of all beef and cattle exports, that only one abattoir was practicable, that its remote location was unalterable and that holding grounds were diffi ult to run economically (viz. the Molopo holding grounds experience of the CDC). All of these factors had made marketing of small mobs of cattle difficult and maintained an important role for middlemen.

The locational problem was exacerbated by the severely drought-depleted national herd of the late 1960s which ruled out a northern abattoir for the time being and precipitated the controversial decision by BMC in 1967 to end all live exports to the north from Ngamiland and Chobe and reroute them through Lobatse, in order to raise the abattoir's throughput – a decision which some allege favoured one or two large speculators with holding grounds near the railhead at Francistown (one of them the then vice-chairman of BMC). But Ngamiland cattle exporters claim that they were not disadvantaged by the decision.[7]

Other BMC policies were more clearly a matter of the commission's discretion. The pricing system, with its annual reviews and consequent bonuses ('agterskot') whenever markets rose, was left unchanged. The grazier scheme (see Section (d)) organized during 1967–69 remained virtually the preserve of freehold ranchers during its initial years. The scheme was financed by Barclays Bank, whose investments in Botswana at the time were mainly in the financing of short-term cattle buying;[8] the retired chairman of Barclays Bank SA, himself a freehold rancher, succeeded to the chairmanship of BMC in 1968, with another freehold rancher as vice-chairman. During 1966–68 the Regional Controller of CDC (the source of all BMC's debenture capital) had remained as chairman, in accordance with the nationalization agreement with CDC.

Breeders and speculators had a common interest as long as the latter could be seen to be serving an essential function at a reasonable price. But the advent of the Lobatse abattoir had made the speculator's function less than essential, in principle at least, and there was widespread dissatisfaction with the high returns they were reputed to reap from marketing imperfections (see Section (d)). Moreover they no longer as a group had the ear of the government as previously[9] nor any public political leverage. The smaller and less established speculators (mainly owners of single trading stores) had already lost most of their cattle business to direct marketing, which was being promoted energetically by the Ministry of Agriculture. The conflict of interests sharpened in the early 1970s: the rapid rise in British meat prices produced record bonuses (32% in 1972) much of which was reportedly retained by middlemen,[10] the drought of 1973 resulted in such throughput pressure at Lobatse that many applicants for quotas could not be accommodated during the flush season, had lost money and the matter had become a political issue.[11] Criticism focussed on the manner in which BMC's operations continued to serve the interests of the large cattle dealer/fattener: the limited production capacity, absence of up-country buying by BMC, the quota system, the seasonal pricing system, annual fixing of producer prices and the bonus system.

The President then put BMC on a shorter rein (Act 7 of 1974), increasing his powers of dismissal of Commission members. He replaced the sitting chairman by the then Permanent Secretary in the Ministry of Agriculture and increased governmental representation of the Commission. Quarterly review of producer prices was introduced so as to minimize annual bonuses, and seasonal price variation was abolished[12] on the grounds that by reducing flush season prices it discriminated against suppliers who did not have the grazing or fodder available to hold animals over in good condition into the off-season. Government also pressurized BMC to take on the newly created BLDC as its subsidiary (p.155 below). At the same time the Ministry of Agriculture pressed ahead with plans for a northern abattoir in order to increase throughput capacity and create a more accessible processing facility for northern breeders.[13]

Thus by 1974 the state had moved to bring BMC's policies more into line with political realities.

(d)   Conduct and performance of BMC

It is argued here that during the first decade after Independence a 'growth industry' was established. The argument is pursued by analyzing BMC's conduct and performance (during the entire post-colonial period) against the background of the contrasting external and internal market structures within which BMC operates. The principal structural characteristic is the combination of an external market in which BMC is almost totally a 'price taker' with a domestic cattle market in which it is a near monopsonist.

(i)   *The influence of market structures*
Although Botswana's beef exports increased rapidly in volume in the post Independence period (86% during 1966–67 to 1976–77), rather faster than world beef exports as a whole (65% increase 1965 to 1975), they still constituted only 1% of the volume of beef in world trade in 1981–83 (Table 2.5). The degree to which Botswana is a 'price taker' in international markets (i.e. does not affect international market prices) is rendered more graphic by recalling that only some 5% to 10% of world beef production enters world trade.

Even taking into account that strictly speaking there is no 'world market' for beef (since disease control regulations, quotas, tariffs and product differences have created a network of bilateral trade flows instead) Botswana still supplies only a minute proportion of her major markets' requirements. Even in the few cases (e.g. Angola, Reunion) where a larger proportion of the market is supplied there is competition from alternative suppliers.

By contrast, BMC's near monopsony within Botswana means that local beef prices are normally ruled by BMC export prices (with corrections for local market imperfections caused by transport difficulties and less than competitive conditions in the butchery trade in some major towns). Although probably only some 50–70% of total cattle slaughtered in Botswana annually pass through BMC, some 75% of *marketed* slaughter cattle do and some 95% of BMC output is exported.[14]

BMC's contrasting external and domestic market environment results from design rather than accident: the export monopsony of cattle and beef which BMC inherited from the BPA and the CDC was designed as a defence against the vulnerability of the export abattoir company through its 'price taking' position in external markets and lack of an internal market. The export monopsony, together with the smallness of the domestic market, ensures that price decreases on external markets can be passed on to the cattle production sector without diminishing (in the short run at least) abattoir throughput. Failure to secure an effective export monopsony in these market circumstances was a main cause of the collapse of the Lobatse export abattoir in the 1930s (see Chapter 5); only through securing an effective monopsony (both legally and *de facto*) was the CDC abattoir enabled to survive the 1950s (see Chapter 7).

The logic for the abattoir company being able through the export monopsony to displace the costs of an external price decrease back onto cattle production has been simply that it ensures its own viability. For the governments of Bechuanaland and Botswana, the implied logic of the monopsony was not only that it kept the abattoir in business but that cattle production (through its very low production costs) could more easily than the abattoir bear the lower prices and remain viable.

The security of BMC's monopsonistic position has been maintained in recent years, despite the rapid expansion of the domestic market for beef (up approximately 200% between 1974 and 1983), by the continuing absorption of the vast bulk of offtake into exports, as indicated in Table A4. BMC has thus been spared the pressures of competition for cattle supplies from domestic demand which can be more cheaply and efficiently supplied from small local abattoirs. In Kenya these pressures caused a crisis in the KMC as soon as KMC's monopoly of beef supplies to the domestic market was abolished in 1972. With little surplus now available for export and unable to compete on the local market, KMC's future has been in doubt.[15] BMC has never had a monopoly of domestic supplies and never needed it, owing to the small size of domestic demand.

The general predictions whch micro economic theory makes regarding the effect of the market structures described above on firms' conduct and performance are that: (1) a small firm in a highly competitive market survives only if it is efficient; (2) a monopsony can remain in business despite inefficiencies (as long as it enjoys protection from competition), because it can to an extent pass on the higher costs to its captive suppliers without losing their supplies.

That these characteristics have been present in BMC's conduct and performance is illustrated below.

(ii) *BMC's conduct*

The impact of BMC's operation within these two contrasting market structures is most apparent in the priority assigned to different aspects of overall management.

Product acceptability and sales effort in the richest markets are the first priority. This is best illustrated by the efforts made to maximize sales in Botswana's best market, the EEC (mainly the UK): the restructuring of the Lobatse abattoir in the mid-1970s to meet EEC product requirements (primarily chilled boneless cuts of beef) and veterinary standards; the adherence to EEC veterinary regulations regarding cattle movement and isolation from the export abattoir after outbreaks of Foot and Mouth disease (despite heavy social costs, see p.168); the forward integration into the UK market through the setting up of Allied Meat Importers.

By comparison, the other end of BMC's activites, cattle purchasing and the organization of abattoir throughput, receives low priority: BMC readily accepted the cattle buying system which it inherited from the CDC (no up-country buying activities, queuing by cattle suppliers via a quota system). It took on the responsibility of BLDC reluctantly in 1973 and was quick to shed it in 1977. This conduct was clearly the result of BMC's near monopsony which made up-country cattle buying unnecessary in order to attract adequate supplies, together with an awareness (possibly) of the difficulty of making holding grounds pay.

(iii) *BMC's performance*

The performance of a firm (its production and productivity) must be assessed in terms of its objectives; in the case of private firms (where the objective is assumed to be short or long run profit maximization) common performance indicators are growth of sales and profits.

However, BMC is not a private, profit accumulating firm but is statutorily instructed to carry on business 'efficiently and economically' (BMC Act para. 7) and '. . . in such a manner as to promote the interests of the livestock producing industry of Botswana, and in particular to secure that so far as is reasonably possible all livestock offered or available for sale in Botswana to the Commission are purchased and that the prices paid therefore are reasonable' (BMC

Act para. 4). BMC clearly has tried to handle, so far as its existing facilities permit, all cattle and small stock *offered* for sale – to the extent of running its plant beyond capacity (1973, 1979, 1983). But inadequate capacity since the mid-1970s means that BMC has not always slaughtered all cattle offered, as witnessed by queuing for slaughter quotas. As regards slaughtering all livestock *available* for sale, marketing imperfections (compounded by the unfavourable location of the abattoir for northern herders) have meant that BMC would have had to involve itself far more in up-country buying activities (both cattle and small stock) to have attained this objective.

For the sales effectiveness of BMC's operations on the one hand, and efficiency and economy on the other, the indicators of (i) growth of sales and of payments to livestock suppliers and (ii) the proportion of net sales absorbed by BMC's production and administration costs (or its residual: the proportion of net sales transferred to livestock suppliers) are respectively suitable. In these terms, BMC's sales effectiveness has been impressive: net sales (sales minus freight, storage and other selling expenses) rose in current prices from P9 million in 1966/67 to P44.5 million in 1976/77, to P96 million in 1983 (Table A2). Export volume was on an upward long-term trend (from some 100 000 head per annum in the early 1960s to over 200 000 head per annum in the early 1970s, and over 230 000 in the early 1980s (Table A2). Average price per 100 kg CDW (current values, including bonus) paid to cattle suppliers increased from P30 to P70 between 1966–67 and 1976–77, to P138 in 1983 (Fig. A1). On comparative and real price trends (1960–83), suppliers to BMC did slightly worse than their South African counterparts (Fig. A2), but increases in cattle prices outpaced rises in the cost of living (with the exception of 1973–78) (Fig. A2). Since the Foot and Mouth disease induced market closures of 1977–1981, net sales and real producer prices have risen continuously (Table A2, Fig. A2).

By contrast, performance on the indicators of economy and efficiency is less favourable. Although the proportion of net sales absorbed by BMC's production, processing and administration costs (Table A2) showed a declining trend to 1976 it increased sharply thereafter. This reflects both rising administrative costs and the expansion of productive facilities (cannery, tannery and pet food unit). The tannery has yet to be developed beyond the reputedly less profitable wet blue stage, and the cannery is arguably an important fall-back facility in the event of disease outbreak. Nonetheless, the comprehensive investigation which brought to light the frequent losses made by these new facilities also complained of inadequacies in BMC's accounting and management information systems for individual departments[16].

This coincidence of strong sales performance combined with weaker performance on efficiency and economy strongly suggests the influence of the contrasting external and internal market structures within which BMC operates. Other features also suggest this influence.

Firstly, some two-thirds of the increase in BMC's net sales during 1966–67 to 1982–83 resulted from increases in export prices with only one-third deriving from increased export volume[17]. Secondly, the increase in BMC throughput (114%) was less than the increase in cattle population (127%) over the same period. The relative lagging behind of volume expansion was coincident with BMC's passive policy on cattle supplies and inadequate capacity at Lobatse; both probably reflect BMC's domestic monopsony.

Thirdly, BMC has been able to make good use of the very few advantages accruing to a very small supplier of large markets: large proportions of total exports have been switched from one market to another (e.g. UK and SA) from one year to the next – a strategy possible in the case of the South African market only because the modest quota given to Botswana (as a proportion of the SA market) is usually a large proportion of total Botswana production. More recently the political concession Botswana secured for her beef from the EEC under the Lomé Conventions (90% rebate of variable levy on a quota amounting to some three quarters of total BMC output) depended for its winning on the very small percentage of EEC beef imports coming from Lomé Convention countries, among which Botswana is the largest beef exporter (see p.158).

(e) Cattle Marketing

Major infrastructural and institutional changes produced during the period an overall trend toward more direct marketing of cattle by breeders themselves to BMC (mostly via agencies), replacing the old buying system based on trading store networks (Table A5). Only the few traders (mainly in Ngamiland) and speculators with well-established buying systems and well-placed holding/fattening facilities continued to deal in cattle by the mid-1970s.

This rising volume and value of BMC throughput has produced rapid growth of marketing agencies (both private and cooperative), improved roads, trek routes and marketing information, making direct marketing by breeders a simpler matter than before, except in the remoter areas where the vestiges of the old system of sales to trading stores remains. It is noteworthy that the more developed marketing structure has not tended to produce much specialization in fattening or finishing, owing partly to the uniformity and low productivity of Botswana's range and its unsuitability to cultivated pastures. Direct marketing has also been substantially encouraged by government since Independence as an alternative to the old system.

In the late 1960s the Ministry of Agriculture began to formulate policy to (i) reduce the number of immature and unfinished cattle slaughtered at Lobatse (thereby raising overall productivity of the industry), and (ii) reduce the difference between up-country cattle prices (auctions and private sales) and BMC prices, in order to secure a better deal for herders not marketing directly.[18] Initial plans involved setting up a parastatal buying organization to act as residual buyer at auction sales, offering a floor price by live grade at which it would be prepared to purchase all cattle offered. The buying organization would operate ranches for the holding and growing out of the purchased cattle. Since this model drew on the activities of the S. Rhodesian Cold Storage Commission and the Zambian Cold Storage Board, BMC was initially cast in the role of the buying organization, but it declined (following the example of CDC twenty years earlier).

In 1973, in the face of misgivings regarding the economic viability of holding grounds,[19] the Botswana Livestock Development Corporation (BLDC) was launched as a subsidiary company of BMC: to buy and hold cattle in Ngamiland and to operate a string of holding ranches in the east of the country on a grazing fee basis. An immediate setback was the scrapping of BMC's higher off-season prices (see p.149), thereby reducing further the viability of holding grounds. BLDC's troubled history has been chronicled recently by Odell (1981): BMC's lack of support and its shedding of BLDC in 1977; the drastic underutilization of the 'grazing for hire' ranches and the mounting debt. In Ngamiland BLDC through its buying operations initially raised prices (1974) but then, through financial pressure, could not sustain them (BMC's prices were also falling to 1976). Then the series of Foot and Mouth outbreaks (late 1977 to

1980) halted buying altogether in Ngamiland. BLDC was rescued in 1979 by the writing off by government of a substantial part of its debt. With the grazing for hire scheme moribund, BLDC's future usefulness will depend on whether its Ngamiland ranches can become effective holding grounds for the Maun abattoir and the planned Francistown abattoir[20]. Other public institutional initiatives in the cattle marketing field have been the BMC's Grazier Schemes and the livestock co-operative marketing societies. The BMC Grazier Scheme was started in 1969, with a stated objective similar to that which motivated the BLDC planners:

'Producers often send to the Abattoir immature animals which, if allowed to develop to maturity, would make a greater contribution to the income from Botswana's livestock industry. The Commission therefore has under consideration a Grazier Scheme which, if finance can be found, would enable the Producer to receive immediate payment and the annimals to grow to maturity before slaughter' (BMC Annual Report 1967 p.10).

But provision of additional funds for cattle buying was probably a major consideration.[21] The design of the scheme was similar to that run in Southern Rhodesia to grow out on private ranches immature cattle bought by the Cold Storage Commission. BMC (with the support of commercial bank funds) buys the immatures and the grazier assumes responsibility for maturing them, reaping the difference between the purchase price plus costs and the final value yielded at the abattoir. Initially the graziers were mainly freehold farmers, but by the mid-1970s substantial allocations of Grazier Scheme money had been made for holding immatures at cattle posts. A breeding stock loan scheme (loans for purchases of heifers) was launched in 1977, and by 1978 cattle valued at P4.5 million were being grown out under the male scheme, while some P0.5 million had been loaned under the female scheme.

New allocations under the schemes were suspended in 1978 following the Foot and Mouth disease outbreaks. It was expected that with the lifting of restrictions on cattle movement in 1980 allocations would be resumed, but 'irresponsible attitudes towards clearing their accounts' by some graziers and poor management of Grazier Scheme cattle (BMC Annual Report 1980:7) have caused the schemes to remain suspended to the present. In 1983 BMC obtained judgements against the few prominent cattlemen who are the principal debtors but has not yet recovered all outstanding debts. This adverse experience has no doubt contributed to the reluctance of the commercial banks to lend under the Hypothecation Act (1980), which had been designed to facilitate lending against the security of cattle.

Livestock cooperative marketing societies during the 1970s showed 'what can only be described as fairly spectacular growth. By 1977 there were 56 active livestock marketing cooperatives which altogether handled 18% of the BMC's total throughput' (McDonald 1979:14), rising to 20% in 1982 (Table A5). The main problems have been the managerial ones typically experienced during the early years of cooperative growth. Despite these, and the formidable difficulties associated with organizing marketing from remote areas, plus the delays in payment which members have to put up with by comparison with sales to a local trader or speculator, the marketing societies have gained at the expense of middle men. Their relative importance in the marketing structure is likely to grow as they enter their phase of consolidation, aided by the easing of marketing difficulties (particularly by more accessible abattoirs); but a condition of further growth will be re-establishment by BMC of control over its quota allocation system which recently has deteriorated to its disorganized state of the early 1970s.[22]

The developments in cattle marketing have reflected the developments in the processing sector and the limitations imposed by the nature of cattle production in Botswana. Specifically: the rapid expansion of BMC value and volume and ascendency of breeder interests through government; the expansion of marketing facilities and institutions; the increasing dominance of direct breeder-to-abattoir marketing and the state's encouragement thereof; the increasing quantities of cattle marketed but the generally stagnant productivity of cattle production (see Chapter 3) making for adverse fattening economies. Together the changes set in motion during 1961–74 are bringing to an end the participation in the cattle business by the old mercantile network; even the largest speculators will find their profits threatened as the process continues. These changes therefore represent at the cattle marketing level the breaking away of the beef export industry from its prior 'reserve' status. Significantly, the trading store network as a whole has expanded rapidly since Independence, to distribute the increasing quantities of imported goods on which Botswana's growing incomes have largely been spent – *but it has lost the cattle business*. It is of further significance for this hypothesis that investment in trading establishments has become the main alternative to cattle investment as an outlet for local capital (see Chapter 9), underlining the point that the rest of the economy (besides the cattle industry) has so far failed to break away from its peripheral status within southern Africa.

(f)   Summary

Owing to favourable world market developments and associated with the ascendancy to political power of cattle-breeding interests, (enjoying the sympathy of the former colonial power, which also provided the major new market), Botswana's beef export industry was enabled during the 1960s and early 1970s to build upon the establishment of the Lobatse abattoir in the previous period and:

1.   Break away from its previous status as a peripheral supplier to regional markets;
2.   Become independent of foreign ownership and control;
3.   Undertake a thorough restructuring of the processing sector and gearing to the standards of its best market.

The impact upon cattle marketing has been to remove it increasingly from the old 'reserve trading system'.

II.   Market instability and the EEC connection

While the 1961 to 1974 period was characterized by internal reorganization and external market growth, the main feature of the post-1975 period has been adjustment to external market shocks through the mid-1970s recession, the entry of Britain into the EEC (meaning that the British market now fell under EEC veterinary and tariff regimes) and the market closures resulting from successive outbreaks of Foot and Mouth disease. The last time the industry had been faced with an external environment as adverse as that of the mid-1970s was in the 1930s; and that had contributed to its collapse. But above all the political circumstances of the mid-1970s were different: in response to the threatened loss of the British market the Botswana government used every diplomatic weapon it possessed – by contrast with the indifference of the British High Commission in the 1930s. Moreover, European political interests now favoured stability in Botswana. Additionally, as argued above in Section I of this chapter, the export industry had now established a viable basis previously lacking.

The nature of the mid-1970s crisis is considered first of all, followed by an examination of the closer ties with the EEC emerging from that crisis. It will be argued that EEC policies have meant that its favours to countries like Botswana are double edged: that although it has been in Botswana's financial interests to accept the favours, the consequences of EEC policies (large scale dumping of beef on world markets) have been to limit other market opportunities.

(a)   The mid-1970s marketing crisis: collapsing prices, Britain's accession to the EEC and Foot and Mouth disease outbreaks

In late 1973 Botswana found herself at a historical peak in her beef export marketing opportunities: a generalized shortage of beef had more than doubled prices since 1971 and shortages of beef were forecast to continue: BMC could pick and choose the best markets (with the exception of the veterinarily exclusive US and Japan); Foot and Mouth disease was a remote memory, there having been no outbreak since 1968.

The crisis which began in 1974 was of a two-fold nature: firstly, an unexpected collapse of prices (due to simultaneous peaking of American and European cattle production cycles combined with slackening demand as income growth slowed in industrialized countries) (Connolly 1976); secondly, Britain's entry into the EEC. Faced with heavy intervention buying in order to maintain domestic prices the EEC suspended all beef imports (except for small GATT quotas). All exporters were hit by the falling market, but those dependent on the British market and without access to alternative markets for chilled and frozen beef were hardest hit: Argentina in particular.[23]

Botswana was saved by the protected South African market – where prices remained high despite the world slump – encouraging the South African Meat Board to increase Botswana's quota. The negotiations for the first Lomé Convention took place in 1974 – the worst circumstances from the standpoint of securing beef import concessions from the EEC. All that was obtained by the time of the signing of the convention in February 1975 was an ACP quota of 23 000 tonnes (of which Botswana was awarded 17 360 tonnes per annum) rising by 7.5% per year, exempt from the EEC common external tariff (CET) of 20%, plus immediate suspension of the EEC import ban which remained in force for all other than ACP exporters (Parris 1978:78, Scott 1978:17). This amounted to hardly any concession at all and was indicative of the EEC's hard-line in Lomé I on commodities falling within CAP: relief from the CET without relief from the Variable Levy (at the time about 100% of depressed world prices) (Scott 1978:17) meant that Botswana effectively had to pay the full cost of the levy, being a price-taker in the British market[24] and therefore facing an extremely elastic demand at the market price. Since the variable levy is designed to raise the price of imports (based on a notion of a 'world price') to the EEC price level, it follows that an exporter to the EEC subject to the levy receives only the 'world price' net. For a small exporter such as Botswana this leaves no advantage in selling to the EEC (a large exporter, such as Argentina, might run some risk of causing a reduction in prices in alternative markets by spurning the EEC).

Botswana succeeded in extracting from the EEC at the last meeting before the signing of Lomé I an undertaking to find means by which ACP beef producers could maintain their position on EEC markets if the CET exemption were insufficient for them to do so (Scott 1978:17). But it was only after vigorous diplomatic efforts at the highest level that Botswana was finally able to secure a 90% reduction in the variable levy (from July 1975), negotiated half yearly in 1976 and then yearly for 1977 and 1978, on a fixed quota of 17 360 tonnes per annum.[25]

The series of Foot and Mouth disease outbreaks in northern Botswana, beginning in October 1977, undermined this gain. The reduction in the variable levy on ACP (principally Botswana's) beef had been a political decision in the face of opposition from the EEC agricultural ministers. Additional technical (veterinary) grounds were now at hand to oppose resumption of imports from Botswana. Moreover, veterinary permission for entry into the British market passed into the hands of the EEC Standing Veterinary Committee from 1st January 1978.

Despite the fact that the outbreaks were successfully confined to the northern veterinary cordon zones (Northern Central District and Ngamiland) and neighbouring zones were sealed off as buffer zones, moves to resume EEC imports from the disease-free south of the country were repeatedly opposed in the Standing Veterinary Committee.

With assistance from Britain and an extensive diplomatic campaign by Botswana in EEC capitals (apparently stressing the likely politically destabilizing impact of a predicted halving of producer prices[26] if access were not restored) permission for resumption of imports from disease-free zones to the British market and the French overseas departments (i.e. Reunion) was obtained from the Council of Ministers in July 1978. From the troubled negotiations of the second Lomé Convention (signed 31st October 1979) Botswana emerged on paper as one of the main beneficiaries of a package little changed from Lomé I (Stevens 1981: Ch. 3) – via the enlarged levy-rebated beef quota of 30 000 tonnes (18 916 tonnes for Botswana) secured for the entire five-year duration of the agreement, and the greater manoeuvrability permitted the ACP beef exporters in altering the total quota allocation among them and rolling over portions thereof into the following year. In addition, Zimbabwe was awarded a quota of 8 100 tonnes in 1981 on joining the Lomé Convention. But although by 1981 Botswana had apparently emerged from a period of stress with a more secure foothold in its best market, structurally its position *vis-a-vis* the EEC had changed, since there was no prospect of the EEC agreeing to resumption of imports from Ngamiland (the most Foot and Mouth disease-prone region), necessitating a major readjustment in export policy. Furthermore, Botswana's diplomatic successes in negotiations with the EEC have masked some of the costs inflicted by EEC agricultural policy and Botswana's privileged access. The situation has not been altered by the third Lomé Convention (Dec. 1984), which increased the ACP levy-rebated beef quota to 38 000 tonnes per annum.

(b)   The costs and benefits for Botswana of EEC Agricultural Policy

The costs and benefits of Botswana's beef marketing link with the EEC can be assessed from two different standpoints: either separating the beef dispensation from the rest of EEC agricultural policy or considering it as one part of that agricultural policy. The latter approach is taken here since the nature of the beef dispensation (exemption from the variable levy particularly) is argued to be determined by EEC agricultural policy as a whole (i.e. domestic price support and subsidized export of surpluses) and should not be separated from the entire policy in assessing its impact on other countries. The direct aid component of the Lomé Convention (access to the EDF) is treated as independent of the beef policy and therefore left out of account.

(i) *Benefits*
The benefits of EEC agricultural policy for Botswana are purely financial and of a two-fold nature:

(i) Higher prices for chilled and frozen beef through exemption from the CET and 90% of the variable levy on a quota of 18 916 tonnes of boneless beef. This is a benefit that has already been realized.

(ii) STABEX payments for exports of hides and skins. This is only a potential benefit since to date (1985) the market for hides and skins has remained sufficiently buoyant as to dis-qualify them from STABEX supplementation. Assuming that this situation will continue this potential benefit is not consi-dered further.

Von Massow (1982) has estimated the nominal protection given to Botswana's beef production through its sales to the EEC by cal-culating for boneless beef exports the extra revenue reaped from the difference between EEC prices and the average of the prices in other markets to which Botswana sold boneless beef, and showing it as a proportion of BMC revenue (Tables 8.3 and 8.4). Boneless beef makes up some three-quarters to four-fifths of total BMC sales value and is the commodity to which all the EEC's beef preferences apply.[27]

Table 8.4, row 6, indicates that the value of EEC beef preferences was at its maximum in 1976 and 1977, declining thereafter. Three factors account for the decline. Firstly, the series of Foot and Mouth disease outbreaks reducing sales to the EEC in 1978 and 1980 particularly. Secondly, the recovery of the South African market from 1980–82 (after its weakness of 1977–79), bringing higher prices and sales volumes which increased the proportion of total sales from this source (thereby decreasing the share from the EEC). Thirdly, the decision by the EEC after the series of Foot and Mouth outbreaks not to readmit beef from the northern Central District and Ngamiland. With approximately one-third[28] of total offtake

Table 8.3: *BMC: Prices received in different markets (Pula per tonne, current)*
(Average quality boneless beef, per tonne, net of selling and distribution costs)

	1972	1973	1974	1975	1976	1977	1978	1979	1980	1981
(1) UK and EEC (including Reunion)	880	1070	1070	1150	1470	1410	1580	2160	2400	2440
(2) South Africa	589	854	1012	800	920	880	960	1500	1700	1970
(3) Other (excluding UK, EEC and SA)	607	879	999	942	1168	816	1128	1679	1612	1777
(4) Local Sales*					778	839	852	800		
(5) Average of all markets (weighted by volume sold in each market)	790	1020	1030	980	1290	1210	1260	1840	1760	2070

Sources: Von Massow 1982 (Table A10) (1975–81); BMC (1972–74); Ministry of Agriculture 'Botswana: A Handbook of Livestock Statistics' (1978 and 1980); for local prices.
*Prices received from local sales were not available for all years.

Table 8.4: *Benefits to Botswana of UK and EEC market preferences*

	1972	1973	1974	1975	1976	1977	1978	1979	1980	1981
(1)Prices received for exports to UK and EEC (pula/tonne) (incl. Reunion)	880	1070	1070	1150	1470	1410	1580	2160	2400	2440
(2)Prices received for exports to other markets (average) (pula/tonne)	589	854	1012	800	920	880	960	1500	1700	1970
(3)Difference (1)−(2)	291	216	58	350	550	530	620	660	700	470
(4)Exports to UK and EEC (tonnes)	10774	17710	5337	11726	18277	18439	10181	16664	1415	5569
(5)Gross benefits (P000) (3)×(4)	3135	3825	310	4104	10052	9773	6312	10998	991	2617
(6)Gross benefits as share of BMC's total payments to producers (%)	21	14	1	15	32	32	29	24	4	5

Source: Reproduced from Von Massow (1982: Table 4) 1975 to 1981 and extended back to 1972 using BMC data.
Note: All prices are net of all selling and distribution costs.

coming from these areas this indicates a substantial reduction in the benefits of EEC preferences, compared to 1976 and 1977.

Turning briefly from the EEC to the South African market, it might be expected that the protected nature of this market (import restrictions, guaranteed 'floor' prices) should similarly make for

Table 8.5: *Benefits to Botswana of South African market protection (boneless beef only)*

	1974	1977	1980	1981
[1]Prices received from SA (Pula per tonne)	1012	880	1700	1970
[2]Prices from other markets (excluding EEC) (Pula per tonne)	999	816	1612	1777
[3]Difference (1)−(2)	13	64	88	193
[4]Exports to SA (tonnes)	7638	5844	4340	11232
[5]Gross benefits (P000) (3)×(4)	99	374	382	2168
[6]Gross benefits as share of BMC's total payments to producers (nearest %)	0	0	0	4%

Source: BMC

Table 8.6: *BMC's boneless beef sales (P000, current prices)*

	EEC	SA	Other	Total
1972	9481	426	3331	13328
1973	18950	503	4042	23495
1974	5711	7730	4543	17984
1975	13485	6926	1853	22264
1976	26867	6062	492	33421
1977	25999	5143	2031	33173
1978	16086	6083	4334	26503
1979	35994	5700	16904	58598
1980	3396	7378	19372	30126
1981	13588	22127	16973	52688

Source: BMC

prices in excess of external prices. But the fluctuations in the South African market mean that this is not always the case (compare rows 2 and 3 of Table 8.3); only in 1974, 1977, 1980 and 1981 were prices fetched by Botswana beef in South Africa better than those in other markets (excluding the EEC); and even then the price difference was so small as to be of insignificant proportional benefit in payments to producers (Table 8.5).

But Botswana has benefited indirectly from the insulation of South Africa from world markets, causing its fluctuations to be out of phase with world markets. Thus in both 1974 and 1981–82 the South African market was strong while world markets were weakening.

Although when the South African market has been strong its *prices* have not been much better (except in 1981–82 – see Table 8.3) than elsewhere, at these times the South African *quota* allocated to Botswana has been raised considerably. The benefits therefore have come mainly through increased sales volume at times when other markets have been weak. Coincidentally, the strong South African market in 1981–82 also provided a convenient outlet for the offtake from the northern areas excluded from the EEC. In sum, South African preferences, while usually (during the past decade) much less valuable than EEC preferences (see Table 8.4) have been usefully counter-cyclical to the world market.

(ii)   *Costs*
The costs incurred by Botswana as a result of EEC beef policy can be classified as avoidable and unavoidable. Botswana can do little to alter the price and trade reducing effects of dumping of exports by EEC. By contrast, some costs arise from the nature of Botswana's political economy in its interaction with EEC policy, and are potentially avoidable. It must be stressed that the costs classified 'avoidable' do not arise from EEC policy but effectively from Botswana government policy and should therefore be omitted if the purpose is to weigh up the costs and benefits for Botswana of EEC policy. They are included here only to indicate that additional costs have in fact been incurred by the country in association with EEC policy.

Unavoidable costs
EEC dumping of beef onto external markets since 1980 has reduced both prices and markets for Botswana's beef outside the EEC and

South Africa. (Von Massow 1982:34). Export restitutions (approximating the difference between EEC prices and realized export prices) are paid to exporters.

For Botswana to date this cost has been largely potential rather than real: in 1980 when the EEC market was still closed the Angolan market was available. In 1981 and 1982 when Angola, Mozambique and Zimbabwe were importing EEC beef the South African market was strong and the EEC was open. Had Botswana tried to sell in West Africa, the Middle and Far East or Eastern Europe, she would no doubt have faced prices lowered by EEC dumping.[29] But better markets were available.

Thus although EEC dumping may not yet have cost Botswana any export revenue, it has made her more dependent on preferential access to the EEC itself and more dependent on the South African market. Whether these costs will be potential or real in the future will depend on whether EEC surpluses persist. EEC policy to date of granting real increases in producer prices (with the brief exception of 1976–78) despite surpluses, suggests a trend to long-term overproduction running through the shorter term beef production cycle.[30] If so then Botswana's main option for marketing exports from the northern areas excluded from the EEC will be South Africa. But the volatility of the South African market suggests that other markets will have to be found periodically; probably at lower prices (since entry into the South African market is controlled by quota).

Whether or not the unavoidable costs of EEC policy increase in future their impact on Botswana's cattle production is unlikely to be structurally significant, as the relations stressed in Chapter 3 indicate: the comparative advantage of much of Botswana's land and labour lies in cattle production and is unlikely to be shifted by marginal (or even rather larger) changes in real prices. This comparative advantage of Botswana's extends internationally, as Von Massow (1982:43–44) has demonstrated.[31]

While a comparative cost analysis is static and oversimplifies it does underline the strength of Botswana's export competitiveness, within the volume limits imposed by the production system.

Avoidable costs
These are costs associated with EEC policy arising from its interaction with Botswana's political economy, and which are therefore

potentially avoidable. Firstly, much of the costs imposed by Foot and Mouth disease closures could have been avoided had a northern abattoir existed in the late 1970s. Secondly, there is the opportunity cost of channelling scarce development funds into an industry which is already subsidized (see Chapter 9 Section II), is already the major focus for private local investment and does not require additional revenue in order to maintain investment in it. The funds in question are the 90% rebate on the EEC levy which (by arrangement with EEC) is subtracted by the Botswana Government from payments for BMC shipments to EEC. So far it has been paid directly back into BMC's general revenue.

This is an internal decision unstipulated in the Lomé agreements. For the four years 1977/78–1980/81 the levy rebate amounted to about P11 million per annum on average – twice the average development budget of the Ministry of Agriculture during the same period.[32]

But this opportunity cost has so far been held down by government's lack of implementation capacity (owing to the continuing shortage of educated manpower), meaning that development funds have not been the constraint on development project implementation (with the brief exception of 1982 when the government's development budget was cut back owing to the slump in diamond export earnings).

The third possible avoidable cost arises from the interaction of the levy-rebated quota with the monopsonistic position of BMC and its alleged control by large well-placed cattle owning interests. The argument, most recently and forcefully put by the Mmusi Commission[33], is that given the difference between 'world prices' and EEC prices, BMC exports in excess of the EEC levy-rebated quota tend to lower the average price to the producer; therefore it is in the interests of large, well-placed cattle suppliers to restrict BMC exports to an amount approximating the EEC quota.

Plausibility has been lent this argument by the composition of the BMC Board, on which large producers are strongly represented, by BMC's unwillingness to involve itself in up-country cattle buying in a situation where, it is sometimes believed, many more cattle are available for sale but do not reach the abattoir because of marketing difficulties,[34] and finally by BMC's long-term opposition to the establishment of a northern abattoir. The northern abattoir proposal, after simmering throughout the 1970s (Hubbard 1981), was finally precipitated in 1979 by the clear inadequacy of Lobatse to cope with the record drought-induced offerings of that year; other factors were the difficulties of yet further expansion at Lobatse and the emerging realization that the EEC would no longer accept Ngamiland beef under any circumstances – implying a complete separation of Ngamiland marketing and processing from the rest of the country.

Whatever the case in the past, the risk of the limited EEC quota encouraging restriction of export volume by BMC seems small for the future, even if BMC's objective is to maximize producer prices. There are four reasons: Firstly, the scheduled increase in BMC slaughtering capacity (Maun abattoir opened early 1983, Francistown to open within the decade) will oblige BMC to maintain high levels of throughput in order to spread overhead costs. Secondly, the decision to produce carcase and boneless beef rather than canned beef at Maun eroded the possibility of totally different and independent price structures for Maun and Lobatse.[35] Maun prices per head presently approximate Lobatse prices minus transport costs per head from Maun to Lobatse. This represents a commitment to 'dilution' of EEC prices. Thirdly, Government has accepted the Mmusi Commission's recommendation that livestock marketing cooperatives be represented on the BMC board, hopefully lessening the domination by large individual suppliers. Fourthly, all the ACP beef exporters (including Botswana) underfulfil their levy rebated quotas.

The third avoidable cost of EEC policy consists of the social costs resulting from the expansion of cattle production – to the extent that the higher prices provided by the EEC market have contributed to the expansion of cattle production. On the assumption that the trend in expansion of cattle production has followed the trend in availability of private investible funds (see Chapter 3 p. 60), higher cattle prices have resulted in expansion of cattle production through their being one source of increased investible funds. The social costs of the expansion of cattle production are the subject of the next chapter.

To conclude this discussion of the benefits and costs of EEC policy for Botswana the future should be considered briefly. On the benefits side, the levels of the mid 1970s will probably not be regained as long as the northern one third of offtake is excluded from the EEC. The revenue benefits will continue to fluctuate inversely with world market prices (i.e. reflecting the level of EEC protectionism through the variable levy). On the costs side the unavoidable cost inflicted by EEC dumping will probably continue in the longer term until CAP is reformed. Concerning the avoidable costs: the opportunity cost of directing the levy rebate back to BMC will increase when government's development funds replace manpower as the constraint on project implementation; any past tendency of BMC's towards restricting the volume of exports will probably not continue in the future; expansion of cattle production as a result of higher EEC prices will be minor if the revenue benefits remain small. In sum, EEC net benefits to Botswana have diminished since the mid-1970s and will probably not recover soon to their former level.

III.   Conclusion

This chapter has stressed two aspects of the post-colonial experience of the beef export processing sector. Firstly, the establishment of a 'growth industry' during the period 1961–74 by completion of the transition begun in the 1950s, at both the political level (nationalization) and economic level (expansion and gearing to the requirements of overseas markets). Secondly, the nature and implications of the industry's preferential ties with the EEC, which has been the main feature of its experience during the troubled marketing climate of the post-1974 period.

In the following chapter, attention is turned to the social and developmental conflicts emerging as a result of the expansion of the cattle industry as a whole during the post-colonial period.

Chapter 9
Post-colonial Period II: Contradictions emerging from a growth industry within a peripheral economy

Earlier chapters (Chapters 4 to 8) have analyzed the dynamic of the cattle and beef export industry culminating in its emergence in the post-colonial period as a 'growth industry' providing a market of paramount political importance in a country where most senior government personnel are prominent cattle owners. This chapter marshals evidence concerning hypotheses 4 and 5 of Chapter 1 (p.7) – namely, that during the post-colonial period the growth in cattle production (as the major industry accessible to local capital), has caused the emergence of conflicts between its further expansion on the one hand and social welfare on the other, in respect of fiscal incidence, resource use and resource distribution.

The context in which these characteristics of a 'staple trap' (in which growth tends to be immiserising, see Chapter 1 p.5) have emerged has been that of the most rapid economic growth in the country's history. The growth has resulted mainly from mining developments (diamonds and copper-nickel) and investment of vastly increased government revenues (from the revised SACUA as well as mining) in urban and rural infrastructure, together with beef exports. The amounts of investible funds available publicly and privately have increased greatly. Yet as a result of the continuing peripheral nature of the economy and its land resource the reinvestment of domestically retained profits and other surplus into production (as distinct from infrastructure) has favoured cattle production and import trading rather than manufacturing. Import trading, together with mining, continues to be the main focus for foreign investment, although a small import substituting manufacturing sector has emerged in the early 1980s.

The argument of the present chapter focuses on the continued concentration of local private investment in cattle production, which has:

(i) encouraged a reversal of fiscal incidence on the industry since colonial times (from net tax to net subsidy);

(ii) brought about an over-expansion of cattle production in some areas at the expense of cattle productivity and future grazing resources, and

(iii) precipitated a land reform programme (the Tribal Grazing Land Policy) whose benefits have so far accrued to only a small group of people yet which threatens to absorb a substantial proportion of the country's land.

Sections I and II deal with private and public resource allocation, Section III with resource use and Section IV with resource distribution, focusing on the TGLP. Section V concludes.

I.   Private resource allocation

The flow of private investible funds into the industry can be divided into those from savings on cattle transactions and those from other sources. These are used to pay for material inputs and imports of breeding stock. To arrive at total investment in cattle production the change in value of cattle inventories during the period must be added to the flow of investible funds. Thus:

$$I_t = \text{Flow of investible funds}_t + \text{Inventory value change}_t$$
$$= Ic_t + Io_t + (S_t - S_{t-1})\ V_t$$

Where I is total investment in cattle production;
  Ic is reinvestment of savings from cattle transactions into cattle
      production;
  Io is investment of savings from other activities into cattle produc-
      tion;
  S is the cattle stock (number and weight)
  V is the average value of cattle per head;
  t and $t-1$ are time periods.

In chapter 3 (p.55) the flow of investible funds into cattle production historically was argued to have been a function of the availability of investible funds domestically. Marginal changes in the rates of
return to cattle and alternative investments were argued not to have
been determinants owing to the much greater returns to cattle
investment and inflexibilities in switching of resources to alternative
uses. Thus, at the level of private investment, the link between
growth of beef exports and expansion of cattle production has been
via the increased investible funds which rising prices and sales
volumes have provided.

By this understanding, the impact of beef export growth on the
flow of investible funds into cattle production has been similar to
that of other factors increasing the savings available to rurally based
households, principally the increased salary and wage earnings
post-Independence as the state was established, plus employment in
mining and infrastructural development. Cattle production investment (water points, breeding stock, medicines and feed) has probably been the main outlet for personal savings of citizens, from
whatever source they have been earned.[1]

But the flow of investible funds $(Ic_t + Io_t)$ has been only a small
proportion of total investment in cattle production since the vast bulk
has consisted of increases in the value of cattle stocks $(S_t - S_{t-1})V_t$.
Column 2 of Table 9.1 shows that increases in the value of cattle
stocks usually account for over 80% of investment in the entire
agricultural sector – the result mainly of the very large size of the
cattle herd relative to other agricultural assets.[2] It follows that the
beef export industry has been the major source of increase in value
of cattle stocks (since BMC producer prices have increased much
faster than the cattle population e.g. 213% against 44% during
1970–80, and increases in V are determined by increases in BMC
producer prices) and thereby the main source of increases in
investment in cattle production.

The increase in value of cattle stocks is not simply a 'paper value' without real significance for private resource allocation, unless such increase is ephemeral – which has not been the case (see the real price trend in Fig. A2). It reflects the pattern of investment decision making to the extent that the increased value continues to be accumulated in the form of cattle in succeeding periods (as has been the case generally) rather than sold off and the proceeds invested elsewhere. At another level, it has encouraged owners of cattle to take action to protect the value of their investments – most notably in efforts to secure private control over pieces of communal land (to keep out competitors for grazing) and to secure state subsidization.

The purpose of Table 9.1 below is to illustrate the proportionate importance of investment in cattle within investment in the agricultural sector as a whole and within all the sectors which provide an alternative to cattle investment (i.e. excluding mining, government, banking, water and electricity, social and personal services).

Table 9.1: *Value of increases in the cattle herd (Pula, current) and their percentage of gross capital formation*

	1.	2.	3.	4.
		As per cent of gross capital formation in:		
			Agric. etc.	
	Value of increases in the cattle herd (P million) (current prices)	Agric., Forestry and Fishing	+ Manufacturing + Building + Trade + Transport	Total
1965	− 5.0	–	–	–
1966	− 3.8	–	–	–
1967/68	3.6	86	68	30
1968/69	6.1	84	63	35
1971/72	− 0.7	–	–	–
1973/74	9.4	87	22	10
1976/77	14.8	88	36	15
1977/78	19.2	96	58	16
1978/79	15.7	99	37	8
1979/80	12.5	76	23	4
1980/81	9.0	67	12	3
1981/82	2.0	33	2	1

Source: National Accounts of Botswana (various years)

Column 1 of Table 9.1 shows changes in the value of the national herd, reflecting changes in both cattle numbers and cattle prices. The mid-1960s drought caused the negative figures of 1965 and 1966 and a price fall that of 1971/72. Column 2 indicates the major proportion of total agricultural investment accounted for by increases in the value of cattle (except in drought years like 1981-82). Column 3 tries to provide a rough idea of increases in the value of the national herd as a percentage of investment in the sectors which provide an investment alternative to cattle; it can only make the point that investment in cattle (which are owned overwhelmingly by nationals) is a substantial proportion of total capital formation in all alternative investment areas even including foreign and parastatal investment. Thus Column 3 understates the degree of concentration of local private capital investment in cattle. Both column 3 and column 4 indicate that relative investment in cattle production fell during the mining and infrastructural boom of the early 1970s, and then rose once more with the end of that boom and the onset of the Foot and Mouth disease outbreaks (restricting BMC throughput, and therefore total offtake of cattle, in 1977/78 and 1980). The Jwaneng mining boom underlies the fall from 1979, together with the 1979 and post 1981 droughts.

It is not clear from Table 9.1 (or other available data) whether alternative investment opportunities for local capital have become more competitive with cattle during the post-colonial period. They probably have – particularly in the expanding import trading sector (bottle stores notoriously!) which, like cattle production, is an activity for the household supplementary to wage or salary employment. Even so, there has been no obvious letting up in investment in cattle production (allowing for the herd decreases in the mid-1960s and 1980s droughts). Moreover, long-term accumulation of cattle is not determined by the trade-off facing investible funds alone. In Chapter 3 it was argued that in the long term net accumulation of cattle, in aggregate over the long term, could continue in the face of rising rates of return in other sectors – owing to the continuing superiority of returns to cattle investments and to the barriers against switching investment out of cattle. Furthermore, savings from incomes generated in other sectors have partially flowed back into cattle production.

As regards alternative uses for the land and labour used in cattle production, little has happened to make them more competitive – a conclusion drawn from the fact that the *absolute* level of investment in cattle production has risen rapidly, thereby absorbing increasing quantities of land and labour rather than less. The returns to the major alternative use for *both* these inputs i.e. crop farming, *declined* relative to those of cattle production until the late 1970s, if indexes of market prices (Table 9.2 below) provide an indication thereof (which they do provided unit costs of cattle keeping have not risen faster than unit costs of crop production). Since 1979 producer prices for grain have risen quickly but, in the face of a major drought, grain production has not responded positively.

Table 9.2: *Cattle prices, grain prices and farming costs (current): indexes*

Year	BMC producer price	Botswana sorghum price	SA farm input prices: all items
1960	100	100	100
1965	152	98	106
1970	217	113	121
1975	429	199	239
1980	645	464	429
1982	844	602	559
1983	863	692	na
1984	na	909	na

Sources: BMC producer prices: Fig. A.1
Cereals producer prices: SA summer cereals prices until 1975; thereafter sorghum prices offered by Botswana Agricultural Marketing Board (BAMB).
SA prices: Abstract of Agricultural Statistics 1983. Division of Economic Services, Dept. of Agriculture, Pretoria.

Note: No domestic farming costs indexes are available for Botswana. SA indexes are regarded as a good proxy owing to the extensive farm goods trade with South Africa.

Not only has the proportion of rural resources in arable farming fallen but there has also been no trend to increasing *absolute* levels of resource use (labour and land) (Opschoor 1981:3 and Table 1) by arable farming, despite increasing population. In short, with the noteworthy exception of the Baralong farms[3], arable agricultural production has stagnated in the post-colonial period, with total production ranging (with rainfall) widely around an average which is an increasingly small proportion of domestic requirements. Smallstock production has had neither the market nor the veterinary support to compete with cattle for land use.

In summary, prior to 1970 the beef export industry was the 'leading sector' of the country's economy ('leading sector' being used in the staple theory sense of the sector with most linkages, and the focus of investment and economic growth). Thereafter mining (as Colclough & McCarthy 1980:63 argue convincingly) and government (via the more than doubling of revenues from the revised SACUA) became the leading sectors. But at the level of local private resource allocation, the cattle industry has remained the focus for investible funds from all sources. As such the growth of cattle production post-Independence is the result of a transfer of private resources from other sectors (notably mining and government employment) to cattle production, as well as being the result of increased generation of investible funds within the sector itself, from market expansion and a rising price trend. Increased allocation of public resources to the cattle industry has been a further factor, as the next section argues.

II. Public resource allocation: fiscal incidence

Although the historical evidence available concerning fiscal incidence upon the cattle industry is incomplete, it suggests:

(i)   that during the colonial period taxes on revenues from cattle and beef exports constituted at least 20% of government revenue from domestic sources, the bulk of the rest coming from payments under the 1910 customs agreement with South Africa.[4] This is based on the estimates in Table 9.3 below. By contrast, at the present time the cattle industry usually contributes only some 5% to 10% of total domestic revenue.

(ii) that during the colonial period government revenues from cattle were usually more than double government recurrent expenditures on the industry (Column 3 of Table 9.3). By contrast, in the post-colonial phase state expenditures on the industry began to exceed tax revenues from it, especially if after 1975 the EEC levy rebate (see Chapter 8) is included as state expenditure. (Table 9.4).

Table 9.3: *Estimated public revenues and recurrent expenditures related to the cattle industry: colonial period*

	1. Recurrent expenditures on cattle^A (P000 current prices)	2. Revenues from cattle^B (P000 current prices)	3. 1÷2 ×100 %	4. Cattle revenues as % of total domestic revenues	5. Recurrent expenditures on cattle as % of total expenditure %
1922/23	15,4	58,8	26	32	9
1930/31	26,7	78,6	34	26	9
1935/36	43,8	58,6	75	22	10
1940/41	53	113,5	47	27	12
1945/46	84	223,2	38	27	12
1950/51	131	302,7	43	27	12
1955/56	192	394,4	49	20	9
1960/61	609	484,7^C	126	19	13
1965/66	655	1 504,3^C	44	28	6

Source: Hermans 1974, Tables 1, 2, 3.

Notes:
A   Agricultural and Veterinary Services (3/4 of this after 1940 when Agricultural Department is started);
B   Based on following assumptions: Revenues deriving from cattle=0.5 Hut/Native/Graded Tax+0.5 personal income tax+1.0 Export duties
C   Includes tax revenue from Lobatse abattoir.

Table 9.4: *Estimated public revenues and recurrent expenditures related to the cattle industry: post-colonial period*

	Revenue^A	Expenditure^B	(EEC levy rebate)
1971–72	1.4	1.3	
1977–78	7.0	17.3	(10.6)
1978–79	6.6	27.7	(17.6)
1979–80	5.2	27.4	(14.9)
1980–81	11.1	19.0	(0.0)

Sources: Republic of Botswana 'Annual Statements of Accounts' 1971-72.
Republic of Botswana 'Report of the Presidential Commission on Economic Opportunities' May 1982: Table 5.3.1.

Notes:

A *Revenue* categories:
Dept. of Animal Health revenue
Dept. of Agricultural Field Service revenue
Tax on BMC
Tax collected on farming companies and individuals

B *Expenditure* categories
Dept. of Animal Health recurrent
Dept. of Agricultural Field Services recurrent (50%)
Min. of Agriculture Development budget (cattle related projects)
Rebate of EEC levy

The shift in the fiscal position of the industry post-1970 reflects firstly the alteration in the industry's status from being the leading sector overall in the economy while remaining the focus for private local investment. The result is that the industry has contributed a declining proportion of public revenue while attracting an increasing amount of public expenditure as infrastructural support for the private investment (veterinary fences and requisites, stock route maintenance, breeding and management research, bull purchase subsidies, artificial insemination subsidies, water point subsidies and subsidies to BLDC). World Bank loans for implementation of TGLP (on-loaned and administered by government) provide a further element of subsidy – potentially large if TGLP ranches are unable to repay the loans (see p.190–1). The declining proportion of public revenues contributed by the cattle industry is above all the result of extremely rapid growth in other revenue sources (customs and excise and minerals). Public revenue from agriculture (virtually all from cattle) and BMC have themselves increased (P1 million in 1971/72, P3.8 million in 1975/76, P4.7 million in 1978/79) (Lewis and Mokgethi 1981: Table 5).

A second reason for the shift in the fiscal position of the industry is the alteration in the tax structure of the economy. With indepen dence the 'African' personal taxes (mainly fixed sum taxes) were abolished and replaced by a unified income tax. This meant tax relief for the majority of cattle-owning households, since their incomes now fell below the taxable minimum (Hudson 1981:67). It also meant effectively the abolition of a tax on cattle incomes and migrant earnings – since historically these were the only sources of cash income for payment of the colonial 'African' personal taxes. At the same time, Local Government tax was introduced to compen sate local governments to an extent for the loss of 'African' taxes (an increasing proportion of which had been paid to Tribal Treasuries in the post-war period) (Hermans 1974:97). But the amounts col lected under Local Government tax have been relatively small.

A third reason (closely related to the first) has been the power of the cattle industry lobby in government to turn the changing struc ture of the economy to advantage. The cattle export tax (over which there had been so much debate in the 1940s), rose from P1 to P2.25 per head exported between 1951 and 1965[5] amounting to some 7% of domestic revenues in that period. But it has remained at the same level since then, and Hermans (1974:99) remarks that there had been 'considerable public opposition to any upward revision of the rate of duty'. In real terms (and relative to cattle prices) the rate of this tax had dwindled to insignificance, as have the proceeds in their proportionate contribution to the fiscus.

Taxation of income from cattle farming was set on a lenient basis by the Income Tax Act of 1973 and made even more so by the amending Act of 1979. Government justified this as an emphasis on rural development by providing 'valuable incentives for farming development' (Government Paper No. 1 of 1973, Para. 29). The tax concessions include allowance for averaging of income over three years (to iron out income variations); 'standard values' (for calcula tion of income from inventory charges) which were only about a quarter of market values in 1981 (Hudson 1981:b:4) but have recently (1983) been raised; deduction of farming losses from tax able income from other sources (including employment); deduction from farming income of purchase of land from a non-citizen and

180

deduction of the entire costs of capital improvements (e.g. a borehole) in a single tax year. Furthermore, collection of farming taxes is probably inefficient: Hudson (1981a:76) estimates that taxes are collected from only one in eight tax-liable farmers. Tax yield is not affected to this extent since the largest farmers and farming companies pay the most tax and are the easiest for the Tax Department to trace. In 1978/79, the five farmers with the highest taxable incomes paid 41% of all taxes received from unincorporated farmers, and the four farming companies with the highest taxable incomes paid 64% of all taxes received from farming companies.[6] In overview, the leniency of farming taxation lies not in the rates charged on taxable income (these being the same as for all other individuals or companies) but in the generosity of the deductions allowed in order to arrive at taxable income from net income and in inefficient collection.

Given the political power of cattle farmers, it is perhaps surprising to note that the taxation of BMC's revenue has risen considerably during 1966–81; from some 5% to 11% of net sales, and from 8% to 16% of payments to cattle suppliers, at which levels they are now stabilizing, as indicated by Fig. 9.1 below. The reason for the increase is that the tax basis of BMC[7] was fixed in 1965 when the beef industry was the leading sector (and therefore cast as the main generator of public funds) and when annual beef sales were only some P7 million, and probably thought unlikely often to exceed greatly the P9 million mark – above which additional net sales (i.e. gross sales minus marketing expenses) were taxed at the maximum rate i.e. approximately 11%.

The tax base set in 1965 represented a compromise between the Ministry of Finance and cattle farmers. The Ministry of Finance's proposal (that BMC's taxable income should be 30% of its net sales) was designed to ensure that tax receipts remained at the level of those received previously from BPA[8], from ECCO profits and from Mr Cyril Hurvitz as minority shareholder in ECCO (approximately P1 million per annum).

The farmers and cattle traders for their part (as represented by resolutions in the Livestock Industry Advisory Committee) protested that ECCO's and Hurvitz's profits had been superinflated by receiving BPA's beef at fixed 1961 prices instead of current prices, and therefore provided no realistic basis for future taxation; furthermore, they had suffered heavily in the drought and were already paying export taxes and income taxes (raised in 1964 by the raising

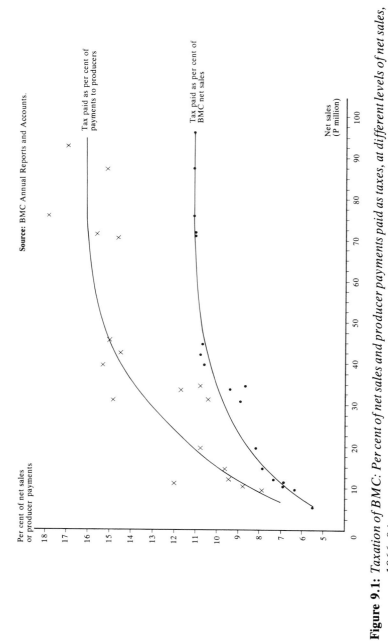

Figure 9.1: *Taxation of BMC: Per cent of net sales and producer payments paid as taxes, at different levels of net sales, 1966–84.*

of the 'standard values' for livestock inventory valuation) on their livestock earnings.

At the time government was motivated by '. . . the need to ensure, on the one hand, that government does not overtax the livestock industry and thereby discourage production and investment in the territory, and on the other that government must make every effort to bridge the wide gap between revenue and expenditure . . . bearing in mind the unfortunate fact that the livestock industry is the only industry that can yield any significant amount of tax in the Territory and that most people in one way or another derive their livelihood from it'.[9] In the event government settled in favour of the farmers in the short and medium term by imposing a 'sliding scale' by which immediate tax yields from the abattoir were halved (by comparison with the P1 million received from ECCO and Hurvitz previously) and did not surpass previous levels until 1971. Probably neither farmers nor government expected that in the 1970s net sales would rise to so high a level that taxable income would tend towards one third of net sales, as the proportion of net sales below P9 million per annum dwindled. (See Fig. 9.1). BMC did protest in 1969 and 1971[10] that the 'sliding scale' tax basis meant that cattle suppliers would receive no benefit from the economies of scale on higher levels of throughput at the abattoir since these would be absorbed by increased taxes; but this had no impression on a government then preoccupied with achieving budgetary independence from Britain. In the booming prosperity of the industry accompanying the more than doubling of the cattle price between 1970 and 1974 the increased taxation apparently became a minor concern for individual cattle owners, enjoying, as they were, increased subsidization of livestock services.

Recently the topic of taxation of the cattle industry has returned to public debate. Hudson (1981a and b) and the Presidential Economic Opportunities Commission (Mmusi Commission) (Para. 5.11) have recommended a raised slaughter tax at BMC and an increased contribution to the fiscus from the industry. While rejecting the increased slaughter tax proposal, government has committed itself to a '. . . speedy examination of the possible means of raising more revenue from this sector. This will take account of the present incidence of taxation of, and subsidies to, the cattle sector, with the objective of ensuring that the sector as a whole is not a net recipient of government funds' (Government White Paper 'National Policy on Economic Opportunities' 1982).

This guarded intention of fiscal neutrality for the sector which is the main depository of Batswana wealth suggests a possible continuation of the post-Independence trend to favouring the cattle industry fiscally. To date the opportunity cost of this policy has been low, owing to implementation capacity rather than public funds having been the constraint on development projects. But in future, as the shortage of skilled manpower lessens, the cost will escalate.

III. Resource use

It was argued in Chapter 3 that cattle production has expanded mainly through geographical extension of a fundamentally unchanged system of cattle production into the sandveld and areas of the eastern hardveld previously not grazed perenially. Together with the expansion of cleared fields, this process has resulted in increasing shortage of land in several of the more densely populated parts of the country (notably Tlokweng, Kgatleng, Malete, Southern Ngwaketse, Rolong and the North-East). In the sandveld, new grazing lands with accessible ground water are increasingly few.

Future expansion of cattle production along the same lines must ultimately undermine itself in the face of land shortage, as the nutritional status of cattle worsens – particularly during droughts. [11] The heavy losses in the North-East in the current drought (1982–85) may indicate that this stage has already been reached there.

The process of self-undermining growth of the cattle population is further hastened by the damage it inflicts on the grazing land itself – self-evidently through trampling and denudation in the immediate vicinity of water points, more contestably through destruction of perennial grasses and bush encroachment further afield. No other single issue has attracted more attention in writings on cattle production in Botswana. [12] At the root of any solution is the political question of access to land and control of its use, a question which has become increasingly vexed as the frontier of virgin grazing land ends and individuals strive to lay claim to land surrounding water points in order to prevent encroachment of new water points and herds upon it. The issue has come to a head in the Tribal Grazing Lands Policy.

IV. Resource distribution: The impact of the tribal grazing lands policy (TGLP)

The TGLP was launched in 1975 with the objectives of raising the productivity of cattle production and halting the negative side-effects of its path of expansion, namely the increasing concentration of cattle holdings and overgrazing. The provision of secure legal claim to land for larger cattle owners was not an explicit objective of the policy except in so far as this was assumed to be a precondition for more productive cattle-raising and conservation of the range. The main results of the first decade of the policy have been the strengthening of district land use planning machinery (mainly Land Boards), extensive allocation of land and credit to ranchers and scrapping of the policy's communal area proposals.

(a) Outline of the Policy

The TGLP was launched in Government Paper No. 2 of 1975. It set out the problem as follows:

'Increased herds, under the system of uncontrolled grazing, have led to serious overgrazing around villages, surface water sources and boreholes. Overgrazing has led to sheet erosion and bush encroachment which reduces the amount of good grazing. This is worst for the small cattle owners, most of whose herds graze in the village areas'. (para. 10).

'Under the present system, the wealthier cattle owners secure virtually exclusive rights to the land around their boreholes. More and more grazing land gets taken up by a few large cattle owners. Meanwhile those who only own a few livestock stay where they are in the village areas with little hope of improvement. . . .' (p.11).

The alternative, which the Tribal Grazing Land Policy was supposed to realize, was billed as '. . . improved grazing and livestock management, much more money, better distributed to more people'. (Title of Part III). The basis of the policy was the division of existing grazing land into 'commercial' and 'reserved' areas. 'Commercial' areas were to be blocks of fenced ranches owned by individuals or syndicates (groups). 'Reserved' land would remain idle 'so that there will be some left for our children and for those of us who have no cattle now' (Fig. 1). 'Communal' land would remain unfenced and be for 'traditional grazing' (Ibid). The theory was that the policy would ensure greater productivity of cattle and a halt to overgrazing in both 'commercial' and 'communal' zones by:

In the 'Commercial' zones
   (1)   Associating private cost with private benefit through conferring leasehold title therein.
   (2)   Putting into practice 'an improved system of range management' which although 'it is simple to use allows us to raise many more cattle on the same amount of land' (Ibid.).

In the 'Communal' zones
   (1)   Removing from the 'communal' zones all large cattle herds to the 'commercial' zones, thereby ensuring 'better grazing for the cattle left there'. (Ibid.).
   (2)   Limiting the quantity of cattle which may be in the 'communal' areas by law, to bring stocking rates 'into line with the carrying capacity of the land'. (Para. 29).

The policy was drawn along grand lines, ('It will change the Botswana way of life; it will affect, directly or indirectly, virtually every Motswana' (para. 2); it was launched as the centrepiece of a mass public awareness campaign[13]. However, implementation has been halting and piecemeal, with major changes wrought in the policy during implementation (consisting mainly of the stripping away of idealism regarding its impact on cattle productivity, overgrazing and redistribution). No restatement of policy in the light of these *de facto* revisions has been issued to date, and (as will be discussed below), the policy on the basis of its present implementation and direction has political, legal and social significance (especially for non-stockholders in 'commercial' areas), but little immediate significance for cattle management (except insofar as it is likely to result in the drilling of more boreholes).

(b)   Implementation of the policy

(i)   *Land use and tenure*
Figure 9.2 summarizes the state of implementation of TGLP's 1975 White Paper proposals in 1984. Since none of the proposals for the 'communal' areas has been implemented, the focus has been on the

'commercial' areas. The 'commercial' lease comes very close to granting freehold tenure rather than leasehold – particularly since non-payment of rent is not a condition for cancellation of the lease, and lessees are free to ranch the land more or less as they choose (subject only to the general provisions of the Natural Resources Act) and have the right to renew the fifty-year leases.

PROPOSAL	IMPLEMENTATION
A. 'COMMERCIAL AREAS'	
Land tenure Fifty-year lease, renewable inheritable, sub-leasable, sub-dividable subject to approval of Land Board (para. 45).	Implemented.
Rent To be charged and effectively collected (para. 45).	4 thebe per hectare, or approximately P250 per annum for an 8 km² ranch. Up to 5 years without rent allowable. Non-payment of rent not a condition for lease termination.
Allocation Priority to groups, non-ranch holders and those from over-grazed areas (paras 22–24, and 42f).	Incorporated into principles of allocation.
All cattle owners in 'commercial' areas would, in time, have to take out leases (para. 42a).	Dropped (Sandford 1980:9).
Amount of land to be occupied by any one owner to be limited (para. 41).	Implemented. No more than two TGLP ranches per person.
Allocation of 'commercial' land only after taking 'communal, reserved and national needs' into account (para. 38).	No reserved areas allocated (see B below).
All owners of livestock currently using boreholes in 'commercial' areas to have satisfactory alternative arrangements made for them before being excluded by grant of a lease (para. 42).	Carefully implemented. But rights of non-stockholders omitted from 1975 White Paper and became subject of major controversy, with real risk of rights of non-stockholders being extinguished. (Hitchcock 1981:6).

PROPOSAL	IMPLEMENTATION
A. 'COMMERCIAL AREAS'—cont.	
Cattle management Ranch development to be encouraged, including fencing and piping of water (para. 22).	Low rates of return on ranch development suggest that ranches may remain essentially cattle posts for some time to come with minimal fencing, unless capital investments are heavily subsidized.[14]
Resident management at ranches will be encouraged (para. 41e).	This is not being pressed, presumably because of the unattractiveness financially of the ranch development package.

PROPOSAL	IMPLEMENTATION
B. 'RESERVED AREAS'	
Areas to be reserved for future use for those with few or no cattle at present, also for mining, wildlife and cultivation.	Not implemented as regards 'reserved' areas for future grazing since amount of land available was originally over-estimated.

PROPOSAL	IMPLEMENTATION
C. 'COMMUNAL AREAS'	
Land tenure Communal, except for 'group ranches' which will be encouraged (para. 30).	Small pilot 'group ranches' being experimented with – but no clear progress.
Cattle management Stock limitation to be enforced (para. 40).	Dropped (National Development Plan V 1979–85: Chapter 6 para. 48).
Private borehole restriction. Borehole owners to be restricted from watering more than the maximum number of stock per borehole laid down by Land Board. New boreholes generally to be permitted only for residence and cultivation (para. 40e).	Dropped. Borehole freeze ended (May 1983) and 8 km minimum distance between boreholes conditionally dropped.
Enlargement of 'communal' areas where there is overcrowding (para. 37c).	Not implemented as yet.

PROPOSAL	IMPLEMENTATION
C. 'COMMUNAL AREAS'—cont.	
Subsidization. Funds from 'commercial area' rents to be used for development purposes.	Revenue from rents too small to make significant contribution in communal areas. Uncertain whether they will be collected at all.

GENERAL

Land allocation: percentage of country (approx.):

6%	freehold farms
10%	'commercial' (700–900 ranches)
32%	'communal'
15%	State land (incl. forests)
11%	Wildlife Management Areas
26%	still to be allocated
	(adapted from Hitchock 1981: 5–6)

Legislation anticipated in White Paper	No sign that this will be implemented.

Figure 9.2: *Proposals of 1975 White Paper on Tribal Grazing Lands Policy and their implementation to 1984.*

In the 'communal' areas tenure has not been changed in any way, with present indications being that privately owned boreholes will not be disturbed or have their stocking rates limited (as was envisaged in the 1975 White Paper, Fig. 1).

(ii) *Cattle management*

The 1975 White Paper's proposals on cattle management (designed to raise productivity and halt range degradation) have suffered the most during the implementation stage. Although ranch development is being encouraged with National Development Bank loans, the pace and extent of such development is likely to continue to be slow. Stock limitation in the 'communal' areas has been dropped as a proposal and there is at present no articulated policy against veld degradation in the 'communal' areas. Revenue from rents on 'commercial' farms will be too small to be of significant benefit in the 'communal' areas, if indeed they are collected at all since their

189

payment is not a condition of the lease. The largest current 'communal areas' livestock programme ('Services to Livestock Owners in Communal Areas') providing funds for infrastructural investments, will serve to increase stock numbers.

(iii) *Reasons for altering the policy during implementation*
The 1975 White Paper's proposals were put forward on a number of assumptions (Sandford 1980) including:

(1) Cattle production technology was available to enable 'many more cattle on the same amount of land' to be raised (para. 1).
(2) That giving individuals or groups control over designated land areas will improve significantly the care they take of the grazing land;
(3) That the stocking rate in 'communal' areas would be reduced significantly by the concentration of large cattle herds into 'commercial' areas;
(4) That sufficient 'unused land' existed to enable 'reserved' areas to be set aside for the future;
(5) That it would be politically feasible to apply compulsory stock regulations in commercial areas.

The revisions made during the execution of the policy are in part the result of the revealed incorrectness of the assumptions, which also accounts for the increasingly likely failure of the policy as it stands to achieve its stated aims of halting overgrazing, increasing livestock productivity and ensuring that further development of the cattle industry benefits small herders.

Assumption (1) Rather surprisingly, the confident prediction of the 1975 White Paper regarding the raising of cattle productivity was made only on the basis of uncosted technical research results. When these technical coefficients (relating to productivity differences between cattle posts and minimally fenced ranches) were applied to budgets, the rate of return on the fenced farm investment emerged as unattractive[15] – even on the basis of the unrealistic assumption that ranch-type productivity levels are achieved immediately the investment is made.

The harsh experience with the ranches of the 'First Livestock Development Project' in the Western Kgalagadi, plagued by high costs, low productivity and overstocking (Odell 1981, Hitchcock 1980, Kgosidintsi and Bekure 1979) underlines the point that increases in productivity over cattle post levels cannot be expected in the short-term on a ranching project. (Indications from Livestock I ranches are that productivity levels there have been actually lower than on surrounding cattle posts, Hitchcock 1980:65).

Understandably many potential leaseholders on TGLP 'commercial' ranches have been unwilling to incur the risks involved in taking out a loan for ranch development, and it seems likely that most 'commercial' ranches will be farmed basically as traditional cattle posts for a long time, distinguished only by the firebreaks and beacons at their perimeters, or with only perimeter fencing.

Assumption (2) That private control of land does not necessarily mean no overgrazing is evident from a number of experiences besides that of the 'Livestock I' Nojane ranches discussed above. Experiences with the freehold farming blocks bears witness (Chambers and Feldman 1973:62; Samboma 1982:55).

Acute financial pressure leading the farmer to maximize short-term gain at the risk of long-term ruin, or poor management resulting from absentee ownership, are two common factors that can break the link between private control and veld conservation. If the land is held under leasehold, subject only to a small rental, and can be surrendered without prejudice by the lease-holder in worse condition than that in which he took it up, (and with compensation for 'improvements' made),[16] then the risk of misuse occurring is increased (since overgrazing and then disposing of a piece of land can then become a sensible accumulation strategy).

The TGLP lease agreement has these characteristics and puts its entire hopes for preventing overgrazing in clause 7(c) of the agreement:

'The Grantee shall farm the leased land in accordance with
the principles of good husbandry and the laws of Botswana
and in particular the Grantee shall comply with the
provisions of any laws concerning the conservation of natural
resources and good husbandry', [presumably referring to the
Natural Resources Act].

This clause is theoretically enforceable by a Land Board, but unlikely to be practically enforceable, given the difficulties of defining overgrazing legally and since leaseholders will frequently be among the most influential people in the community. There is thus a real risk that the land tenure arrangements in the 'commercial' areas will combine the worst aspects of freehold and leasehold tenure: freedom both to use and abuse, combined with freedom from paying the costs of any such abuse.

Assumption (3)   One of the early discoveries in the research underlying the land use plan (1976/77) was that most of the large cattle holders had already moved their herds out to the Sandveld and that the movement of the rest would not affect significantly the stocking rates in the 'communal' areas (Jenness 1978:8).

Assumption (4)   That this was not the case was another early discovery during the land use planning exercise. Much land was found to be unsuitable (Jenness 1978:7) or populated by hunter-gatherer groups (National Development Plan V: Chapter 6 para. 50). The latter has proved the major point of controversy in TGLP implementations in the form of a struggle over non-stockholders' rights in the 'commercial areas'. This was the great omission of the 1975 White Paper (only the rights of existing stockholders were taken into account). The issue has been characterized by constitutional disagreements over the status of hunter gatherers and impatience of potential TGLP leaseholders.

A legal opinion by the Attorney-General's litigation consultant suggested that 'the true nomad Basarwa (the principal stockless group involved) can have no rights of any kind except rights to hunting', thereby excluding Basarwa from the constitutional rights of tribesmen to land, on ethnic grounds alone (Hitchcock 1980:22). At the same time the Attorney-General (November 1979) forbade the attachment of appendices to the TGLP ranch leases by individual land boards seeking to ensure that rents were collected and reasonable stocking rates maintained (Hitchcock 1981:7).

Given the acknowledged unattractiveness of the profitability of ranch development investment packages, what is the interest of potential leaseholders in the ranches, most of which (to begin with) will be set up on existing private boreholes in the Sandveld?

Hitchcock found in his survey of the Western Sandveld of the Central District:

'. . . that the most commonly voiced reason for wanting exclusive rights was so that the "squatters" could be forced off the land. In this way the TGLP is playing into the hands of those who wish to remove unwanted people who live around the boreholes but who, under traditional Tswana law, cannot be forced to leave' (Ibid, p.72).

Among those intent on fencing, the primary purpose seems to be to keep other cattle off the ranch by erecting a perimeter fence.[17]

Assumption (5) The 1975 White Paper did not state how the limitation of stock numbers in communal areas was to be achieved. The dropping of this proposal means that the principal issue involving the future of smaller stock owners is not (as yet) confronted by the policy.

By late 1980, the basis of TGLP in the 'commercial' areas had been set: the terms of the lease; the decision to set up 'communal service centres' (communal living spaces with services for people evicted from the enclosed farms) in the 'commercial' areas; the practice of dezoning individual ranches from 'commercial' status where contesting claims to the land made compensation too thorny an issue. Since then attention has been turned to the communal areas where 'First Development Areas' are currently being identified in which a wide variety of services (chiefly water facilities, trek routes, drift fences) will be upgraded. Although still formally coming under the TGLP title the policy is as much concerned with issues of land use planning between arable and livestock and with building and reinforcing cooperative institutions (the movement to form Agricultural Management Associations in particular) as it is with livestock alone. This 'gradualist' approach is prominent in the Third Livestock Development Project (1985) to be financed by the World Bank.

By the standards and arguments of the 1975 White Paper TGLP has failed to date – productivity has not been raised, stocking rates have not been lowered or controlled, the 'communal' areas have not benefited from the creation of the 'commercial' areas by removal of cattle thereto; the opposite seems rather to have occurred due to movement of people and stock to the communal areas. Although 'commercial' ranches have by no means been allocated only to the wealthiest stockowners (Bekure and Dyson-Hudson 1982:23–25), the land concerned is being taken away from thousands of non-stockholders (Hitchcock 1981:6) who now face a real risk of eviction. If much of the remaining 25% of the country is given over to increasing the 'commercial' zones and they continue to expel both people and cattle, then the social costs of the policy will be deepened further through additional stress being placed on the 'communal' areas.

V.   Conclusion

In the post-colonial period to the mid-1980s cattle accumulation has remained a substantial proportion of aggregate household investment. The associated political influence of cattle owners and the much increased availability of public finance from other sectors (notably mining) caused the industry to become an increasing net recipient of public funds, whereas in the colonial period it had been a net contributor. The major policy initiative in cattle production has brought substantial privatisation of grazing land but as yet has failed in its production, conservation and equity objectives. These social costs are symptomatic of a 'staple trap' in cattle production—a conclusion which is elaborated in Chapter 10.

Chapter 10
Conclusions: The 'staple trap' and the impending land shortage

In the chapters on the history of Botswana's beef export industry (Part II: Chapters 4 to 9) evidence was presented concerning hypotheses 1 to 5 of the study, as outlined in Chapter 1 (pp. 6, 7). This evidence is summarized in Section I below. Section II reviews the case for hypotheses 6, 7, 8 (Chapter 1, p.7) on the basis of the evidence presented in the study as a whole.

I.   Summary

The history of Botswana's beef export industry can be divided into two long periods in accordance with long-term trends in British colonial policy and the world beef trade. Both disadvantaged the industry until after the Second World War when they turned in favour of it, through British investment in commodity production in the colonies and expansion of world import demand for lean beef.

In the first long period (c.1900–1949), dealt with in Part IIA: Chapters 4, 5 and 6, the beef cattle export trade from the Protectorate emerged in response to the demand for meat from the labour compounds of the Witwatersrand and Copperbelt mining complexes. Under an imperial power which viewed the territory as an appendage to South Africa which should cost the exchequer as little as possible and which would officially be transferred to South Africa at some stage, the Protectorate in this period was little different from any 'native reserve' in South Africa – its economy made subservient to the interests of South African industrialization and agriculture (through exports of labour and cattle principally and imports of manufactures, organized through a 'reserve trading system' which became established in the territory during the first twenty years of the century). Accordingly, the Protectorate's cattle and beef export industry was a 'reserve industry' – fully exposed to the vagaries of the regional market and foreign machinations; in short, it provided a regional reserve of cattle, to be drawn on when required and shut down when not required.

In the slump following the First World War and the continuing market instability culminating in the depression of the early 1930s, the industry was forced to bear the costs of efforts by farmers and meat companies in South Africa and Southern Rhodesia to regain their profitability. The one gain that emerged from the Protectorate – an export abattoir put up at Lobatse by the Imperial Cold Storage Co. (ICS) – was viewed by the local administration as a golden chance to set the industry on a more stable footing by reaching overseas markets. But devoid of political muscle with which to secure markets from Britain or South Africa, lacking any capital with which to subsidize its infant industry and unable to extract the capital from the live export trade, it failed completely. Caught in the mid-1930s by a major drought, the loss of the Copperbelt market and a South African import embargo, the industry descended into a turmoil of smuggling and stock theft when subjected simultaneously to the shock waves of the sudden expansion of South African gold mining – drawing in migrant labour and meat supplies on an unprecedented scale. The abattoir collapsed and the cattle population recovered to its 1933 level only by 1950. It was a case of market forces prevailing, but in circumstances of poverty and social dislocation; so that while individuals benefited in the short term (through selling off stock and earning wages) the cost was borne in the undermining of the territory's agriculture and the destruction of the base for a more stable beef export industry. The interventions by the colonial government in the 1940s to try to regulate cattle marketing and export, and thereby prevent a recurrence of the collapse, were inappropriate and no more effective than earlier ones.

The second long period (Part II B: Chapters 7, 8, 9), during which the industry was transformed from a 'reserve industry' to a 'growth industry' (see p.8), began in 1949 with the entry of the Colonial Development Corporation (CDC) to expand the Protectorate's production of beef and maize, in accordance with Britain's post-war policy of increasing the sterling area's commodity production. Through a combination of favourable export markets in the early 1950s and a great deal of capital, plus good fortune, CDC succeeded (in spite of its own incompetence) in establishing a viable export abattoir at the expense of northern producers' short-term profits through the live export trade. By doing so, it effectively broke the hold of the 'reserve trading system' on the industry through creating the basis for direct marketing from breeder to abattoir, which the country's cattle production conditions favour. In time only the largest and best-placed speculators and cattle traders continued to prosper as the trend towards direct marketing set in – encouraged by the new post-colonial government. The creation of the abattoir, the concentration of its surpluses in the country (through nationaliza-tion), the transformation of its production facilities and the coun-try's veterinary standards to meet the requirements of overseas markets, the forward integration into cold storage in Britain, the successful defence of the industry's British market by the Botswana government in the Lomé Convention negotiations – all point to the establishment of a 'growth industry' (i.e. robust and relatively stable).

But the prosperity of the beef export industry, together with the massive expansion of incomes through mining developments in the 1970s, were overlaid on an economy in which the main investment opportunities for the private savings generated by economic growth have been cattle production and import trading. Not only the small percentage (5%–10%) of farmers with very large herds (to whom probably about half of BMC producer payments went)[1], but also newly formed households seeking to build their economic base, channelled much of their savings into construction of water points, supplies of diesel and repairs of pump engines, watering fees, wages for herdsmen (in kind if not cash), cattle feed, medicine and vehicles.

The result was that the expansion of cattle production in the post-colonial period was accompanied by growing social costs in terms of public resource allocation (growing public subsidy of the industry, despite the industry's comparative advantage in land use), resource use (overstocking in some areas at the expense of both grazing land and herd productivity) and resource distribution (particularly the exclusion of prior users from land enclosed under TGLP).

II. The 'staple trap' and land shortage

Hypothesis 6 (p.7) states that the above conflicts are in part symptoms of a 'staple trap' in cattle production i.e. continuing specialization in cattle production despite mounting social costs, with no prospect for alleviation of those costs created either by the growth of the industry itself or by the dynamic of the economy as a whole. In Chapter 2 (pp.24–28) it was argued that these characteristics appear to be shared by several 'new beef exporting countries' of Central and South America, with similar adverse impact on resource use and distribution. But Botswana's position within the 'staple trap' seems to be different in three respects. Firstly, poverty and inequality as contradictions of economic growth seem not yet to have proceeded as far; secondly, conflict between exports and local subsistence is not likely to become a major issue since local demand for beef will probably remain small relative to supply (Table A4); thirdly, Botswana's extremely arid climate over most of the country (and hence inferior adaptability to more productive forms of land use) means that the comparative advantage of stock production in land use will not easily be lost. This last difference is particularly crucial. Given (i) the labour-extensive nature of 'extensive' cattle production, and (ii) the suitability of stock raising as an activity supplementary to off-farm employment, investment in cattle may be sustained or increased by economic growth in any sector of the economy (Hypothesis 7). Thus even if diversified manufacturing production were successfully established, decreasing rural unemployment and raising wages generally, this would neither stop the flow of funds into cattle production (see p.44) nor bring about a widespread rise in agricultural production to compete with cattle for land – no matter whether it shifted the balance of political power from cattle farmers.

Therefore the impact which the imminent ending of the frontier of expansion of cattle production (as the supply of unused grazing land runs out) is allowed to have, will be crucial in determining the future costs, and the distribution of benefits, from cattle production (Hypothesis 8); simply because it is the only development arising from economic growth which will affect the future course of cattle production. In terms of resource use, growing scarcity of land has the potential for improving land management – particularly if the productive potential of the land is high (therefore high opportunity cost of abuse or neglect). Even under unregulated communal tenure increasing scarcity of land generates agitation for its more efficient use – thus the conflict in the more fertile communal areas between grazing land and the expansion of fields which has produced the widespread establishment of drift fences between fields and grazing land, financed and erected by the farmers themselves.[2]

But increasing scarcity of land also encourages speculative scrambles for land – already evidenced in the pressure for privatization on 'give away' terms in the TGLP 'commercial' areas and in the pressure on land boards in some communal areas (e.g. in Kgatleng) to begin allocations of new fields in the names of young children. Where the productive potential of land is as low as it is in most of Botswana (alternatives being either low yielding high-risk crop farming and 'extensive' cattle production) there is a real risk that such scrambles if allowed to take their course will only mean (in the case of grazing) more land and wealth for already wealthy absentee cattle owners, with no incentive for them to improve their herd or land management. For the remaining communal grazing areas the prospect would be further deterioration in herd productivity and grazing land. In all areas (grazing and arable) the consequences for poverty and income distribution would be most adverse.

It follows that if a land scramble, accompanied by widespread landlessness, is not to be the main result of the growing scarcity of land a major initiative is required in the building of local institutions for the management of communal grazing. The goal would be to provide the basis for (i) preventing the further alienation of

199

communal grazing land (ii) expanding the communal areas rather than the 'commercial' areas into the presently unzoned land, in order to provide grazing land for the stock whose acquisition by the present and future rural poor will probably be their chief means to a more secure future.

Footnotes

Chapter 1

1. Kay's analysis is implicitly structurally based when he argues:

   '. . . when industrialization finally started in the underdeveloped world in the 1930s and picked up steam in the post-war period it was a process altogether different from that which had taken place earlier in the developed countries. *It took place in conditions of established underdevelopment* which it could not overcome but only reinforce'. (Kay 1975: 124; emphasis added).

2. Commerce grew as a proportion of GDP through 1965, 1971–2 and 1976. *Source:* National Accounts of Botswana.

3. With the exception of the recessionary conditions in 1982 during which banks' excess cash was quickly depleted.

Chapter 2

1. The historical material for the first period is drawn mainly from Hanson (1938) and Smith (1969).

2. Sunday Times (UK) November 2 1980: 'The Gilded Tax Dodgers'.

3. Foot and Mouth disease is thought to remain active longer in bones, offal and lymph glands than in flesh. Imports of bone-in beef are therefore not permitted into the EEC from countries where Foot and Mouth disease is endemic (Hill 1972: 5).

4. Crotty argues that the slower rise in demand for milk, and therefore reduced dairy herds, has also caused the price of calves to rise by reducing the supply of calves (calves being a joint product with milk) (Crotty 1980: 33).

5. The following figures of beef production per head of the national cattle herd provide an approximate indication of relative herd productivity in beef production:

Tonnes of beef per thousand head of cattle

	1969/71	1979/81
Australia	45	64
New Zealand	44	57
Central America	27	30
Latin America (all)	31	31

Source: FAO Production Yearbook 1981, Tables 80 and 83.

6. Identification of linkages to a specific industry is not straightforward where the linkages are not solely dependent on that specific industry or are not viable without subsidy or protection (the problem of 'bad' linkages) (Thoburn 1977: 39–44). Empirical evidence, in the form of measures of linkages to beef production in different countries relative to linkages created by other industries, is also lacking. On *á priori* grounds alone, beef seems to be a relatively poor generator of diversified growth: ranching and other 'extensive' cattle production use much land and little labour per unit output, use few material inputs, have little capacity for input intensive innovation, and incomes from beef production tend to be concentrated (thereby further limiting final demand linkages). Beef processing, though using much labour on the production line, has backward linkages, mainly to high technology engineering (especially given modern veterinary hygiene standards in slaughtering for export), which is most easily imported. Forward linkages (beyond canning, packaging or grinding) are confined to leather and soap.

7. 'Accounts of cattle interests decimating tribes for their lands in Paraguay and Brazil have been related by missionaries, human rights advocates, scientists, ranch workers and the cattlemen themselves' (Shane 1980: 28).

Chapter 3

1. Compiling of time series figures of total vaccinations against fatal diseases is hazardous owing to gaps in the reports available at the Department of Animal Health and uncertainty regarding the number of vaccinations obtained privately from other sources and regarding the number of vaccinations actually injected. What information is available (i.e. time series for Kanye, Ghanzi, plus a rough overall comparison of figures for 1975–81 with the total vaccinations for 1969 quoted in the Department of Animal Health report for that year) suggests no sizeable increase in total vaccinations; therefore possibly a reduction in vaccinations per head since cattle numbers increased by almost 50% 1969–80. I am indebted to Mr George Akafekwa of the Department of Animal Health for his assistance with this information.

2. The 'banking' role of cattle in African pastoral societies has been identified by, among others, De Wilde (1967: Vol. 1: 55–56), Fielder (1973: 351) for Barotseland, Raikes (1981: 94) for Tanzania and Kenya.

3. Low, Kemp and Doran (1980: 31) have argued that their analysis of Swaziland shows a negative price responsiveness even in the long term – but this only with regard to offtake *percentage* which is not the relevant variable in a supply curve analysis. Their conclusion is furthermore based on shaky assumptions (see p.51–52).

4. Jerve (1981: 20) argues that high fixed costs of boreholes are an important reason for continuing accumulation of cattle in the Tsabong area. But this is to put most of the cart before the horse: the boreholes are invested in *in order* to accumulate cattle, no matter whether accumulation then becomes essential to pay for the investment or not.

5. 'Ruin is the destination towards which all men rush, each pursuing his own best interest in a society that believes in the freedom

of the commons. Freedom in a commons brings ruin to all' (Hardin 1968).

6. Contrast the observations of De Ridder & Wagenaar (1984) with those of Van Vegten (1982). As regards perception of veld degradation, rural people in Botswana are far more inclined to blame low carrying capacity on drought rather than veld degradation.

7. The Walker and Hobday report (1939: 5) estimates offtake at 7% but notes that the 'popularly accepted' figure is 10%. Historical data for other beef productivity indicators, such as age at slaughter and killing-out percentage (= CDW/Live weight) are even more scanty. BMC throughput tends to average about five years (oxen) and to slaughter out at 40% to 50% (see BMC Reports and Accounts and 'A Handbook of Livestock Statistics' Ministry of Agriculture 1978 and 1980). Figures for up-country slaughter (were they known) would probably be less favourable from the beef productivity standpoint.

8. Without evidence of whether Swaziland's cattle population has also been subject to major changes independent of herders' offtake decisions (i.e. particularly rapid growth rates after a major drought) it is not possible to comment on how this affects Low, Kemp and Doran's results.

9. Herd composition data from Department of Animal Health reports for various years between 1942 and 1968 indicate no long-term trend to change: of total cattle numbers bulls were 3% to 4%, cows 50% to 55%, oxen 23% to 27% and calves 17% to 22%. Sources: Vet. Department Figures in Ryan (1958: Appendix A).

10. With the important exception of the late 1930s owing to greatly depleted cattle numbers after the great drought and cattle selling of the mid-1930s.

11. The exception is during the recent period of Foot and Mouth disease outbreaks (1977–80) when restrictions on cattle movement became a very influential 'marketing imperfection' determining offtake numbers from the north of the country.

12. The Water Points Survey (Bailey 1981: Table 5.16) included questions on reasons for selling, from which the conclusion was

drawn: 'It is apparent that once subsistence household needs have been met, the cattle holder has more scope for using cattle sales as a tool of herd management' (*ibid.* 251). The herd size necessary for meeting subsistence requirements 'without significantly depleting the capital stock represented by the herd' (*ibid.* 244) was estimated to be 60 head. But since the data in Table 5.16 do not break down clearly into investment and consumption related reasons, they do not bear substantially on the present argument.

13. The Carl Bro International report (1981: 4.87–89) carries over uncritically to Botswana from Swaziland the arguments of Doran, Low and Kemp 1979 (an earlier version of Low, Kemp and Doran 1980).

14. Roe also examines the relation between the volume of migrant labour and the ratio of cattle prices/migrant wage rates, noting that while a rise in this ratio may reduce the need to migrate for those who possess cattle, it may *increase* the need to migrate for those who do not.

15. These criticisms do not detract from the usefulness of Emery Roe's pioneering study, of which offtake motivation formed only a small part. Moreover, I myself must bear some of the weight of these criticisms having read through the manuscript and not picked these points up at the time!

16. The Department of Water Affairs is not responsible for drilling all government boreholes. In the period three years (1978–81) none had been put down for stock watering. Source: Department of Water Affairs.

17. Comparisons of the returns to capital invested in farming are complicated by variable inclusion of imputed costs for family labour and land. Comparisons over time are complicated by the need to revalue cattle inventories continually with current prices as part of the capital stock; when cattle prices are rising the formal calculations of return to capital are depressed. This also complicates comparisons with returns to investment in arable agriculture since '. . . in any given year conventionally calculated "returns to capital invested" are often much higher for crops than for cattle, because of the low level of capital in arable agriculture and the fact that the value of the cattle herd is included as capital' (Heisey 1981: 42).

There are presently three sources of calculations of returns to cattle investment. The annual Farm Management Survey (Ministry of Agriculture) excludes family labour and management costs and found returns to capital of 12% to 13% in 1978, 1979 and 1980. Returns to crop investments were calculated as 17%, 7% and 88%, for the same three years (Farm Management Survey Results 1980: Table 23). The livestock project evaluation report (Carl Bro International 1982 p.4.131) also excludes any charge for family labour or management showing returns to cattle investment in 1980 of 22% to 26%. While gross margin per head did not show any marked relation to herd size, the amount of value generated in cash by small herds was only marginal. Finally, the Water Points Survey results presented in Bailey (1981: Table 5.19) included an imputed family labour input cost and on this basis showed a negative net revenue to cattle keeping for herd sizes below 30 head. Excluding family labour costs, net revenue relative to capital stock varied from 6% to 13% with no relation to herd size.

18. The ratio of crop/cattle prices fell during the period 1960–75 and since then has risen sharply through government policy to encourage crop production. But crop production has been bedevilled by drought recently. (*Sources:* Cattle prices: Fig A2; Crop prices: SA summer cereals prices 1960–75 in '1983 Abstract of Agricultural Statistics', Dept. of Agriculture, Pretoria; Botswana Agricultural Marketing Board prices 1974–84, in Miller & Miller (1984: 8). *Note:* there is no crop price series for Botswana before 1974, therefore South African prices are used as a proxy, owing to the fairly free trade in grains and Botswana's large imports of South African grains).

19. The Rural Income Distribution Survey (1976) contains some valuations of types of farm capital and investment (not in the report but on the computer tapes). While they indicate that net accumulation constitutes the overwhelming proportion of investment the data is too limited for more detailed breakdown.

20. Contrast Pim's description of the lack of managerial innovation on the freehold farms: the farms were characterized by 'a general want of interior fencing and of watering facilities. Most of the farmers interviewed appeared to be apathetic towards the former; some of them are definitely opposed to fencing as a sheer waste of money'. (1933: 123).

21. See BP African Advisory Council: Minutes of the 21st session 1940 pp.58–62 and BP European Advisory Council 'Summary of Minutes of Full Committee Meeting on Report on Cattle Industry by Messrs Hobday & Walker' 1939, p.1.

22. Neil Parsons argues (personal communication) that although real wages may not have risen the nature of herding labour has changed (at least for those less wealthy households not using semi-vassal labour) through migrant labour drawing young men away from herding and their place being taken by boys and the infirm.

Chapter 4

1. The earliest recorded visit is that of the commissioners Trüter and Somerville 'who had been sent to the interior by the Government of the Cape Colony to procure draught oxen to replace local stocks depleted by drought'. A. Sillery, 'Botswana: A Short Political History', p.1.

2. N. Parsons, 'The Economic History of Khama's Country in Botswana 1844–1930' p.118, in Palmer R. and Parsons N. (eds.). 'The Roots of Rural Poverty in Central and Southern Africa'. Heinemann 1977.

3. The trade of the Rolong with the Ovambo is one of the earliest documented cases of long-distance cattle trading in the region. 'Between 1885 and 1895 regular trading caravans, backed by the chief men of the Rolong reserves, set out . . . across the desert with horses, saddlery, clothing and firearms to exchange for Ovambo cattle' (Shillington 1981: 278). This trade across the Kgalagadi through Lehututu still took place in the early 20th century (Stals 1962: 75–76).

4. 'Official Yearbook of the Union of South Africa'. No. 8, 1925. Union office of Census and Statistics. Map of cattle distribution in South Africa 1925.

5. By the 1920s Africans owned about half of South Africa's nine million cattle, despite being confined officially to only 13% of the land ('Union Statistics for 50 Years' Table 1–4). Much white-owned land was at the time occupied by African 'squatters' and employees.

6. 'Report of the Commission of Enquiry into Abattoirs and Related Facilities'. Government Printer, Pretoria, 1964, p.10.

7. These firms had even gone to the lengths of purchasing an Argentinian *frigorifico* to supply South African imports: 'La Plata', the subsequent sale of which to the US firm Swift and Co. is of historical significance since it signalled the entry of US firms into the Argentine-UK meat trade. Hanson 'Argentine Meat and the British Market', Stanford, 1938 Chapter V and SA Board of Trade and Industries 'Meat, Fish and other Foodstuffs. An Inquiry into Trade Combinations, Supplies, Distribution and Prices', Report No. 54, 1925, provide material on the early history of the Imperial Cold Storage and Supply Co.

8. As it had earlier in the case of the Rolong cattle traders (see note 3 above).

9. A. Best (1970: 601) discusses discrimination against Asian and African applicants for trading licences.

10. This was still the case in the 1940s. 'Facts tend to show that the majority of European farmers still give more attention to acquiring livestock for export than to rearing livestock. This has been the case for some years past and there seems little doubt that the farming of smaller farms today provides insufficient income and consequently the exchange and purchase of livestock with the native community constitutes the mainstay of European cattle farming operations in this country'. (Source: Annual Report of the Department of Veterinary Services, undated but from period 1940–47. BNA S.261/9/1).

11. I am grateful to Mr Tom Kays of Maun (who started farming and trading in Ghanzi in 1912) for this information on the early Ghanzi trade. See also M. Russell and M. Russell 'Afrikaners of the Kalahari: White Minority in a Black State'. Cambridge 1979.

12. Gold exports were as much as £56,000 worth in 1909 but were on a declining trend. (Colonial Annual Reports, Bechuanaland Protectorate).

13. Ibid.

14. As reflected in the poor profits made by ICS in this period

which were also partly due to temporarily sharp competition (SA Board of Trade and Industries, Report No. 54 1925, p.7).

15. Meat slaughtering and handling conditions in Johannesburg prior to the opening of the municipal abattoir were primitive, consisting of '. . . a number of insanitary and filthy ramshackle wood and iron slaughter poles . . . dotted around the city'. With the advent of the abattoir '. . . all the old slaughter poles were closed down' and a by-products plant was opened – converting waste material into commercial fats, fertilizers and other farm foods.
Source: Col. I. Smith 'Transforming a City's Meat Industry: The Growth of the Johannesburg Livestock Market' in *Municipal Magazine* Johannesburg 1938.

16. Ibid.

17. Colonial Annual Report for Bechuanaland Protectorate 1909–10.

18. Colonial Annual Report for Bechuanaland Protectorate 1911–12.

19. 'Native taxes' totalled 25s per adult male per annum in 1923. These taxes provided almost half of BP government domestic revenue during the period 1899 – 1925. Through providing cash for both 'Natives' taxes' and income taxes (on 'non-Natives', introduced in 1922) cattle exports were the source of probably about one-third of government's domestic revenue in the early 1920s. See Table 9.3.

20. 'Official Yearbook of the Union of South Africa' No. 8 1925, p.1063. Even so, the Union did suspend briefly imports other than for immediate slaughter in March 1919 owing to a feared southward spread of 'lung sickness'. (Res. Magistrate to Chief Linchwe 20 March 1919. Linchwe I papers, Phutadikobo Museum, Mochudi).

21. Figure for 1916/17 from Colonial Annual Report for Bechuanaland Protectorate 1916–17; figure for 1920/21 from BNA S.274/1.

22. 'Report of the Commission of Enquiry into Abattoirs and Related Facilities', Government Printer, Pretoria, 1964, para. 43.

23. The bulk of beef marketed in South Africa at the time came from retired trek oxen and was therefore lean, hence low-grade. See Board of Trade and Industries, Report No. 54 1925, p.38, and *Cape Times* editorial 19 August 1924: 'What is chiefly wrong with our cattle trade is not that it suffers from unfair competition but that it produces so much bad beef. It will never get good (export) markets until it grows better beef'.

24. 'Official Yearbook of the Union of South Africa' No. 8 1925, p.1063.

25. 'Union Statistics for Fifty Years' Table H9.

26. SA Board of Trade and Industries, Report No. 54 1925, pp.7–8.

27. Reports of farmers' meetings, *Cape Times,* 18th August 1922, 23rd March 1923; *Rand Daily Mail*, 22nd August 1924; *Star*, 19th August 1924.

28. *Rand Daily Mail*, 22nd August 1924.

29. SA Board of Trade and Industries. Report No. 54, p.10.

30. Parliamentary debate, reported in *Cape Times*, 19th August 1924.

31. SA Board of Trade and Industries. Report No. 54 op. cit.

32. Ibid. p.41.

33. Ibid. p.42.

34. Italy became the major market for Southern African beef exports until UK market quotas for chilled beef were obtained by the Ottawa Concessions of 1932.

35. South African bounties were payable on exports from South West Africa, and South Africa had reached agreement with the British High Commissioner that bounties paid on cattle slaughtered for overseas export originating in the High Commission territories (Botswana, Lesotho and Swaziland) were recoverable from the territorial governments. A similar arrangement seems to have existed with Southern Rhodesia. BNA File S.18/4. The bounties were payable even on lean third-grade meat.

36. Parliamentary debate. *Cape Times* 18th August 1924, and Board of Trade and Industries, Report No. 54, p.47.

37. Statement by Graaff to the Board of Trade and Industries enquiry. Report No. 54 p.11. The support of the mining companies was crucial owing to the magnitude of their meat requirements.

38. Union of South Africa 'Findings of the Board of Control in an Enquiry into the Meat Trade'. UG 21 of 1922, p.6.

39. *Cape Times*, 18th August 1922.

40. Board of Trade and Industries, Report No. 54 p.13. The manner of take-over of FCMI repeated ICS's much earlier experience with the formerly state-owned Transvaal Koelkamers Beperkt. Ibid. p.15.

41. Petition prepared by Isang Pilane, Chief of the Bakgatla, to be presented to Prince Arthur of Connaught on the occasion of the opening of Mochudi National School in August 1923. (Source: Isang Pilane papers, Phutadikobo Museum, Mochudi. I am grateful to Sandy Grant for bringing this petition to my attention).

Chapter 5

1. Union Department of Agriculture to Chairman of Farmers' Cattle Conference Committee. August 1923. BNA S.18/4.

2. Imperial Secretary to RC (BP) 29/8/23. BNA S.18/4.

3. 'Their technical advisers probably realised as well as our own that the 800lb weight limit would not produce a great effect but the mere fact of the imposition was a sop to public opinion. Strength is lent to this supposition by the fact that the Government in power was the SAP under General Smuts'. 'Memorandum on Fiscal Relations between the Bechuanaland Protectorate and the Union of South Africa with special reference to the export of cattle and meat'. RC (BP) 1934. BNA S.420/7.

4. Ibid.

5. RC (BP) to HC October 1924. BNA S.18/4.

6. The SWA agreement granted ICS a fifteen-year monopoly of overseas beef exports and a large tract of land. See SA Board of Trade and Industries, Report No. 54 1925, p.11.

7. The manager of FCMI, by then under ICS control (see p.77 above) was *both* a member of the three-man steering committee of the farmers' conference which interviewed the Prime Minister to discuss the form which import restrictions should take *and* initiated discussions on behalf of ICS with the BP government about ICS setting up in the territory. BNA S.18/4. That the weight restrictions on live cattle export to Johannesburg favoured the interests of any export abattoir setting up in BP is evident from Bovril's refusal in 1940 to set up works in BP because there was no certainty that SA weight restrictions on live cattle would be maintained. Bovril argued that what was required for an export abattoir to be profitable were SA restrictions on *live* cattle imports and no restrictions on *beef* imports BNA S.316/9.

8. Marnock to RC (BP) 7/2/24 BNA S.18/4.

9. McKenzie to RC (BP) 18/3/24 BNA S.18/4.

10. *Star* Johannesburg. 7/2/24, 'Factory to Can Scrub Cattle'.

11. Lobatse had been decided upon as the site for the factory after the first choice of Mahalapye was refused land by Sekgoma Ngwato Paramount Chief, on the grounds that the last grant of land made (the Tuli Block, to the British South Africa Company) had resulted in the surveyors granting, in most part 'double the decision's miles'. BNA S.18/4.

12. Thomas cited the precedent set by the despatch of his predecessor W. S. Churchill on the subject of alienation of Crown Lands in the Protectorate which read as follows: 'I am anxious to give the white settlers all the assistance possible in improving conditions in the Protectorate, but . . . I feel compelled to adhere to the view that any extensive alienation of Crown Lands would not be in accordance with the responsibilities which HMG have undertaken towards the native population, which in their opinion make it generally necessary to avoid disturbing natives at present in occupation of such lands or diminishing the quantity of land available for those who are at present not sufficiently provided for' (Despatch 24/3/22). Thomas's over-riding of this precedent to provide 'holding grounds' for ICS released this land along the Molopo River for ultimate settlement by white farmers in the 1950s. Secretary of State to HC 21/5/24. BNA S.18/4.

13. Secretary of State to HC 31/1/25. BNA S.18/5.

14. RC (BP) to Secretary of State 20/1/25. BNA S.18/5.

15. HC to Secretary of State 26/9/24. BNA S.18/5.
    Hertzog raised the weight restrictions in order to make them effective (particularly against Southern Rhodesia, the main source of imports, at the time). In reply to the High Commissioner's complaint of the hardship that BP would suffer Hertzog suggested incorporation of BP into South Africa as a means of avoiding the weight restrictions altogether. (Hertzog to HC 23/10/24; quoted in 'Basutoland, Bechuanaland Protectorate and Swaziland: History of Discussions with the Union of South Africa 1909–1939'. London, Commonwealth Relations Office. Cmnd. 8707, 1952, p.15). With South Africa pressing continually for incorporation at this time it is likely that South Africa's eagerness to impose trade embargoes against BP (p.99), its prolonging of quarantine periods after Foot and Mouth disease outbreaks and of the weight restrictions (until 1941), were partly in order 'to demonstrate the costs . . . of remaining outside the Union' (Colclough and McCarthy 1980: 16).

16. Ibid.

17. 'If the Imperial Cold Storage bought the interests of three or four of the big traders, the Company would be able to buy direct from the natives, thereby eliminating the profits of middlemen'. BP trader quoted in *Cape Times* 1/11/25.

18. The chiefs were '. . . one and all very perturbed. They dwelt on the theme that the past High Commissioners had promised that they would not be disturbed in the possession of this land as long as they behaved themselves and that seeing that they had done nothing wrong they were of the opinion that the Government had not kept its promise'. Lobatse Magistrate's report. June 1925. BNA S.18/4.

19. When finally ordered to provide men for the purpose, N. Ratshosa, Acting Paramount Chief, replied: 'I am willing to send the required assistance, unless something happens as the Bangwaketse are sick and dying'. BNA S.18/5.

20. Tshekedi's displeasure was caused by ICS's employing George Smith of Serowe as cattle buyer. Smith was formerly of the

ill-fated Garrett Smith & Co., the trading concern in which Khama III had had an interest and in the winding up of which he lost over £3,000. BNA S.242/11. Tshekedi refused grazing rights to ICS in the Ngwato quarantine camp, the erection of which ICS had partly financed (as part of the abattoir agreement) in the campaign against Pleuro-Pneumonia. The Resident Magistrate at Serowe backed Tshekedi's denial since '. . . practically every water worth having in the reserve is in the hands of Mr Geo. Smith, the local representative of the Cold Storage'. BNA S.18/4.

21. The name of the Farmers' Co-operative Meat Industries (FCMI) was apparently changed later to Federated South African Meat Industries (FSAMI).

22. Imperial Secretary to BP Cold Storage Co. Ltd. 20/4/28. BNA S.18/4.

23. Imperial Secretary to SA Department of External Affairs. April 1928. BNA S.18/4.

24. Union government to HC, May 1928, BNA S.18/4.

25. The South African compensation to Southern Rhodesia was the result of her concern to avoid retaliation. When Hertzog announced his intention in 1924 to raise the weight restrictions against imports of S. Rhodesian cattle the main anxiety expressed in the South African parliament by SAP (Opposition) members concerned Rhodesian retaliation against SA manufactured exports. *Cape Times.* 19/8/24.

Thus the 1925 customs agreement between South Africa and Southern Rhodesia compensated S. Rhodesia for SA restrictions on cattle, beef and tobacco imports by: (1) reimbursing 12% of value to Rhodesia in respect of re-exports (to attract S. Rhodesian import trade to Union harbours); (2) reimbursing 6% on goods of Union manufacture imported into S. Rhodesia. As regards transport costs, 'Rhodesian livestock and produce enjoyed the Union's lowest railway rates on similar goods' (Van Biljon 'State Interference in South Africa'. 1938, p.192). These apparently amounted to a 50% reduction on normal rates. BNA S.274/1–3.

26. The report of the South African Egg Export Commission, March 1926, before which the ICS had refused to give evidence,

accused the ICS of harmful monopolistic practices in even
stronger terms than those used by the Board of Trade and
industries (Report No. 54) in the previous year, leading the
South African Party press to complain that: '. . . the Commission started on its researches with the purpose of bringing
nearer a State system of cold storage . . . (T)he name of Gen.
Smuts is dragged into the body of the report for no conceivable
purpose unless indeed it is to arouse political prejudice'. *Cape
Times* 3/4/26, 'A Flavour-Tainted Easter Egg' (editorial). The
Report of the Livestock and Meat Industries Control Board
1934–39, discussing the reasons for the setting-up of the body
by the Government states: 'From the period 1929 to 1932 . . .
Government became seriously perturbed by the low prices paid
for livestock . . . and an investigation by the Department of
Agriculture took place over a wide portion of the Union. It was
found that the Johannesburg market which set the tone and
level of values in South Africa was in effect not a free market.
Control of competition amongst wholesale butchers was the
order of the day. . . . In Cape Town there was no market and the
greater portion of the trade was dominated by one set of interests. . . . The necessary investigations having been made, it was
realised that a position of emergency existed and that it was
essential to do something to raise the income of the industry to
prevent its insolvency' (pp.7–8).

27. ICS to Imperial Secretary. 4/5/28. BNA S.18/4.

28. HC to RC (BP) 21/12/28. BNA S.242/11.

29. ICS to HC 8/12/28. BNA S.242/11.

30. HC to RC (NP) 21/12/28. BNA S.242/11.

31. ICS to HC 8/12/28. BNA S.242/11.

32. HC to ICS 21/12/28. BNA S.242/11.

33. The machinery was removed to East London to process cattle
from the Transkei. The reluctance of the Dominions Office to
make such a large grant of land was a further factor blocking the
establishment of the meat extract plant. They cited as a precedent the refusal of land to Bovril in 1919.

34. Mr J. G. van der Horst, ousted in 1921 by Graaff, was re-
appointed chairman, amid allegations of gross mismanagement

against the previous directorship under Sir David Graaff. *Star*, Johannesburg, undated but ca. 1930, in BNA S.242/11.

35. RC (BP) to HC, September 1931. BNA S.243/1.

36. CVO Hay to RC (BP) October 1931, BNA S.243/7.

37. The principal company involved was Compagnie d'Elevage et d'Alimentation du Katanga (ELAKAT).

38. There were four principal meat supply contracts in the Congo at the time, the largest of which were Union Minière, Katanga Railways and the Government. Together they accounted for over 90% of beef imports. RC (BP) to HC 24/11/31. BNA S.243/8.

39. Among the Directors of Smith's companies were 'Count Lippon, ex-Governor of the Congo and one of the Rothschild family, M. Carton de Wiart and others'. RC (BP) to HC 24/11/31. BNA S.243/8.

40. Also known as the Union Fresh Meat Company. Source: *South Africa Board of Trade and Industries*. Report No. 54, 1925 'Meat, Fish and Other Foodstuffs: and Inquiry into Trade Combinations, Supplies, Distribution and Prices', p.28.

41. The French contract was at 2½d per lb and the Italian at 3⅓d per lb. The lowness of this tender may be judged by the fact that South African wholesale beef prices were around 3⅓d per lb in 1931 (Source: 'Union Statistics for Fifty Years' Table H9. *South African Bureau of Census and Statistics* 1960).

42. RC (BP) to HC 30/9/31. BNA S.243/2.

43. Southern Rhodesia Department of Agriculture to Bongola Smith, October 1931. Copy of letter included in RC (BP) to HC 24/11/31. BNA S.243/8.

44. South of an east-west line drawn through Palapye-Serowe.

45. While cattle from Ngamiland (north-west Botswana) were marketed on the hoof to Northern Rhodesia, this market was not accessible to cattle from south of the Botete River, owing to lack of water on possible trek routes at the time. Moreover the abundance of cattle in Ngamiland meant that cattle traders to the north had no need to seek supplies from further south.

46. To add to its infringements of the 1925 agreement with Bechuanaland Protectorate, ICS had in 1931 bought only half of its contracted annual quota of 10,000 head. The most likely reason was reduction of ICS's overseas market through Union Cold Storage competition.

47. HC to Secretary of State 10/9/31. BNA S.243/2.

48. RC (BP) to High Commissioner 28/9/31. BNA S.243/2.

49. RC (BP) to HC 18/10/31.

50. When reminded of their obligation to buy the 600 head, ICS argued that there were not the cattle available – despite abundant evidence from the veterinary department to the contrary.

51. RC (BP) to HC 24/10/31. BNA S.243/9.

52. In 1923 the British Government had tacitly conceded the principle of South African infringement of the South African Customs Union Agreement by permitting the imposition of weight restrictions on cattle imports from Bechuanaland Protectorate. South Africa took advantage of this concession to raise the weight restrictions (1926) and ban the import of beef (1928). See pp.118 and 123 above.

53. A month earlier Smith had, undeterred, predicted losses of £20,000 to £30,000 on the 1931 contracts. He intended to fulfil them in order to obtain a more substantial share of the 1932 contracts.

    As for the 'exchange situation' problem this referred to Britain's leaving the gold standard in September 1931, with the result that sterling depreciated in value against gold and other currencies (such as the South African pound) which adhered to their gold parity. Although Smith's overseas contracts were payable in depreciated sterling, his interests were predominantly in Southern Rhodesia whose currency had depreciated in line with sterling, and on exchanges of sterling for which, therefore, Smith would not lose.

54. Smith had represented to the South African Minister of Agriculture that insufficient cheap South African cattle were available to fill the contracts entirely so that the winning of the contracts depended on being able to fill a proportion of them with Bechuanaland Protectorate beef.

55. Telegrams of Union Secretary of Agriculture Williams to B. Smith 26/11/31 and 27/11/31. Quoted in B. Smith to RC (BP) 27/11/21. BNA S.256/1.

56. RC (BP) to Imperial Secretary 10/11/31. BNA S.243/8. Bechuanaland Protectorate did not receive 25% of future Italian contracts. In 1932 South Africa (by now emboldened in her ability to infringe the Southern African Customs Union agreement with impunity) gave notification that 75% was to be fulfilled in South Africa, leaving 25% for Bechuanaland Protectorate and Southern Rhodesia *together*. *Source:* RC (BP) 'Memorandum on Fiscal Relations between the Bechuanaland Protectorate and the Union of South Africa with Special Reference to the Export of Cattle Meat'. 1935. BNA S.420/7.

57. Ibid.

58. 'In view of Mr B. Smith's change of front I no longer considered that I could fairly apply further pressure to the Imperial Cold Storage Company'. HC to Secretary of State, 11/11/31. BNA S.243/8.

59. Mr Russell England.

60. 'Financial and Economic Position of the Bechuanaland Protectorate' HMSO 1933. (Pim report on Bechuanaland) p.28.

61. Ibid. Appendix VI.

62. The two creameries operated during the embargo period only on a subsidized basis.

63. Report of the Union Superintendent of Dairying on his visit to BP in 1933. BNA S.388.

64. The Dairy Board was set up in South Africa to stabilize dairy prices in a falling market, primarily by organizing their export overseas at a loss (met from a levy fund derived from taxes on domestic sales of milk). South African prices were thus held above those in principal export markets, mainly Britain. See Van Biljon (1938: 116, 133–134).

65. Treatment was not in fact equal, a case in point being the attempt by the Union Department of Agriculture in March 1933 to make re-admission of BP dairy produce after the Foot

and Mouth outbreak conditional upon incorporation of BP into South Africa. BNA S.243/13.

66. Mr Richard Glover, who was farming in the Tuli Block at the time, avers that the great drought of the mid-1930s was mainly responsible for the breaking of the dairy export industry. (Personal communication.)

67. Chief Bathoen to Resident Magistrate, Kanye 24/4/35. BNA S.428/3.

68. Chief Medical Officer Dyke. BNA S.428/3.

69. BNA 4/6.

70. BNA S.428/3.

71. BNA S.338/4.

72. RC (BP) to HC 19/4/39. BNA S.388/1/2−4.

73. 'Union Statistics for 50 Years'. Table Q6.

74. Ibid. Table H9. The mid-1930s were the turning point after which South Africa became a net importer of meat, owing to the expansion of gold mining and industrialization in the Second World War and after. Policy for raising the incomes of livestock farmers then switched from export promotion to securing maximum returns from the domestic market through the controlling of meat supplies to the cities by the newly created Livestock and Meat Industries Control Board. See Union of South Africa, Department of Agriculture and Forestry, 'Report of the Department Committee on the Problem of Meat Export from the Union of South Africa'. 1936.

75. No comparative cattle price indexes for BP and SA could be found. But the following comparison illustrates the price gap in late 1934 to early 1935.

	Shillings per 100 lb CDW
1. Trader's expenses on sale of beast to Johannesburg (including 10/− per head export levy)	8.33
2. Realized in Johannesburg (April 1935)	26.00
3. Price paid by FSAMI (October 1934) at Lobatse	5.80

Sources: 1 & 2: RC (BP) to HC 30/9/1935. BNA S.274/1–3.
3: RC (BP) 'Memorandum on the Cattle Trade in the BP' Para. 31 1939. BNA S.388/1/4.

76. The Union claimed that Pilane had leases of five Rustenburg farms which he used to receive 'smuggled' cattle. They asked the HC to prohibit foreign ownership or leasing of land by BP Africans. He declined. BNA S.18/4.

77. See 'Colonial Annual Report: Bechuanaland Protectorate' 1933 and 'Memorandum on Fiscal Relations between the Bechuanaland Protectorate and the Union of South Africa with Special Reference to the Export of Cattle and Meat' 1935. Para. 36. BNA S.420/7. It is very likely that these extensive embargos were a political manoeuvre by Hertzog and Smuts in their renewed attempts to secure transfer of BP to the Union.

78. 'Smuggling of cattle from the Protectorate to the Union, for long a profitable hobby, rapidly became an established business in which it is believed considerable capital became invested. . . . The Protectorate cattle producer, though not engaged in smuggling himself, sells his cattle in the market which offers him the highest price, and this market is provided by the smuggler'. RC (BP) to HC 19/4/39. BNA S.274/1–3.

 H. C. Bosman, revisiting Marico in the 1930s, wrote: 'And on the train that night on my way back to the Bushveld, I came across a soldier who said to me, "As soon as I am out of this uniform I am going back to cattle smuggling". These words thrilled me. A number of my stories have dealt with the time-honoured Marico custom of smuggling cattle across the frontier of the Bechuanaland Protectorate. So I asked whether cattle smuggling still went on. "More than ever" the soldier informed me. He looked out of the train window into the dark, "And I'll tell you that at this moment, as I am sitting here talking to you, there is somebody bringing in cattle through the wire".' (from 'Marico Revisited', in H. C. Bosman, 'A Cask of Jerepigo', Human and Rousseau 1964, p.159).

79. Susman Bros., in particular.

80. Evidence of Veterinary Officer Holmes. BNA S.244/11.

81. Annual Report: Bechuanaland Protectorate 1932. Bongola Smith had managed to get his way in South Africa in 1932 (entire Italian contract plus railway subsidies) perhaps aided by ICS's prevailing unpopularity with the government. In November 1932 the Chairman of ICS complained that the South African Government had recently been making it impossible for ICS to export beef, possibly '. . . in order to keep the price of beef low here so as to allow Union Cold Storage to get through with their Italian contract . . .'. Van der Horst to RC (BP) 14/11/32. BNA S.273/9.

82. ICS Chairman to RC (BP) 14/11/32. BNA S.273/9.

83. RC (BP) relating South Africa's position as told him by Union Veterinary Department. BNA S.273/9.

84. RC (BP) reporting on the chilled Beef Conference, Pretoria, November 1932. BNA S.273/9.

85. South Africa's purpose in suggesting stringent minimum quality standards was, firstly, to pursue the abortive policy of trying to establish herself as a major exporter of quality beef; secondly, to confine the benefits of the higher priced chilled market to white cattle breeders cf. Minutes of the Chilled Beef Conference, November 1932 and RC (BP)'s comments thereon. BNA S.273/9.

86. Dominions Office to HC February 1934. BNA S.303/3. By this stage Britain was trying to renege on the Ottawa beef concessions, viz. the Roca-Runciman pact with the Argentine, by which Britain agreed to impose no further restrictions on imports of Argentinian meat which were not imposed against all imports of meat. Hanson 'Argentine Meat and the British Market' 1938, Chap. X.

87. Although South West Africa was under South African mandate it had its own administration.

88. Isang Pilane, Acting Paramount Chief of the Bakgatla, objected to the BP Stockowners Association being confined to white membership. The instigators claimed that racial exclusiveness was essential because of future plans to link up with the Rhodesian Stockowners Association. BNA S.372/12.

89. 'Memorandum in reply to Sir Edward Harding's Letter.' BNA S.388/1/1.

90. A negative repercussion for southern Africa of the Ottawa chilled beef concessions, and of the further decline of the British market, was that South American beef exporters were forced to seek markets other than the UK. South Africa found itself cut out of the frozen beef trade (effectively the Italian and Belgian contracts) and thereafter made a point of reintroducing generous subsidies (approximately 50% of final price realized) on frozen beef exports, in order to support the local price of 'low grade' cattle. Sources: SA Livestock & Meat Industries Control Board, Report 1934–39. SA Department of Agriculture and Forestry, 'Report of the Departmental Committee on the Problem of Meat Export from the Union of South Africa' 1936.

91. RC (BP) 'Memorandum on the Cattle Trade in the BP' Para. 31. 1939. BNA S.388/1/4.

92. In October 1935 the League of Nations imposed economic sanctions on Italy against Mussolini's invasion of Ethiopia. Referring to FSAMI's proposed beef exports to Eritrea from Lobatse in 1936 the Secretary of State for Dominion Affairs cabled in November 1935 '. . . it would be difficult to agree to use UK funds to subsidize export of meat to Italian army there'. Secretary of State to HC 13/11/35. BNA S.274/1–3.

93. The first cattle export levy (5/– per head) imposed in 1916 (Proc. 12 of 1916) had been reduced to 2/6 in 1923 and then abandoned in 1925 (Proc. 10 of 1925) on grounds of hardship. Source: Hermans 1974: 97.

94. This is certainly an error; a larger *proportion* of cattle raised by Europeans may have been 'prime', but even this generalization should probably be confined to the largest freehold farmers.

95. RC (BP) to HC 30/9/35. BNA S.274/1–3.

96. EAC Chairman to RC (BP) 9/8/35. BNA S.240/9.

97. Minutes of the 20th Session of the EAC. 3–8 February 1936.

98. HC to RC (BP) 8/2/36. BNA S.274/4.

99. The measures limiting the power of the chiefs were the Native Administration Proclamation and the Native Tribunals Proclamation, both of 1934. In early 1936 Tshekedi Khama was preparing his unsuccessful contestation of these measures.

100. 'Aphthization' refers to putting the disease through the herd i.e. infecting all the cattle with Foot and Mouth disease virus in order to get the outbreak over and done with as quickly as possible, the cattle recovering after two to three months. The danger is that the disease may spread from the aphthized area. Aphthization is considered outmoded by comparison with modern vaccination.

101. The much enlarged quota was a result of the change in British farmer support policy from reliance upon import control to direct subsidization, cf. 'Imports of Meat into the United Kingdom: Statement of the Views of His Majesty's Government in the United Kingdom'. Cmd. 4828, HMSO 1935.

102. 'Memorandum' on the state of the cattle trade. CVO. BNA S.274/6.

103. *Bulawayo Chronicle* 10/9/37.

104. Source: 'South West Africa: Report of the Long-Term Agricultural Policy Commission' 1949. SA Department of Agriculture (copy in Meat Board library, Pretoria).

105. The Protectorate enjoyed a clear comparative advantage regionally in extensive production of cattle owing to its very low population/land r'.ao, good grazing, comparative freedom from stock diseases and the unsuitability of these resources for alternative uses. But its lack of infrastructure and a domestic beef market, together with the unfavourable economics (at the time) of transporting meat rather than live animals and the poor world market for lean beef, all favoured live export as opposed to the establishment of an export abattoir in the territory.

Chapter 6

1. Both countries had been surplus zones until the late 1930s and their beef industry policies had been geared to export promotion. In Southern Rhodesia the increased domestic demand was ascribed to 'the influx of immigrants, the mounting needs of a rapidly growing urban African population, and a change to beef in the dietary in reserves' (from 'Report of a Commission of Inquiry into the Cold Storage Commission of Southern Rhodesia', Salisbury 1952).

2. *Cattle and Beef Prices in BP, S. Rhodesia and SA (index)*

	BP	SA	S. Rhodesia
1938/39	100	100	100
1949	163	205	235

Sources: BP cattle exports $\frac{value}{volume}$ from colonial annual reports.

'Report of a Commission of Inquiry into the Cold Storage Commission of S. Rhodesia' 1952.
'Union Statistics for Fifty Years' 1960.

3. There were Foot and Mouth outbreaks in 1944, 1947 and 1948 each of which resulted in only a brief suspension of cattle exports. In the 1930s outbreaks occurred in 1933–34 and 1937. BP had to wait sixteen months after the last outbreak in 1934 before cattle were re-admitted to South Africa. BNA S.420/7.

4. Source: BNA S.231/2/1.

5. The creation of more widely spread water points was generally seen at the time as the solution to overgrazing, which was concentrated in the east (Roe 1980:25). The amount of Colonial Development and Welfare funds available for water development increased rapidly during the period:

1935–37	£25,300
1937–46	£127,312
1946–55	£348,057 (ibid: 18)

Besides the water-point development programme the only other government initiative on the cattle production side was the Livestock Improvement Centres, a series of demonstration ranches concentrating on bull improvement, which were set up in the 1930s. They operated on too small a scale to have a genetic impact on Tswana herds. See Watermeyer 'Memo on the Livestock Improvement Centres' p.19. undated, BNA V.6.

6. 'Price control by means of ceiling prices failed and, in consequence of the findings of the Meat Commission of 1943, it was decided to resort to full price control or the Meat Scheme of 1944. In terms of this scheme, the Food Control Organization became the sole buyer of meat in the nine main consumer centres or "controlled areas" at fixed prices according to the

grade and weight of carcases . . . Ceiling prices and slaughter-ing quotas remained in force in the "non-controlled" areas'. 'Report of the Commission of Inquiry into Abattoirs and Allied Facilities'. SA 1964, p.13.

7. Compulsory destocking in the reserves was introduced into S. Rhodesia in the 1940s under the banner of range conserva-tion but principally in order to alleviate the beef shortage. In the late 1940s it almost tripled the number of cattle sold from the reserves – much to the benefit of white farmers who received good supplies of immatures for growing out under a grazier scheme financed by the Cold Storage Commission (see 'Report of the Commission appointed to inquire into the marketing of slaughter cattle and the products thereof' S. Rhodesia 1942, and 'Report of a Commission of Inquiry into the Cold Storage Commission of Southern Rhodesia' 1952). Compulsory de-stocking had already been introduced beforehand in the South African reserves, but accounted for only a very small percen-tage of total offtake from African-owned stock (Ryan 'Report . . . on the Livestock Industry of the Protectorate' 1958, p.17).

8. The measures contained in Proc. 1 of 1940 to curtail 'smuggling' and to provide funds for subsidizing overseas exports were:

   A. *Licensing* Cattle buying licences had been originally introduced in 1911 (see p.71 above) but were then abolished by Proc. 43 of 1923. Under the new licensing regulations:
      (i) only licence holders could buy and sell stock to each other (excluding 'Natives').
      (ii) licences were issued free to holders of butcher, hawker, or general dealer's licences and to freehold farmers for purchase of a limited number of stock for farming operations. Others were subject to a £100 deposit.
      (iii) each licence holder could nominate only *one* other person to acquire stock on his behalf.
      (iv) export allowed only by holders of buyers' licences or producers' licences (issued only to freehold farmers breeding and fattening their own cattle). 'Natives' could export without a licence.

B. *Export Levy*   Reintroduced at five shillings per head. Proceeds to be used only to subsidize overseas export of beef (see footnote 31 below).

C. *Monthly Returns*   Every licence holder to submit returns monthly of all cattle transactions to the Veterinary Services Department.

D. *Compulsory Rebranding*   Within 72 hours of purchase.

Proc. 1 of 1940 was amended successively during the next decade: by Procs. 23 and 67 of 1941, 21 of 1944, 86 of 1948, 21 and 22 of 1950. There were further minor amendments during the next 20 years. Only the export levy survived effectively; the licensing provisions remained on the statute book into the post-colonial period, but were at no time thoroughly enforceable.

9. Source: RC to HC 16/6/37. BNA S.388/1/2–4.

10. 'In 1935 an undertaking was given by the Protectorate authorities to the Union government that in return for the quota of 10,000 head a year . . . every effort would be made to put a stop to smuggling. The Union authorities have urged time and again that stronger measures be taken in the Protectorate to suppress smuggling and the Union Secretary for Agriculture has recently gone to the length of suggesting that the Union Veterinary Department should assume control of a buffer strip within the Territory along the common borders. For ethical, administrative and political reasons it is the obvious duty of government to suppress smuggling . . .' R. C. Arden-Clark 'Memorandum on the Cattle Trade in the Bechuanaland Protectorate' 1939. BNA S.388/1/4.

   But as was pointed out by an independent observer in 1946, the practice of an *exporting* country taking measures to suppress smuggling rather than the importing country itself was unheard of internationally. Since South African nationals (farmers and cattle buyers providing finance to procurers in the Protectorate) were the instigators of 'smuggling', only South Africa itself could ultimately end it. South Africa set up a veterinary cordon along the border for this purpose from 1937 to 1940.

11. RC to HC December 1939. BNA S.388/3/1.

12. 'Business experts in the meat industry consider that the only really reliable meat market in the world is the United Kingdom,

since its arrangements in regard to supply may be depended upon and are not likely to be upset at short notice; as a result prices are more or less stable'. Memo by Chief Veterinary Officer Hobday, May 1937. BNA S.274/6.

13. The Cold Storage Commission ran a 'Feeder Scheme' whereby cattle suitable for export as 'chillers' were allocated to farmers in the Southern Rhodesian maize belt for finishing on grain preparatory to slaughter. Increasing domestic demand created a shortage of supply of suitable 'feeder' cattle, thereby inducing the offer to BP.

14. 'Cattle of good quality fetch a higher price when manufactured into chilled beef but it might be advisable, in consonance with the policy adopted in the Union and in S. Rhodesia to pay a small export subsidy on improved cattle, the majority of which in the Protectorate would be produced by the European farmer, and for this funds should be available'. R. C. Arden-Clarke BNA S.388/1/4. R. C. Rey had opposed the use of levy funds for this purpose since they were paid mainly by African cattle owners who would not benefit therefrom (see p.106 above).

15. The scheme had a curious beginning in that it originated in the visit by Sir John Harris of the 'Anti Slavery and Aborigines Protection Society' to BP where he had talks with Tshekedi who had expressed interest in the erection of a meat extract factory. Harris then took up the suggestion from a philanthropic standpoint (thinking of it as a 'Bechuana Industries' in which a certain percentage of the profits would go to a trust for African education) by contacting Lord Luke of Bovril, who, he claimed, was an 'ardent Christian'. Luke agreed to investigate the scheme by sending Walker out – provided the Dominions Office paid his fare! BNA S.316/9.

16. 'Report on the Cattle Industry of the Bechuanaland Protectorate with Recommendations for Improving its Organization and Assisting its Future Development' H. Walker and J. Hobday 1939.

17. A levy fund of £15,000 had been accumulated unused since the 10/– per head levy was introduced in 1935. In June 1939 the levy was abolished in order to stabilize the fund at this level. See also note 31 below.

18. African Advisory Council meeting April 1942. The system of removal permits for cattle had been set up by Government Notice No. 28 of 1926 in order to curb stock theft and the spread of animal diseases.

19. 'So long as there is doubt as to whether the cattle are to remain in Bechuanaland for industrialization there, or be sent to Johannesburg because the import restrictions have been removed, it would be a very speculative venture to put up a meat works in the Protectorate' Lord Luke, chairman of Bovril, to Dominions Office, 8/1/1940. BNA S.388/3/1.

20. *Source:* Meeting of the SA Livestock and Meat Industries Control Board 20/10/39, as reported by BP's observer, the Chief Veterinary Officer. In response to this threat the CVO suggested that if increased supplies of BP cattle were needed on the Johannesburg market the SA weight restrictions should be removed. 'It was indicated in confidence, that when supplies of cattle are required, the weight embargo is not insisted upon since the Board is asked to comment before action is taken. I pointed out that the BP government was responsible to the Union government for observing the regulation'. BNA S.274/7.

21. White farmers and traders in the Gaberones and Lobatse blocks complained that the legislation 'will bring poverty and attendant hardship' and pleaded that 'ways and means of disposing of tollies and underweight better class cattle . . . be explored as soon as possible'. BNA S.388/1/1.

22. EAC member Glover to RC January 1941. BNA S.389/1/1.

23. The weight restrictions were lifted only during the off-season (August–December) but were never re-imposed. BNA S.389/1/1.

24. The reasons given for the BP government's minimum export weight restrictions were: 'In order (a) to limit within reasonable proportions cattle offered by Protectorate producers for sale on the Johannesburg market, and facilitate allocation of the quota; (b) to ensure that undersized animals are not sent to the market and thus damage the Territory's reputation and jeopardize the suspension of the weight embargo; (c) to ensure that small animals which travel less successfully and are liable to be injured in trucks are not sent forward; it has been decided that

the minimum weight of cattle which will be permitted to go forward until further notice will be 900 lbs.' for oxen, 760 lbs for cows. Producers with animals in prime condition but weighing less than these embargo weights could make special application to the Veterinary Services Department for export permission.

Associated correspondence indicates that the real anxiety was that export of immatures would run down cattle numbers again as it had in the mid-1930s. BNA S.389/1/1.

It is not clear whether the sharp increase in official exports to South Africa between 1941 and 1942 (a 50% increase – see Table A3) was due to the relaxation of the weight restrictions or to increased demand from South Africa plus a larger quota. Even if the relaxed weight restrictions were the cause, much of the increased official exports were probably accounted for by a diversion of cattle from unofficial (i.e. 'smuggling') to official channels, meaning that the overall increase in BP's export volume was probably much less than 50%.

25. HC to Dominions Office 5/6/44. BNA S.388/3/2.

26. The anxiety over a possible post-war beef surplus in South Africa was engendered by a report forecasting that slaughter of draught animals (used in place of tractors) following renewed availability of petrol, would result in a short-term beef glut, and that longer term indications were towards a return to the pre-war surplus conditions. SA Livestock and Meat Industries Control Board 'A survey of the supply with regard to slaughter stock and meat in the Union, and probable future trends' 1945. BNA S.388/3/2.

27. The proposed use of the levy funds had thus come full circle back to the original 1935 plans.

28. *Source:* Agricultural Adviser Thornton to HC. February 1946. BNA S.388/3/2.

29. Owing to continuing lack of offtake availability the Congo market was not supplied at all from BP during the 1940s.

30. In the early 1950s the Livestock Industry Advisory Council was set up to allocate monies in the Cattle Export Levy Fund, which had lain unused since 1936. The levy was raised to £1 to provide additional funds towards Veterinary Department expenses.

31. The stop-go history of the Cattle Export Levy: Proc. 33 of 1935 introduced the levy at 10/– per head, but was repealed and replaced by Proc. 26 of 1936 which imposed an *ad valorem* levy up to a maximum of 14/– per head. This was repealed and replaced by Proc. 2 of 1937 which reintroduced the 10/– per head levy, for oxen, and 7/6 for cows. But this was suspended by Proc. 17 of 1939, and Notice 95 of 1939, only to be reintroduced at the level of 5/– per head by Proc. 1 of 1940. But during the entire period 1936 to 1953 the levy funds were not used at all!

32. For further details of Northern Rhodesian marketing regulation in this period see 'Report of the Federal Committee on Cattle and Beef Marketing' (Murray Committee), Federal Department of Conservation and Extension, Salisbury 1954, p.47.

Chapter 7

1. During the war years and until the mid-1950s UK beef prices were controlled (i.e. fixed). With meat shortages the fixed price was effectively a maximum price; thus decontrol raised prices and stimulated increased domestic beef production.

2. Australia and New Zealand supplied mainly lean, frozen beef whereas imports from Argentina were predominantly chilled and of higher quality, according to the 'Committee of Inquiry into Fatstock and Carcase Meat Marketing and Distribution' (UK Cmnd. 2282 1964) p.62.

3. As a result of the heavy tariffs on imports from other sources boneless beef supplies to the UK were coming almost exclusively from the Commonwealth. Ibid. p.61.

4. Ibid. p.61.

5. Comparative price figures (f.o.r. Lobatse) could not be found to assess the validity of the belief in BP in the early 1950s that regional prices were higher than UK prices. But the 'Report of the Long Term Agricultural Policy Commission' 1949 (South West Africa) supports this belief.

6. Secretary of State for the Colonies. Outward telegram. Circular, Private and Personal. Secret. 15/6/47. BNA S.495/3/1.

7. Colonial Office circular 17/12/47 by Creech Jones. BNA S.495/3/1.

8. Colonial Office circular 5/4/49. BNA S.495/3/2.

9. Colonial Office circular 17/12/47. BNA S.495/3/1.

10. Ibid.

11. Ibid. Cowen (1981:153) quotes Myint's interpretation of the failure of CDC projects: '. . . the root cause of failure lies not so much in the wrong choice of men and inefficient methods of administering the ventures but in the vagueness of the mandate itself which tries to compromise between the principle of obtaining economic returns and the principle of needs'. (Myint 1954:139).

12. Roe (1980:22) states 'In short, almost as many boreholes had been drilled between 1956 and 1960 as had been drilled between 1946 and 1955'.

13. Letter to District Commissioners, January 1949. BNA S.495/3/2.

14. Circular by RC (BP) Sillery, September 1947. BNA S.518/4.

15. From a CDC memorandum dated 1949, in BNA S.518/4.

16. The old ICS works building had been bought and used for dairying by a firm 'Lobatse Milk Products', from whom they were bought for £20,000 by CDC.

17. The allocation of this land to CDC led to immediate conflict with people already living there (ICS had never made use of the land). An investigation recommended that the river frontage west of Mabule be reserved for African occupation and that an additional 450,000 acres from the Kgalagadi be allocated to CDC to make up the promised acreage, plus a narrow corridor along the northern edge of the Barolong farms in order to afford access for cattle trekked to Lobatse from the holding grounds. BNA S.518/2.

18. From the report by CDC Regional Controller Robinson on his visit to BP. BNA S.518/4.

19. No formal agreement was made with CDC until 1956. The undertakings quoted were given in meetings with government and cattle suppliers. BNA S.518/4.

20. Securing commitment from South Africa and Northern Rhodesia to accept beef instead of live cattle was eased by the acute shortage of beef regionally in the early 1950s, which strengthened the CDC/BP government bargaining position. The South African meat supply system to the cities was at the time based on transport of live animals to city abattoirs; Lobatse beef supplies were allowed as an exception. Northern Rhodesia had to invest in increased cold storage capacity in order to accept beef instead of cattle.

21. 'The Ngamiland Cattle Exporters' Association consisted of a group of Ngamiland traders, Christos and Deaconos, Weskob and Odendaal. . . . The Association was formed to put cattle on the Bushmen Pits ranch, to fatten them . . . and then to sell them to CDC at Pandamatenga for futher fattening before sale for slaughter. . . . The Agreement between CDC and NCEA was a fairly complicated document restricting rather tightly the activities of the Traders . . . The NCEA was to purchase Ngami-land cattle at less than 700 lbs, keep them at Bushmen Pits until they weighed 800 lbs, sell them to CDC who took them to Pandamatenga for final fattening and sale. . . . From the very beginning the CDC/NCEA joint operation was a failure. . . . (CDC) attacked the traders for exploitative dealings (by paying breeders) less than half the market price (and) selling to CDC at prices that reduced the profitability of the Pan-damatenga operation. NCEA . . . claimed that the CDC was trying to recover its earlier losses at Bushmen Pits by "squeez-ing" the NCEA. . . . The NCEA fell into financial chaos and as part of the handover of the BECCAT package, the NCEA/CDC agreement was terminated'. Excerpts from 'Report of visit to Commonwealth Development Corporation to examine files and records of the CDC ranch development project at Pandamatenga, Nata and Bushmen Pits'. Botswana Ministry of Local Government and Lands, LG 2/20/9, 1975.

22. Ibid.

23. CDC Regional Controller, January 1954. BNA S.518/7.

24. BNA S.495/3/2.

25. Without holding grounds there was no alternative but to carry on on the pre-existing basis whereby South Africa (experienc-ing the same seasonal variations as BP) displaced the cost of

enjoying a year-round availability of cheap cattle for the mines and industrial compounds onto the export supplier in BP by restricting import quotas in the 'flush' season, when cattle were in good condition on the summer rain pasture and domestic supplies therefore strong, and increasing quotas in the dry spring months when cattle were in their worst condition. The result was a perverse seasonal export pattern from BP to South Africa from the point of view of cattle condition. '(T)he quotas are low in the flush season when it is difficult to dispose of all cattle on offer in the Territory and high in the scarce season when cattle are not readily available'. G. Ryan 'Report to the BP Government on the Livestock Industry of the Protectorate'. June 1958, p.30.

26. BNA S.518/7.

27. BNA S.518/8.

28. The probable loss on sales to South Africa was estimated at £56,000 per annum by the Resident Commissioner. This was thought to be too great to be covered by profits on sales to the north. 'Memorandum on Operation of Colonial Development Corporation Abattoir at Lobatsi'. R. C. (BP) McKenzie 10/4/54. BNA S.518/8.

29. The campaign was led by Russell England, a prominent cattle rancher with trading interests, and had the support of Tshekedi Khama, Acting Chief Pilane of the Bakgatla, the Director of Veterinary Services and the qualified support of the Resident Commissioner himself ('All in all . . . it does not appear that the operation of the abattoir on a permanent basis will be to any-one's advantage'. R. C. (BP) McKenzie April 1954. BNA S.518/8).

30. BNA S.518/7.

31. The appointment as CDC General Manager in BP of Mr J. Hobday, a respected former Director of BP Veterinary Services, was a further palliative. Hobday's new role as advo-cate of the abattoir project was curious in view of the opinions he expressed in June 1953 while Director of Veterinary Services in N. Rhodesia: 'There is no doubt in my mind that compared with the existing method and system of marketing live cattle . . . the economics of the Lobatse abattoir venture are very unsound indeed'. (Hobday to DVS (BP) 29/6/53). BNA S.518/7.

32. The Northern Cattle Export Pool, as it was known in BP, appears to have consisted of the N. Rhodesian Federation of Meat Distributors, a monopoly buying and importing association of the two principal butchery groups in N. Rhodesia, under the overall supervision of the Cattle Marketing and Control Board of N. Rhodesia – a statutory body composed of producers', distributors' and consumers' representatives:

> 'That Board had as its principal function the allocation of import permits for slaughter stock from Bechuanaland Protectorate among the various competing butchers in N. Rhodesia. These butchers were entirely private concerns organizing their own supplies, killing in their own or municipal abattoirs . . . and retailing through their own chains of shops. There were two principal groups, Werner & Co Ltd and Copperfields Cold Storage Ltd. The former was operating in conjunction with Lusaka Cold Storages Ltd and Susman Bros & Wulfsohn Ltd at Livingstone. No permit to import cattle was allocated . . . until a butcher had proved his ability and willingness to support the local cattle industry at the "Fair Indicated Prices for Cattle" which were published by the Board'.
> *Source:* 'Report of the Commission of Inquiry into the Beef Cattle Industry of Southern and Northern Rhodesia'. (Horwood). Fed. Govt. 1963, p.17.

The firm ELAKAT had practically monopolized meat imports into the Congo since the 1920s and had incorporated further strong Southern Rhodesian interests since 'Bongola' Smith's time:

> 'ELAKAT operates in the Katanga, Ruanda-Urundi and Lake Kivu provinces; it is closely linked with a firm of perishable products dealers named Profrigo who supply meat to Leopoldville and Stanleyville. ELAKAT runs 130,000 head of cattle on its own ranches . . . redistributes meat within a radius of 800 miles of Elizabethville and sends a lot by air to Leopoldville, a distance of 1,000 miles'.
> *Source:* Ryan 1958: 40–41.

33. The only evidence of Lobatse's processing costs at this time is from Ryan (1958: 66). The only other possible source of abattoir profits was on sales of the 5th quarter (i.e. hides, offal and

other by-products). But since CDC sold these on the South African market more was not realized for them than had to be paid out to the producer as part of 'Johannesburg parity'.

34. By 1957 most large Batswana cattle owners were marketing direct to Lobatse. (RC to HC July 1957, BNA S.558/2). Also see Ryan 1958:18 who states that 117 registered suppliers in June 1956 were African and 218 in Dec. 1957.

35. For northern cattle interests the price comparison before and after the advent of the abattoir was worsened by the last-minute buying up of large numbers of cattle by the Northen Export Pool at premium prices, just before the opening of the abattoir put an end to the trade altogether.

36. 'Report of the Federal Marketing Committee on Cattle and Beef Marketing' (Murray) October 1954, p.48.

37. The adjective 'exploitative' is the only fitting description of a marketing system for African-owned cattle which imposed a single buyer (CSC at its own auction sales) sales channel, forced sale of African cattle by imposing stock limitation, directed the immature stock so bought to white ranchers (at the expense of a levy on African cattle sales) for fattening, and then subsidized producer prices of high grade fatstock above their market value by fixing prices for lower grade stock at African auction sales below their market value. See Appendixes XI and XII to 'Report of a Commission of Inquiry into the Beef Cattle Industry of Southern and Northern Rhodesia'. Fed. Govt. 1963, and 'Report of the Federal Committee on Cattle and Beef Marketing' (Murray), Fed. Govt. 1954, Part VI.

In Northern Rhodesia attempts to maintain low prices for lower grade cattle were repeatedly defeated by the overall deficit in marketed cattle. Thus the maximum prices set in the 1940s were abandoned as ineffectual in 1953 and replaced by 'Calculated Fair Prices' designed to be indicative to the trade but which, despite the butchers' cartel, had limited effect: 'Purchases made by the Federation of Meat Distributors are distributed by it to its members in the same proportion as imported cattle. . . . The Federation . . . does not pay above the Calculated Fair Price except by agreement among its members, though this is frequently permitted in times of shortage'. Murray Commission 1954, p.43.

38. 'Report of the Commission of Inquiry into the Beef Cattle Industry of Southern and Northern Rhodesia' (Horwood) Fed. Govt. 1963, p.19.

39. CSC and the Federal Government were believed to be behind the press campaign in Northern and Southern Rhodesia discrediting Lobatse beef.

    Northern News 1/3/57: 'Copperbelt butcher calls for S.R. beef – "hit and miss" Lobatsi meat not wanted'.

    The Chronicle, Bulawayo 9/3/57: 'Keeping business at home' (editorial).

    The latter wrote: '(W)e find it difficult to reconcile ourselves to the Northern Rhodesian Cattle Marketing & Control Board's action in granting permits for the import of some 14,000 beef carcases from Bechuanaland. . . . It is true that for some considerable time, the Cold Storage Commission of Southern Rhodesia was not in a position to meet the needs of the North. . . . The situation has, however, changed . . . the Commission is now in a position to supply the whole Federation with meat. . . . There is a strong argument in favour of the Federal Government's intervening and giving encouragement to the local cattle industry by making sure that when there are some big orders going in the Federation, the Rhodesian farmer gets the first opportunity to benefit from them'.

40. 'Report of the Commission of Inquiry into the Beef Cattle Industry of Southern and Northern Rhodesia' (Horwood). Fed. Govt. 1963, p.20.

41. 'Decontrol' of beef prices in South Africa was consequent upon the 'Report of the Beef Marketing Enquiry Committee' May 1955, which argued that the fixed price system was not allowing the price of beef to rise as fast as it should given the growing SA beef deficit, in order to stimulate domestic production.

42. Although cattle slaughtered in South Africa did not register a marked increase. (Slaughter figures from annual reports of the SA Meat & Livestock Industries Control Board.)

43. The general manager of the Union Farmers' Meat Marketing Co-operative alleged in 1959 (BNA S.521/1/2) that the SA Meat Board was unwilling to enlarge BP's quota owing to the price reducing and destabilizing use made of it by Lobatse's Johannesburg agents Byrne, Cooper & Gluckman (allegedly

one of a ring of five meat firms cornering the Chamber of Mines meat supply contracts, known as the 'Compound Pool') by putting it on auction at moments of over-supply.

The allegations are impossible to assess owing to the secrecy surrounding quota allocations. In regard to the other allegations, Ryan found that all the Johannesburg wholesalers (about fifteen) regularly bought Lobatse beef and the Compound Pool 'has had to pay substantially more than the floor price for Mine 3 grade meat, although there is a limited demand for "compound" meat in the retail market' (1958: 60).

44. CDC had concluded a ten-year supply contract for the Congo with ELAKAT in 1950 for the supply of some 3,000 tons per year with effect from the opening of the abattoir.

45. Applications for slaughter quotas at Lobatse:

1955	54,506
1956	88,915
1957	105,064

Source: Ryan 1958: 22.

46. The loss in price for grade by BP beef on the Johannesburg market resulting from auctioning Lobatse's chilled beef against freshly killed South African beef (known in BP as the 'slip') fell most heavily on the higher grades. Further losses occurred through the differential grading of 3rd grade Lobatse beef into 'Trade 3' and 'Mine 3' (a differential which did not exist in South African supplies and was a focus of producer dissatisfaction in BP) and the stricter grading at Lobatse (said to be half a grade lower) adhered to partly in order to make BP beef acceptable in the Federation in view of CSC's strict standards for the lower grades. (BNA S.521/1/1).

47. BNA S.520/3/4.

48. S. Rhodesian exports of cattle to N. Rhodesia were 100 head in 1956 and 7,000 in 1957; beef exports were 550 carcases in 1953 and 12,000 in 1957. *Source:* Ryan 1958:32.

49. See Note 46 above.

50. See discussion in 57th session of EAC. 21/11/55.

51. With the limitation of CDC profits to 6% the payment system to producers was altered. Producers were paid the value of the

beef yielded by that grade on the Johannesburg market (with monthly 'agterskot' or bonus) while the abattoir retained the 5th quarter. Profits in excess of 6% were paid into a fund administered for the general benefit of the industry by the producer-dominated Livestock Industries Advisory Board (constituted by the Livestock and Meat Industries Proclamation of 1957).

52. BNA S.558/2.

53. Notes by DVS (BP) Roe, titled 'Prices paid for cattle' 1959? BNA S.521/1/3.

54. RC (BP) June 1958. BNA S.521/1/2.

55. It is not clear whether Hurvitz's interests in Namibia were acquired before or after those in BP.

56. CDC Regional Controller Cater to RC (BP) Fawcus 17/1/61. BNA S.267/3/1.

57. In 1959 BP turned down on Hurvitz's advice a proposal from the Kenya Meat Commission to set up a joint sales organization along with CSC in London, on the grounds that the three firms were competitive in overseas marketing. KMC had argued that they had common interests, all being marginal suppliers to a very large market. BNA S.521/1/3.

58. From the CDC response to the Tati farmers' meeting Dec. 1958. BNA S.521/1/2.

59. For the CDC regional head office in Johannesburg, the Lobatse abattoir was one of a number of projects and not the largest. At Lobatse the managerial staff consisted only of the manager and his assistant.

60. The main conditions of the Hurvitz contracts:

I *30/7/58 to 30/9/59*
Quantity: Maximum 30,000 head.
Price: Johannesburg floor price (i.e. support price) as at August 1958. plus 5s. per 100lb. CDW f.o.r. Lobatse. Roughly a price slightly below that actually realized by BP exports to Johannesburg during 1958.

II *October 1959 to October 1960*
Same basic conditions but prices set compare less favourably with Johannesburg floor prices i.e. now paying below Johannesburg floor prices.

III *ECCO contract*

Quantity: ECCO entitled to all quantities above a certain allocation to traditional markets.

Prices: Ruling Johannesburg prices (net of marketing expenses to Johannesburg) but subject to price ceilings rising 2% annually. Overseas marketing expenses borne by BPA. Hurvitz puts up half the capital for ECCO and receives managing agent fee, personal expenses, 10% of ECCO profits and 40% of dividends.

61. Hurvitz's profits on his contracts 1958–60 were variously estimated at £50,000 to £200,000. As a result of the January 1959 increase alone in the Johannesburg floor price he was losing £10,000 *per month* in January–February 1959. BNA S.521/1/2.

62. Hurvitz to Government Secretary 16 April 1959. BNA S.521/1/4.

63. See Ryan 1958: Chap. 14.

64. See Chapter 8 p.145 for government's argument as to why nationalization was inevitable.

65. Excerpts from the press campaign:

'The Cattlemen are angry: A hundred angry, bitter
Bechuanaland farmers demanded a new deal on Friday
when they voted no confidence in their only source of
meat distribution – the Colonial Development
Corporation . . .'
Sunday Times (SA) 12/10/58.
'Glazer Brothers in Big Fight with British Government:
Tshekedi joins in row over Bechuanaland meat
monopoly'
Sunday Express (SA) 12/10/58. In BNA S.267/3/1.

66. Government believed there were *prima facie* grounds for having nothing to do with Glazer Brothers: their apparent shortage of liquid capital (making it unlikely that the abattoir would materialize), their alleged ties with the South African 'political financial' group Volkskas, and their alleged 'unsavoury reputation' BNA S.558/3.

67. The ECCO contract was only shown briefly to the members of the Livestock Industries Advisory Board in confidence.

68. The Congo market had temporarily vanished with the onset of war. The outbreak of Foot and Mouth disease in mid-1960 had closed the South African market and Federation demand was only 5,000 head, while the country was drought stricken. Overseas sales on a large scale were essential and the only marketing possibility.

69. Discussions concerning cannery, July 1960. BNA S.521/1/4.

70. As a result of deboning and packaging into individual cuts the grading differences between carcases are lost for all parts except the hind-quarters. Prices per lb for deboned beef were higher in the early 1960s than for bone-in beef in the UK market.

71. This is a personal opinion, gleaned from the correspondence relating to BPA affairs. Along with Russell England, Seretse Khama was BPA's representative on the ECCO board.

Chapter 8

1. See Ryan 1958 (Chapter 16 p.68) for a discussion of these points. Inspection of the associated correspondence indicates that this reflects the Administration's viewpoint, restated in the Edwards report 1963 (Section III).

2. The Livestock Producers' Trust was set up by Proc. 55 of 1960 to accumulate funds from share ownership in BPA with a view to buying out CDC holdings eventually. Trustees were drawn from the (then) Livestock Industry Advisory Board which also supplied board members to BPA. By these means it was hoped that farmers' and traders' representatives would acquire experience in administering the affairs of the abattoir in co-operation with a professional manager.

3. The appeal to the Secretary for Commonwealth Relations was a united effort of trading and breeding interests in the industry. (See BNA S.521/1/4, item 102, 22/2/63). It culminated in a motion passed in the Legislative Council in April 1963, calling upon government to investigate BPA Ltd immediately and to recommend on the best form of management and control of the abattoir.

4. See the memorandum 'Proposed lines of Negotiation with CDC and Circumstances to be Considered' (1961). BNA S.519/2/1–5.

5. These were (i) the 'Preliminary Enquiry into Meat Processing and Export Industry', Development Division of BP Government 1963, (this is an amended version of the 'Edwards report' 1963); (ii) the 'Report to the Government of the BP on the Beef Cattle and Meat Industry' by G. Purnell and W. Clayton (1963), (supplemented by a financial report on BPA and ECCO by Price Waterhouse 'The Livestock Industry of the BP'). These reports reached similar conclusions – the latter pair clearly reflecting the views of the former (the BP Government's). Their views are summarized in a paper prepared by government for the Legislative Council, 'Conduct and Development of the Livestock Industry' (April 1964), which formed the basis for the BMC Act of 1965.

6. An example of government's support for the relative autonomy of BMC from government machinery is provided by the Parliamentary debate concerning the workers' strike at BMC in late 1966 and associated allegations of racial discrimination (investigated in the 'Report of the Commission of Inquiry . . . into Certain Matters Relating to the Botswana Meat Commission' National Assembly Paper No. 13 of 1967). While the opposition held that BMC is a 'state industry' which government can control directly, government stressed its statutory inability so to intervene. (Republic of Botswana, National Assembly, Hansard 20, pp.106–115, 1966).

7. According to Ngamiland cattle trading firms which I interviewed in Maun in August 1978.

8. Barclays investments in cattle trading were still in 1977 a substantial portion of their total investments in Botswana. Source: Mr Brian Egner, then Agricultural Loans Manager for Barclays; personal communication 1977.

9. Perusal of the affairs of the cattle industry in colonial government files reveals quickly the much greater attention devoted to relations with European Advisory Council members than African Advisory Council members on issues that arose. Examples are the discussions in the 1940s concerning the level of the export levy and the plans to introduce the CDC abattoir, and the setting up of the white settlement project on the Molopo in the mid 1950s.

10. BMC Annual Report and Accounts 1974, p.3.

11. See statement by Minister of Agriculture Masisi in the 'Minutes of the Conference on Mr G. Bond's report on Livestock Marketing in Botswana' December 1974. Included as an appendix to the Bond report in its final version.

12. But slight differences in seasonal prices were reintroduced in 1982 in order to encourage holding of cattle into the off-season.

13. The northern abattoir issue in the 1970s is discussed in Hubbard 1981. Its roots lie in the 1950s (see Ryan 1958: Chapter 14 and Chapter 7 above). The 1973–74 plans for the northern abattoir were aborted owing to the mid-1970s marketing crisis and BMC's resistance to the project.

14. Source: Table A4.

15. See a discussion paper entitled: 'Policy issues for Livestock Marketing' Nairobi, November 1979, issued by the Marketing Development. Phase II (KEN-78/006) UNDP/FAO p.13.

16. ANZDEC 'Feasibility Study on the Expansion of Livestock Slaughtering Facilities in Botswana' 1981, Annex IV.

17. Defining average export price per head as

$$\frac{\text{Net BMC sales}}{\text{No. of head slaughtered}}$$

the following identity can be used to approximate the relative contribution of price and volume increases to the increased value of net BMC sales:

$$\frac{\text{Net BMC Sales}}{\text{No. of head slaughtered}} \times \text{No. of head slaughtered}$$
$$\equiv \text{Net BMC Sales}$$

From 1966/67 to 1982/83 average export prices increased 379% and number of cattle slaughtered 114%. Since $\frac{379}{114} = 3.32$, the relative contribution of price and volume increases is 3.32 : 1, or about 70% and 30%. The method is only valid where price and volume for the dates compared are representative of a trend i.e. when price and volume have not been fluctuating greatly in the interim.

18. See for example, a report entitled 'Cattle Marketing' issued by Division of Planning and Statistics, Ministry of Agriculture, 14

October 1970, emphasizing the need for a new policy initiative in cattle marketing.

19. The Ministry of Agriculture had based the anticipated yields of the planned holding grounds on the yields obtained on government demonstration ranches and thereby projected a favourable return. Ansell (1971: 51) questioned this basis and concluded: 'A plan to embark on a programme as ambitious as the construction of these nine holding grounds seems premature when . . . so little is known of their long-term performance in improving the quality of slaughter stock' (1971: 54).

20. See Rutherford 1982: 33–34.

21. Pressure for additional funds for cattle buying had been put onto the CDC and the Administration ever since the opening of the Lobatse abattoir had stopped the old live trade to Johannesburg and thereby cut local cattle buyers off from the finance they had previously received from SA agents and auctioneers. See BNA S.518/3–4.

22. Through failure to enforce liquidated damages (whereby unfulfilled quotas are fined) quota applications have been greatly inflated recently, undermining efficient and fair quota allocation and forcing BMC to make up the shortfall in throughput with increased 'shortcalls' i.e. requests to suppliers operating near the abattoir (effectively large speculator/fatteners) to deliver immediately. (I am grateful to J. S. Morrison for pointing this out to me).

23. Australia and New Zealand, with veterinary access for their fresh beef to Japan and the US are in a more flexible position than Argentina which can only sell cooked beef in these markets.

24. Botswana's levy-rebated EEC quota was equivalent to some 7% of UK beef imports in 1979 (FAO Trade Yearbooks).

25. See Jeske (ed.) 1978: Appendix 2 for a selection of newspaper reports from 1975 to 1978 which tell the story of the negotiations.

26. The South African market was depressed in 1978 and Botswana's quota reduced below its usual weekly level of 1,000 carcase equivalent, and confined to manufacturing grade beef.

27. BMC's other meat exports to EEC are in canned form. There is a 26% tariff barrier against entry of canned meat but no variable levy or quota (Tangermann & Krostitz 1981: Table 1).

28. See 'A Handbook of Livestock Statistics' 1980. Animal Production Division, Ministry of Agriculture. Table 1.4.

29. In 1980 the EEC's principal beef export markets were:

Mediterranean European countries	20%
East European countries	36%
Middle East countries	17%
African countries	10%

Source: Agricultural Commission of the EEC 'The Situation of the Agricultural Markets' 1981.

30. A long-term trend to excess production in agricultural products is suggested both by the growing excesses of milk production (itself a factor increasing beef production in the form of cull cows and calves) and sugar production, and by long-term data on beef production and consumption in the EEC:

EEC's PER CENT SELF SUFFICIENCY IN BEEF AND VEAL (IRRESPECTIVE OF NUMBER OF MEMBER COUNTRIES) $= \dfrac{PRODUCTION}{CONSUMPTION} \times 100$

1960	92%	1970	89%	1980	103%	1985	105%
1962	92%	1972	86%	1982	101%		(projected)
1965	85%	1975	100%	1983	105%		
1967	90%	1977	93%	1984	112%		

Sources: The Economist April 1 1978: 60 (for 1960 to 1978 figures);
International Market Review No. 1982 Table 4, p.15, published by the Meat and Livestock Commission, UK, and personal communication with Meat and Livestock Commission.
For the first time in twenty years EEC attained self-sufficiency in beef and veal in 1975 and since then (with the exception of 1977 and 1978) has continued in surplus.

31. Von Massow (1982:41–44) estimated Botswana's comparative advantage in beef production by calculating the ratio of domes-

tic resource costs to foreign resource costs (at border prices); or, in other words,

$$\frac{\text{Domestic value added (at shadow factor prices)}}{\text{Value added of imports (at the border)}}$$

If this ratio $\leqslant 1$ it indicates that the commodity can, under free market conditions, be produced as cheaply or more cheaply than in other countries, in terms of resource costs. Von Massow estimated it at 0.93 for Botswana (p.43). Whatever the reservations concerning the accuracy of this estimate, the basis for Botswana holding a comparative advantage in beef production is non-controversial: 'that opportunity costs of using the resources in dry areas for extensive beef cattle production tend to be very low' (p.41). I would add only that any comparative advantage of eastern Botswana in extensive cattle production reflects also the spatial dimension of capital accumulation in Southern Africa (see Chapters 1 and 3).

32. 'Report of the Presidential Commission on Economic Opportunities' (Mmusi Commission) May 1982, Table 5.3.1.

33. Ibid. para. 5.08.

34. See the summary of recommendations of 'A Study of drought relief and contingency measures relating to the livestock sector of Botswana', McGowan and Associates, Australia, May 1979.

35. With the Maun abattoir producing only canned beef as was originally planned, the basis for a lower price structure in Ngamiland would have been created since the returns on canned beef are generally lower than on chilled or frozen (see ANZDEC 1981: Annexe IV).

Chapter 9

1. Conclusive evidence is not available.

2. The proportions of increased value of cattle inventories in agricultural capital formation indicated in Table 9.1 are probably over-estimates owing to the under-valuing or under-reporting of capital works for arable agriculture (field clearing, granaries, threshing floors) performed with unpaid household labour.

3. While the claims of Comaroff (1977) that an agricultural trans-formation has taken place in Barolong since the mid-1960s have been modified by more recent work (Heisey 1982) it is not questioned that total production of the Barolong farms has increased markedly over the period.

4. The 1910 Customs Agreement fixed the shares of customs and excise revenue to be paid to each member state as the propor-tion of total imports accounted for by each state in 1906–07. Thus revenue from this source did not vary with changes in Bechuanaland's economy until the agreement was revised in 1969.

5. I was unable to trace the exact date when the levy was raised from P2.00 to P2.25. At the June 1951 meeting of the Joint Advisory Council, it was agreed that the levy be raised from P0.80 to P1.00 on the condition that the extra P0.20 would be paid into the Cattle Export Levy Fund which was (and still is) to be used 'for the general benefit of the livestock industry' (Proc. 21 1950), as administered by the Livestock Industry Advisory Board (set up by the Livestock and Meat Industries Proclamation of 1957) subsequently replaced in 1962 (after the abolition of the advisory councils) by the extant Livestock Industry Advisory Committee.

6. From annual reports of the Commissioner of Taxes.

7. The taxable income of BMC is taxed at the standard rate of company tax (35%). The taxable income for any year is equal to B where:

A = gross sales − direct marketing costs + insurance recovered from loss or damage to products;

B is determined from A on the following sliding scale:

If A is:	then B equals:
≤ P3 million	A ÷ 10
> P3 million but ≤ P6 million	(A − P3 million) ÷ 5 + P0.3 million
> P6 million but ≤ P9 million	(A − P6 million) ÷ 3.33 + P0.9 million
> P9 million	(A − P9 million) ÷ 3 + P1.8 million

Source: The Bechuanaland Meat Commission Law, No. 22 of 1965, Para 22.

8. Taxes paid by BPA Limited:

1961	P69,244
1962	P20,613
1963	P188,000
1964	P500,000

    Source: Annual Reports and Accounts BPA Ltd.

9. Cabinet Memorandum, Ministry of Agriculture, Bechuanaland Government. Cab. Mem. 229/1965.

10. BMC to Permanent Secretary, Ministry of Agriculture. 14 August 1969 and 4 February 1971.

11. Declining nutrition will lead to increased mortality, either gradually or, as Van Vegten (1982: 104) maintains, suddenly, with the decline in grass cover below a critical threshold.

12. The debate over ecological degradation is complex and burdened by problems of both definition (degradation, maximum stocking rate) and evidence (since the alleged process is of a very long-term nature only). The degradation thesis is propounded forcefully in papers presented to a 1971 conference on sustained production from semi-arid areas of Botswana. (Botswana Notes and Records, special edition 1971). It is repeated in Chambers and Feldman (1973) and in Government Paper No. 2 of 1975 which sets out the basis of TGLP. It is stressed in successive reports of the Animal Production Research Unit, Ministry of Agriculture, and its long-term impact is projected most dramatically by Van Vegten (1982). It is questioned by Sandford (1980), (1983) and De Ridder and Wagenaar (1984).

13. See the report 'Lefatshe la Rona – Our Land', Ministry of Local Government and Lands, 1977.

14. See 'An Application by the Government of Botswana for a loan to finance a Second Livestock Development Project', Ministry of Agriculture, November 1976, p.67; 'Livestock and Range Research in Botswana 1979', Animal Production Research Unit, Ministry of Agriculture, Chapter 10; S. Bekure and N. Dyson-Hudson 'The Operation and Viability of the Second Livestock Development Project: Selected Issues', Ministry of Agriculture 1982, pp.13–21.

15. See note 14.

16. Regarding compensation for improvements made, the TGLP lease agreement reads as follows:

    'the Grantee may terminate this lease upon giving six months written notice to the Grantor. On termination of the lease by the Grantee, the Grantor shall, unless the Grantor approves a sale to any qualified citizen buyer, compensate the Grantee for improvements left on the land' (Clause 11a).

17. From my interviews with prospective TGLP ranchers in Ngamiland.

Chapter 10

1. This assumes that the distribution of sales to BMC among households is similar to the distribution of cattle ownership among households found by the Rural Income Distribution Survey, Central Statistics Office 1976, p.111.

2. With government doubling the funds raised by the farmers themselves. See Willett 1981: Chapters 9 and 10 for a discussion of progress in communal fencing.

Appendix: Tables and Figures

Table A1: *Botswana's cattle population and offtake: available historical statistics*

	1. CATTLE POPULATION (000)	2. Exports and all Lobatse abattoir slaughterings	3. OFFTAKE Local consumption	4. % of cattle population
1904/5	139			
1905/6				
1906/7		3 622		
1907/8		3 084		
1908/9				
1909/10				
1910/11				
1911/12	324	14 132		
1912/13		15 673		
1913/14				
1914/15				
1915/16		17 664		
1916/17		18 876		
1917/18				
1918/19		26 571		

Table A1: continued

	1. CATTLE POPULATION (000)	2. Exports and all Lobatse abattoir slaughterings	3. OFFTAKE Local consump- tion	4. % of cattle population
1919/20		23 569		
1920/21		32 450		
1921/22	495(426)	25 884		
1922/23		26 046		
1923/24		32 706		
1924/25		25 162		
1925/26		34 434		
1926/27		31 889		
27		19 870		
28		30 060		
29		30 673		
1930		28 177		
31		26 209		
32	777	25 103		
33	800	715		
34	1 400(1 200)	2 871		
35		24 577		
36	541	19 022		
37	602	8 515		
38	649	21 570		
39	647	24 461		
1940	733	33 928		
41	790	33 009		
42	812	44 933		
43	837	42 931		
44	897	35 159		
45	920	42 024		
46	959	46 994		
47	967	53 983		
48	979	42 403		
49	983	70 403		
1950	1 050	70 169		
51	1 027	77 995		
52	1 054	73 168		
53	1 098	71 116	7 546	6.8
54	1 104	74 603	3 803	7.1

Table A1: (continued)

	1. CATTLE POPULATION (000)	2. Exports and all Lobatse abattoir slaughterings	3. OFFTAKE Local consump- tion	4. % of cattle population
1955	1173	71895	6503	6.3
56	1236	70534	8051	6.1
57	1310	64425	6908	5.4
58	1315	69026	9707	6.0
59	1317	97115	13297	8.4
1960	1272	85150	13100	7.7
61	1319	89208	12312	7.7
62	1352	109029		
63	1350	127467	12755	10.3
64	1347	123051	12721	10.1
65	1481	155982	23000	16.3
66	1237	148654	17000	13.4
67	1492	95902	18000	7.6
68	1688	103776	20000	7.3
69	1945	93074	23000	6.0
1970	2017	128199	26000	7.6
71	2092	167430	31000	9.5
72	2177	156510	40000	9.0
73	2138	209443	34000	11.4
74	2249	186041	38000	10.0
75	2384	188440	42000	9.7
76	2512	211987	50000	10.4
77	2600	196850	50000	9.3
78	2717	149346	70000	7.6
79	2817	229000	45000	9.7
1980	2911	140783	40000	6.2
81	2967	202000	46000	8.4
82	2979	237135	59000	9.9
83	2818	233000	62000	10.5
84	2685	239000		

Sources: Column 1 – to 1965 Great Britain 'Annual Report on the BP'
(as quoted in Roe 1980: Table 1).
– from 1965 National Development Plan 1979–85,
Table 6.5 and Botswana Agricultural Statistics
1984.

Column 2 – to 1920/21 Great Britain 'Annual Report on the BP' (as quoted in Roe 1980: Table 1)
– 1920/21 to 1956 Ryan 1958: Appendix C.
– 1956 to 1965 Great Britain 'Annual Report on the BP'.
– 1966 to 1984 BMC Annual Reports and Accounts.

Column 3 – 1953 to 1964 Department of Veterinary Services in BNA S 521/1/3 and annual report of the department; *Note:* These figures are for slaughter by butchers only.
– 1956 to 1978: Carl Bro International (1982: 2.19). These figures include local abattoir throughput, home slaughter plus an allowance for consumption from animals that die.
– 1979 to 1983: Rows 1 and 2 of Table A4.

Table A2: *Operations of the BMC 1966–1984*

	1. Throughput (000 head)		3.	4. Total producer payments (P000) (rounded)	5. Producer payments as proportion of net sales	6. Per cent of throughput of cattle deboned
	Cattle	Small stock	Net sales* (P000)			
1966	132	3	6805	6900	1.02	74
67	88	7	11120	6300	0.57	39
68	104	32	10593	8000	0.76	31
69	93	35	9334	7400	0.80	27
1970	127	34	11916	9000	0.78	56
71	167	42	14962	12000	0.81	61
72	157	23	19547	15000	0.77	66
73	209	9	31297	27000	0.85	83
74	186	59	34711	28000	0.81	62
75	188	22	33889	27000	0.81	76
76	212	8	44814	32000	0.71	85
77	197	5	42042	30700	0.73	92
78	149	1	32694	21700	0.69	98
79	229	1	77496	45200	0.60	98
1980	141	–	44031	27600	0.69	94
81	202	–	71799	50200	0.70	94
82	237	1	87549	64109	0.73	94
83	234	7	96286	63398	0.66	96
84	239	16	96745	59533	0.62	98

* Net Sales=sales less freight, storage, levies and other selling expenses.

Source: BMC Annual Report and Accounts.
Note: See Fig. A1 for prices paid by the Lobatse abattoir.

Table A3: *Beef Prices: Botswana, South Africa and World
1960–83 ($US per tonne f.o.b. and 1959/60/61 = 100)*

| | 1. | 2. | 3. | 4. | 5.
BMC
producer
payments
(per 100 kg
CDW)
Index |
| | World fresh
bovine meat | | World
canned
meat | SA
slaughter
stock | |
	Price	Index	Price	Index	
1960	603	100		100	100
1965	770	134		140	169
1970	910	158	1130	174	219
1974	1686	296	1863	366	456
1975	1553	269	1952	337	431
1976	1477	257	2003	377	431
1977	1655	288	1979	382	469
1978	1899	330	2275	401	444
1979	2340	409	2589	489	594
1980	2587	453	2811	625	606
1981	2470	430	2641	844	719
1982	2396	410			844
1983	2201	365			863

Sources: Column 1, 2, 3 calculated from volume of exports and value for
'Meat Bovine Fresh' (011.1) in *FAO Trade Yearbook* (various
years).
Column 4 – from *Abstract of Agricultural Statistics 1983,* Pre-
toria.
Column 5 – from BPA and BMC *Annual Report and
Accounts.*

Table A4: *Proportions of domestic consumption and exports in offtake 1979 to 1983 and 1990 (projected) (000 head)* [1]

	1979	1980	1981	1982	1983	1990
1. Homeslaughter and consumption from deaths	26	22	24	30	33	47
2. Local abattoir slaughter	19	18	22	29	29	51
3. BMC local sales	10	22	19	13	14	15
4. Domestic consumption (1+2+3)	55	62	65	72	76	113
5. Exports	219	117	182	224	203	257
6. Total offtake[2] (4+5)	274	179	247	296	279	370
7. Domestic consumption as % of offtake $\frac{4.}{6.} \times 100$	17	34	26	24	27	31
8. Exports as % of offtake $\frac{5.}{6.} \times 100$	80	65	74	76	73	69
9. Domestic consumption from marketed offtake as % of exports $\frac{2.+3.}{5.} \times 100$	13	34	23	19	21	26

Sources: Row 1 *Agriculture in Figures (1979–83)* Botswana, Ministry of Agriculture.

Row 2 *A Handbook of Livestock Statistics 1981–82,* Table 7.1, Ministry of Agriculture.

Rows 3 and 5 BMC *Annual Report & Accounts.*

Notes:
1. This table should be used with caution since Row 1 is only an estimate.
2. Offtake here includes mortality partly (Row 1).

Table A5: *Marketing of cattle to BMC: By category of supplier 1973 to 1982*

	1973	1974	1975	1976	1977	1978	1979	1980	1981	1982
Means of supply										
Cooperatives %[1]	10	13	15	16	19	16	16	15	21	20
Direct %[2]	15	17	15	14	15	17	13	22	na	15
Agents %	75	70	70	70	66	67	71	63	na	65
Supplier										
Freehold ranches, traders and speculators %	62	56	54	46	42	41	36	na	na	na
Cattle posts %	38	44	46	54	58	59	64	na	na	na

Source: BMC as quoted in Carl Bro International (1982: Table 2.5.F.)
Notes: (1) Cooperatives per cent for earlier years:

1968	3
1971	6
1972	8

Source: Ansell (1971:23), Bond (1976:51).
(2) In 1978 74% of cattle marketed direct were from cattle posts and 26% from freehold ranches, traders and speculators.
Source: A Handbook of Livestock Statistics, Ministry of Agriculture; 1980 (Table 5.6), 1981/82 (Table 5.1).

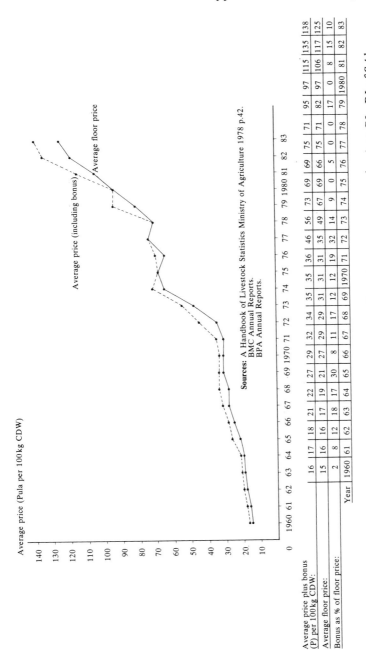

Figure A1: *Lobatse abattoir: prices paid to cattle suppliers (current money values) at PI=RI=£SA‡*

Year	1960	61	62	63	64	65	66	67	68	69 1970	71	72	73	74	75 1970	76	77	78	79 1980	81	82	83
Average price plus bonus (P) per 100kg CDW:	16	17	18	21	22	27	29	32	34	35	35	36	46	56	73	69	75	71	95	97	115	135	138
Average floor price:	15	16	16	17	19	21	27	29	31	31	31	35	49	67	69	66	75	71	82	97	106	117	125
Bonus as % of floor price:	2	8	12	18	17	30	8	11	17	12	12	19	32	14	9	0	5	0	0	17	0	8	15	10

Sources: A Handbook of Livestock Statistics Ministry of Agriculture 1978 p.42.
BMC Annual Reports.
BPA Annual Reports.

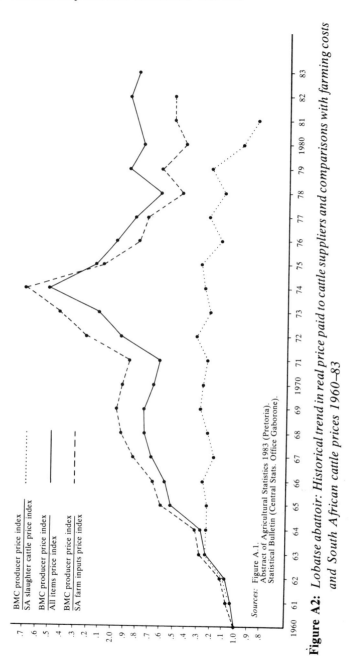

Figure A2: *Lobatse abattoir: Historical trend in real price paid to cattle suppliers and comparisons with farming costs and South African cattle prices 1960–83*

Select Bibliography

Note: References cited in the text will be found under Articles (published), Books and pamphlets (published and unpublished) or Consultancy reports.

Articles (Published)

AMIN S., 'Underdevelopment and Dependence in Black Africa – Origins and Contemporary Forms'. *Journal of Modern African Studies* Vol. X No. 4, December 1972, pp.503–524.

BAKER P., 'The Social Importance of Cattle in Africa and the Influence of Social Attitudes on Beef Production'. In SMITH A. (Ed.) 'Beef Cattle Production in Developing Countries', University of Edinburgh Centre for Tropical Veterinary Medicine 1976.

BERLAN J., 'Croissance de Longue Periode de L'Economie Agricole Americaine et Les Echanges Internationaux'. Institute National de la Recherche Agrominique, Paris 1980 (mimeo).

BEST A., 'General Trading in Botswana 1890–1968'. *Economic Geography*, October 1970, pp.598–612.

BOSMAN H. C., 'Marico Revisited'. In BOSMAN H. C. 'A Cask of Jerepigo', Human and Rousseau 1964.

CLIFFE L. and MOORSOM R., 'Rural Class Formation and Ecological Collapse in Botswana'. *Review of African Political Economy*, 15/16 1979: 35–52.

COWEN M., 'The British State and Agrarian Accumulation in Kenya'. In FRANSMAN M. (Ed.), 'Industry and Accumulation in Africa', Heineman 1982, pp.142–169.

DE RIDDER N. and WAGENAAR K., 'A Comparison between the Productivity of Traditional Livestock System and Ranching in Eastern Botswana'. ILCA Newsletter, Vol. 3 No. 3, July 1984. International Livestock Centre for Africa.

DENBOW J., 'The Toutswe Tradition: A Study in Socio-Economic Change'. In HITCHCOCK R and SMITH M., (Eds.) 'Proceedings of the Symposium on Settlement in Botswana', Heinemann and Botswana Society 1982.

DEVITT P., 'Drought and Poverty'. In HINCHEY M. (Ed.) 'Symposium on Drought in Botswana', Botswana Society and Clarke University Press 1978: 121–127.

DORAN M., LOW A. and KEMP R., 'Cattle as a Store of Wealth in Swaziland: Implications for Livestock Development and Overgrazing in Eastern and Southern Africa'. *American Journal of Agricultural Economics* 61, No. 1 1979: 41–47.

DOS SANTOS T., 'The Crisis of Development Theory and the Problem of Dependence in Latin America'. In BERNSTEIN H. (Ed.) 'Underdevelopment and Development', Penguin 1973.

ETTINGER S., 'South Africa's Weight Restrictions on Cattle Exports from Bechuanaland 1924–41'. *Botswana Notes and Records* Vol 4, Gaborone 1972.

FALCONER J., 'History of the Botswana Veterinary Services 1905–66'. *Botswana Notes and Records* Vol. 3, Gaborone, pp.74–78.

FAY C., 'The Toronto School of Economic History'. *Economic History* III Jan. 1934, pp.168–171.

FIELDER R., 'The Role of Cattle in the Ila Economy'. *African Social Research* 15, June 1973: 327–41.

HARDIN G., 'The Tragedy of the Commons'. *Science* 162: 1243–1248 1968.

HARRINGTON G., 'Problems of Marketing Beef Cattle in Developed Countries'. In SMITH A., (Ed.) 'Beef Cattle Production in Developing Countries', University of Edinburgh, Centre for Tropical Veterinary Medicine 1976.

HECKSHER E., 'The Effects of Foreign Trade on the Distribution of Income'. *Economisk Tidskrift* XXI 1919.

HEDLUND H., 'Contradictions in the Peripheralization of a Pastoral Society: The Maasai'. *Review of African Political Economy* 15/16 1979: 15–34.

HERMANS Q., 'A Review of Botswana's Financial History 1970–73'. *Botswana Notes and Records*, Vol. 6 1974, pp.89–116.

HERSKOVITS M., 'The Cattle Complex in East Africa'. *American Anthropologist* 28, 1926.

HILL B., 'The World Market for Beef and Other Meat'. *World Animal Review* No. 4 1972, FAO Rome.

HITCHCOCK R., 'Tradition, Social Justice and Land Reform in Central Botswana'. *Journal of African Law* 24 No. 1, Spring 1980: 1–34.

HRABOVSKY J., 'Livestock Development Toward 2000'. *World Animal Review* 40, Oct.–Dec. 1981.

HUBBARD M., 'Botswana's Beef Cattle Industry Since Independence'. In OOMMEN M. (Ed.) 'Botswana's Economy Since Independence', Tata McGraw–Hill, Delhi 1983.

HUBBARD M., 'Notes on Beef in the Lome Convention'. In JESKE J. (Ed.) 'Proceedings of the Seminar on Botswana's External Trade in the Light of the Lome Convention', National Institute of Research, Gaborone 1979, pp.58–75.

HUBBARD M., 'Botswana's Beef Export Industry: The Issue of the Proposed Northern Abattoir'. In HARVEY C. (Ed.) 'Papers on the Economy of Botswana', Heinemann 1981.

HUBBARD M., 'Comparisons of Cattle Herd Performance in Botswana and Their Consequences for Cattle Production Investment Planning; Additional Observations from the 1979 and 1980 Agricultural Statistics'. In HITCHCOCK R. (Ed.) 'Botswana's First Livestock Development Project and Its Future Implications'. National Institute of Research, Gaborone. June 1982, pp.62–74.

HUBBARD M., 'Stock Limitation: Any Economic Alternatives for Botswana?' *ODI Pastoral Network Paper* 14c, August 1982. Overseas Development Institute, London.

HUDSON D., (1981a) 'The Taxation of Income from Cattle Farming'. In HARVEY C. (Ed.) 'Papers on the Economy of Botswana', Heinemann 1981.

HUDSON D., (1981b) 'The Taxation of Income from Cattle Farming' (mimeo). Paper read to a Meeting of the Botswana Society, 13th October 1981.

JARVIS L., 'Cattle as Capital Goods and Ranchers as Portfolio Managers: An Application to the Argentine Cattle Sector'. *Journal of Political Economy* 82 (1974): 489–520.

JARVIS L., 'Cattle as a Store of Wealth in Swaziland: Comment'. *American Journal of Agricultural Economics* 62, No. 3, August 1980: 606–13.

JASIOROWSKI H., 'The Developing World as a Source of Beef for World Markets'. In SMITH A. (Ed.) 'Beef Cattle Production in Developing Countries'. University of Edinburgh, Centre for Tropical Veterinary Medicine 1976.

LEWIS S. and MOKGETHI N., 'Fiscal Policy in Botswana 1966–81'. In OOMMEN M. (Ed.) 'Botswana's Economy Since Independence', Tata McGraw–Hill, Delhi 1983.

LIVINGSTONE I., 'Economic Irrationality Among Pastoral Peoples: Myth or Reality?' *Development and Change* 8 (1977), 209–30.

LOW A., 'The Estimation and Interpretation of Pastoralists' Price Responsiveness'. *ODI Pastoral Network Paper* 10, July 1980.

LOW A., KEMP R. and DORAN M., 'Cattle Wealth and Cash Needs in Swaziland: Price Response and Rural Development Implications'. *Journal of Agricultural Economics*, May 1980: 225–36.

MARINCOWITZ G. and LOW J., 'Extensive Cattle Ranching at Soutpan'. Beef Cattle D. 1.7/1979. Farming in South Africa. Department of Agricultural Technical Services, Pretoria.

MILLER W. and MILLER S. 'Agricultural Pricing Policy and its Effects on Production and Equity, with Special Emphasis on Botswana Farming Systems'. (mimeo) 1984. Presented to Botswana Society for Agricultural Development Seminar on agricultural pricing, December 1984.

MITTENDORF H., 'Factors Affecting the Location of Slaughter Houses in Developing Countries'. *World Animal Review* 25 1978, pp.13–17. FAO Rome.

NDZINGE L., MARSH J. and CLYDE GREER R., 'Herd Inventory and Slaughter Supply Response of Botswana Beef Cattle Producers'. Department of Agricultural Economics, Montana State University 1982 (mimeo).

OPSCHOOR J., 'Crops, Class and Climate: Environmental and Economic Constraints and Potentials of Crop Production in Botswana'. In OOMMEN M. (Ed.) 'Botswana's Economy Since Independence', Tata McGraw–Hill, Delhi 1983.

PARRIS K., 'Beef'. In HARRIS S. *et al*, 'The Lomé Convention and the Common Agricultural Policy', Commonwealth Economic Papers: No. 12 1978, London.

PARSONS N., 'The Economic History of Khama's Country in Botswana 1844–1930'. In PALMER R. and PARSONS N. (Eds.)

'The Roots of Rural Poverty in Central and Southern Africa', Heinemann 1977.

PHIMISTER I., 'Meat and Monopolies: Beef Cattle in Southern Rhodesia, 1890–1938'. *Journal of African History* XIX, No. 3 1978, pp.391–414.

PICARD L., 'Bureaucrats, Cattle and Public Policy: Land Tenure Changes in Botswana'. *Comparative Political Studies*, Vol. 13 No. 3 1980.

PITTI A., 'Protein for Panama: Financing Cattle Production'. *Agribusiness Worldwide*, August–September 1980.

PRAH K., 'Some Sociological Aspects of Drought.' In HINCHEY M. (Ed.) 'Symposium on Drought in Botswana', Botswana Society and Clarke University Press 1978.

PRESTON T., 'Prospects for the Intensification of Cattle Production in Developing Countries'. In SMITH A. (Ed.) 'Beef Cattle Production in Developing Countries', University of Edinburgh, Centre for Tropical Veterinary Medicine, 1976.

ROUX B., 'Expansion du Capitalisme et Developpement du sous Developpement: L'integration de L'Amerique Centrale au Marché Mondial de la Viande Bovine'. *Revûe Tiers Monde* XVI 62, (April–June 1975) pp.355–380.

RUNGE C., 'Common Property Externalities: Isolation, Assurance and Resource Depletion in a Traditional Grazing Context'. *American Journal of Agricultural Economics*, November 1981. pp.595–606.

RUTHERFORD A., 'The Botswana Livestock Development Corporation (Pty) Ltd: A Reassessment'. In HITCHCOCK R. (Ed.) 'Botswana's First Livestock Development Project and Its Future Implications'. National Institute of Research, Gaborone 1982.

SCOTT T. 'The Lomé Convention and Botswana's Trade with the European Community'. In JESKE J. (Ed.) 'Proceedings of the Seminar on Botswana's External Trade in the Light of the Lomé Convention', National Institute of Research, Gaborone 1979, pp.11–37.

SCHNEIDER H., 'Economic Development and Economic Change: The Case of East African Cattle'. *Current Anthropology* 15 No. 3, September 1974.

SIMPSON J. and FARRIS D., 'The Benefits for Economic Development from Selected South American Beef Exports'. *World Animal Review* 13 1975, pp.9–15. FAO Rome.

SIMPSON M., 'Problems of Marketing Beef Cattle in Developing Countries'. In SMITH A. (Ed.) 'Beef Cattle Production in Developing Countries'. University of Edinburgh, Centre for Tropical Veterinary Medicine 1976.

SINGER H., 'The Distribution of Gains Between Investing and Borrowing Countries'. *American Economic Review*, Papers and Proceedings. May 1950.

SMITH Col. I., 'Transforming a City's Meat Industry: The Growth of the Johannesburg Livestock Market'. *Municipal Magazine*, Johannesburg 1938.

STALS E. L. P., 'Die Geskiedenis van die Beesteelt in Suidwes-Afrika Tydens die Duitse Tydperk' (1884–1915). Archives Yearbook for SA History 1962, pp.75–162.

VAN HORN L., 'The Agricultural History of Barotseland 1840–1964'. In PALMER R. and PARSONS N. (Eds.) 'The Roots of Rural Poverty in Central and Southern Africa', Heinemann 1977.

VAN VEGTEN J., 'Increasing Stock Numbers on Deteriorating Rangeland'. In HITCHCOCK R. (Ed.), 'Botswana's First Livestock Development Project and its Future Implications', National Institute of Research, Gaborone 1982.

WATKINS M., 'A Staple Theory of Economic Growth'. *Canadian Journal of Economics and Political Science*. Vol. XXIX No. 2, May 1963.

YOUNG M., 'Influencing Land Use in Pastoral Australia'. *Journal of Arid Environments* 2, 1979: 279–288.

Books and Pamphlets (Published and Unpublished)

AMIN S., 'Class and Nation, Historically and in the Current Crisis'. Heinemann 1980.

ANSELL D. J., 'Cattle Marketing in Botswana'. University of Reading, Development Studies No. 8, 1971.

BALDWIN R., 'Economic Development and Export Growth: A Study of Northern Rhodesia 1920–60'. California 1966.

BEKURE S. and DYSON-HUDSON N., 'The Operation and Viability of the Second Livestock Development Project (1497–BT): Selected Issues'. Ministry of Agriculture, Gaborone 1982.

BIRD R., 'Taxing Agricultural Land in Developing Countries'. Harvard 1974.

BOND G., 'A Report on Livestock Marketing'. Government Printer, Gaborone 1976.

BOSERUP E. 'The Conditions of Agricultural Growth'. Allen and Unwin 1965.

COLCLOUGH C. and FALLON P., 'Rural Poverty in Botswana: Dimensions, Causes and Constraints'. ILO WEP 10-6/WP26.

COLCLOUGH C. and McCARTHY S., 'The Political Economy of Botswana: A Study of Growth and Distribution'. Oxford 1980.

COLLINGWOOD R., 'The Idea of History'. Oxford 1946.

COMAROFF J., 'The Structure of Agricultural Transformation in Baralong: Towards an Integrated Development Plan'. Government Printer, Gaborone 1977.

CONNOLLY L., 'Beef and Veal: World Situation and Outlook'. Republic of Ireland Agricultural Institute: Economics and Rural Welfare Research Centre 1976.

COOPER D., 'How Urban Workers in Botswana Manage Their Cattle and Lands: Selebi Phikwe Case Studies'. NMS Working Paper No. 4, June 1980. Central Statistics Office, Gaborone.

CROTTY R., 'Cattle, Economics and Development'. Commonwealth Agricultural Bureau 1980.

DE BOER A., 'The Short Run and Long Run Position of Australian Beef Supplies and the Competitiveness of Australian Beef in International Trade'. Centre for Research on Economic Development. University of Michigan 1979.

DYSON-HUDSON N., 'Karamojong Politics'. Oxford 1965.

EMMANUEL A., 'Unequal Exchange'. New Left Books 1972.

FEDER E., 'Lean Cows Fat Ranchers'. America Latina, London 1978.

FRANK A., 'Capitalism and Underdevelopment in Latin America'. Pelican 1969.

FRANK A., 'Sociology of Development'. London: Pluto 1971.

GULBRANDSEN Q., 'Agro Pastoral Production and Communal Land Use: A Socio-Economic Study of the Bangwaketse'. Government Printer, Gaborone 1980.

HANSON S., 'Argentine Meat and the British Market: Chapters in the History of the Argentine Meat Industry'. Stanford 1938.

HAYAMI Y. and RUTTAN V., 'Agricultural Development: An International Perspective'. Johns Hopkins 1971.

HEISEY P., 'Agriculture and Target Agricultural Populations in Southern District FCDA: A Preliminary Report'. University of Wisconsin-Madison, Department of Agricultural Economics, Dec. 1981 (mimeo).

HITCHCOCK R., 'Production vs. Equity: Land Reform in Botswana'. Ministry of Agriculture 1981 (mimeo).

INNIS H., 'The Fur Trade in Canada: An Introduction to Canadian Economic History'. Toronto 1930.

JENNESS J., 'Rethinking the TGLP in Light of Land Use Planning Exercise'. Paper presented to the National District Development Conference, Ministry of Local Government and Lands, 1978 (mimeo).

JERVE A., 'Pastoralists, Peasants or Proletarians? An Analysis of the Role of Livestock Production in the Economy of Tsabong Area, Southern Kgalagadi'. DERAP Working Papers A 226, CHR Michelsen Institute, Bergen, July 1981.

KAY G., 'Development and Underdevelopment: A Marxist Analysis'. Macmillan 1975.

LAPPÉ F. and COLLINS J., 'Food First: Beyond the Myth of Scarcity'. Houghton Mifflin, Boston 1977.

McDONALD I., 'A Report on Cattle Marketing in Botswana' 1979 (mimeo).

MTETWA J., 'Man and Cattle in Africa'. München 1981.

MYINT H., 'An Interpretation of Economic Backwardness'. *Oxford Economic Papers* Vol. 6 No. 2 1954.

OHLIN B., 'Inter-regional and International Trade'. Harvard 1933.

OSGOOD E., 'The Day of the Cattleman'. University of Chicago Press, 1929.

PEARSON S. and COWNIE J., 'Commodity Exports and African Economic Development'. Lexington 1974.

PERRINGS C., 'Black Mineworkers in Central Africa'. Heinemann 1979.

RAIKES P., 'Livestock Development and Policy in East Africa'. Uppsala, Centre for Development Research Publications 6, 1981.

RICARDO D., 'Principles of Political Economy and Taxation'. Everyman Edition.

ROE E., 'Development of Livestock, Agriculture and Water Supplies in Botswana Before Independence: A Short History and Policy Analysis'. Cornell University Rural Development Committee, Occasional Paper No. 10.

RUSSELL M. and RUSSELL M. 'Afrikaners of the Kalahari: White Minority in a Black State'. Cambridge 1979.

SAMBOMA L., 'The Survey of Freehold Farms of Botswana 1982'. Ministry of Agriculture 1982.

SANDFORD S. 'Management of Pastoral Development in the Third World'. Wiley 1983.

SCHAPERA I., 'Native Land Tenure in the Bechuanaland Protectorate'. Lovedale 1943.

SCHAPERA I., 'Migrant Labour and Tribal Life: A Study of Conditions in the Bechuanaland Protectorate'. London 1947.

SHANE D., 'Hoofprints on the Forest: An Inquiry into the Beef Cattle Industry in the Tropical Forest Areas of Latin America'. Office of Environment Affairs, US Department of State, Washington 1980.

SIMPSON J., 'World Cattle Cycles and the Latin American Beef Industry'. Staff Paper 129. Food and Resource Economics Department, Institute of Food and Agricultural Sciences, University of Florida 1979.

SMITH A., 'An Inquiry into the Nature and Causes of the Wealth of Nations'. New York, Modern Library 1937.

SMITH P., 'Politics and Beef in Argentina: Patterns of Conflict and Change'. Columbia 1969.

SPRAY P., 'Botswana as a Beef Exporter'. National Institute of Research, Gaborone, Working Paper, 1981.

STEVENS C., 'The EEC and the Third World: A Survey'. ODI/IDS Hodder and Stoughton 1981.

TANGERMANN S. and KROSTITZ W., 'Protectionism in the Livestock Sector with Particular Reference to the International Beef Trade'. Institute of Agricultural Economics, University of Göttingen 1981 (mimeo).

THOBURN J. 'Primary Commodity Exports and Economic Development: Theory, Evidence and a Study of Malaysia'. Wiley 1977.

VALDES A. and NORES G., 'Growth Potential of the Beef Sector in Latin America – Survey of Issues and Policies'. International Food Policy Research Institute 1978.

VAN BILJON, 'State Interference in South Africa'. London 1938.

VIERICH H., 'Drought 1979 – Socio Economic Survey of Drought Impact in Kweneng'. Rural Sociology Unit, Ministry of Agriculture, Gaborone 1979.

VON MASSOW V., 'EEC Agricultural Policy and Developing Countries – The Case of Beef After Lomé I'. Institute of Agricultural Economics, University of Göttingen 1982 (mimeo). (A revised version of this paper is published as 'On the Impacts of EEC Beef Preferences for Kenya and Botswana'. *Quarterly Journal of International Agriculture* No. 3 1983).

WILSON F., 'Labour in the South African Gold Mines 1911–1969'. Cambridge 1972.

Official Publications

Bechuanaland Protectorate Government, Mafeking.

'Agricultural Division, Annual Report 1947'.

'Memorandum on the Livestock Industry of the Bechuanaland Protectorate'. (Edwards Report) 1963.

'Conduct and Development of the Livestock Industry' April 1964. BP Government, Paper Presented to the Legislative Assembly.

'Preliminary Enquiry into Meat Processing and Export Industry'. Development Division 1963.

Minutes of Meetings of the Native (later African), European and Joint Advisory Councils. Various Years.

Bechuanaland Protectorate Abattoirs Ltd. (BPA) 'Annual Report and Accounts', (1960–1964).

Botswana

(a) *Botswana Government, Gaborone*

'Hansard', National Assembly, (Various Years).

'National Policy for Rural Development'. Government Paper No. 2 1973.

'National Policy on Tribal Grazing Land'. Government Paper No. 2 1975.

'National Policy on Economic Opportunities'. Unnumbered Government Paper 1982.

'Report of the Presidential Commission on Economic Opportunities' (Mmusi Commission). Government Printer, May 1982.

'Farm Management Survey' (Annual). Ministry of Agriculture, Division of Planning and Statistics.

'Agricultural Statistics' (Formerly: 'Agricultural Survey') (Annual). Ministry of Agriculture, Division of Planning and Statistics.

'Preliminary Investigation into the Marketing of Crops and Livestock in Botswana'. Ministry of Agriculture, Division of Planning and Statistics.

'A Handbook of Livestock Statistics' (1978 and 1980). Ministry of Agriculture, Animal Production Division.

'An Integrated Programme of Beef Cattle and Range Research'. (Annual Reports 1973–80). Ministry of Agriculture, Animal Production Research Unit.

'The Rural Income Distribution Survey in Botswana 1974/75'. Central Statistics Office.

'Annual Statements of Accounts'. Central Statistics Office.

'District Councils Estimates of Revenue and Expenditure. Recurrent Budget 1974/75'. Ministry of Local Government and Lands, 1974.

'Town Councils Estimates of Revenue and Expenditure, Recurrent Budget 1974/75'. Ministry of Local Government and Lands 1974.

'Report of a Visit to CDC to Examine Files and Records of CDC Rural Development Project at Pandamatenga, Nata and Bushman Pits'. _G 2/20/9 1975 Ministry of Local Government and Lands.

Botswana Parastatals

Botswana Meat Commission (BMC).
'Annual Report and Accounts', 1966–1981.
Botswana Agricultural Marketing Board (BAMB).
'Annual Reports and Accounts' (Various Years).
Botswana Livestock Development Corporation (Pty) Limited.
'Annual Report and Accounts', (1975–81).

Britain

'Annual Reports for the Bechuanaland Protectorate' (Colonial Reports) (Annual to 1965). HMSO.

'Report of the Commission Appointed by the Secretary of State for Dominion Affairs: Financial and Economic Position of The Bechuanaland Protectorate' 1933. (Pim report on Bechuanaland) HMSO.

'Imports of Meat into the United Kingdom: Statement of the Views of His Majesty's Government in the United Kingdom'. CMD 4828. HMSO 1935.

'Basutoland, Bechuanaland Protectorate & Swaziland: History of Discussions with the Union of South Africa 1909–1939'. London, Commonwealth Relations Office. Cmnd. 8707, 1952.

'Reports of a Mission to the Bechuanaland Protectorate to Investigate the Possibilities of Economic Development in the Western Kalahari' (Gaitskell Commission), HMSO 1954.

'Committee of Inquiry into Fatstock and Carcase Meat Marketing and Distribution'. CMD 2282. HMSO 1964.

South Africa

(a) Union of South Africa

'Union Blue Books: Expenditure Estimates' (Annual) (to 1960).

'Official Yearbook of the Union of South Africa' (Annual to 1960). Union office of Census and Statistics.

'Findings of the Board of Control in an Enquiry into the Meat trade'. UG 21/1922.

'Meat, Fish and Other Foodstuffs: An Inquiry into Trade Combinations, Supplies, Distribution and Prices'. SA Board of Trade and Industries, Report No. 54 1925.

'Report of the Departmental Railway Tariffs Inquiry Committee' 1930. South African Railways and Harbours.

'Report 1934–39' (thereafter annual). South African Livestock and Meat Industries Control Board.

'Report of the Departmental Committee on the Problem of Meat Export from the Union of South Africa'. Department of Agriculture and Forestry, 1936.

'A Survey of the Supply with Regard to Slaughter Stock and

Meat in the Union, and Probable Future Trends'. South African Livestock and Meat Industries Control Board, 1945.

'South West Africa: Report of the Long-Term Agricultural Policy Commission'. South African Department of Agriculture (?) 1949. (Copy in Meat Board Library, Pretoria.)

'Report of the Committee Appointed to Inquire into Railway Rating Policy in South Africa'. UG 32/1950.

'Report of the Beef Marketing Inquiry Committee'. South African Meat and Livestock Industries Control Board. May 1975.

'Union Statistics for Fifty Years', 1910–1960. Bureau of Statistics, Pretoria 1960.

(b) Republic of South Africa

'Meat Board: Annual Report' (various years). Meat Board, Pretoria.

'Report of the Commission of Enquiry into Abattoirs and Allied Facilities'. Government Printer May 1964.

'Report on the National Abattoir Planning Project' (two volumes). Abattoir Commission, Department of Agricultural Economics and Marketing, July 1978.

Southern Rhodesia

'Report on the Railway System of Southern Rhodesia', Vols. I and II, 1926. CSR 2 1926.

'Report of the Commission Appointed to Inquire into the Marketing of Slaughter Cattle and the Products Thereof' (Thomas Commission). Salisbury 1942.

'Report of a Commission of Inquiry into the Cold Storage Commission of Southern Rhodesia'. Salisbury 1952.

'Report of the Federal Marketing Committee on Cattle and Beef Marketing'. (Murray Commission.) Salisbury 1954.

'Report of a Commission of Inquiry on the Marketing of Cattle for Slaughter and the Distribution and Sale of Beef in Southern Rhodesia'. Salisbury 1956.

'Report of the Commission of Inquiry into the Beef Cattle Industry of Southern and Northern Rhodesia' (Horwood Commission). Federal Government 1963.

United States Government

'Livestock and Meat Statistics, 1977'.

International Organizations

EEC: Agricultural Commission
'The situation of the Agricultural Markets 1981'. Brussels.

Food and Agricultural Organization
'Meat Trade Intelligence'. No. 7 1974.
'Production Yearbook 1976'. FAO Rome.
'Trade Yearbook'.

General Agreement on Tariffs and Trade (GATT), Arrangement Regarding Bovine Meat
'Status Report on World Market for Bovine Meat'. 26 January 1981, Geneva.

UNDP/FAO
'Policy Issues for Livestock Marketing' (Kenya) Marketing Development Phase II (KEN-78/006). Nairobi, November 1979.

World Bank
'World Tables' (Annual).

Botswana National Archives Files

S.18/4   BP Cattle Entering the Union (1923–28).

S.18/5   Molopo Strip Crown Lands: Re Native Population Living on the (1924–27).

S.229/7   Farm Foods: Control of.

S.240/9   Cattle Export Tax: Proposed Imposition of Levy on Cattle (1935).

S.242/11   Agreement between BP Government and ICS (1928–31).

S.242/14   Cold Storage: Lobatsi (1933–34).

S.242/15–6   Cold Storage: Lobatsi: Question of Purchase by Administration. From ICS (1935).

S.242/17/1–2 Cold Storage: Lobatsi: General (1938–49).

S.243/1–7   Northern Abattoir (1931).

S.243/13   Cold Storage – Lobatsi – Creamery – Amended Agreement 1933. Result of Foot and Mouth Outbreak.

S.244/9–12   Cattle Export to Northern Rhodesia and Congo (1931–32).

S.251/14   Abattoir: Lobatsi (1945).

S.255/2–6   Cold Storage and Creamery: Erection of at Francistown by Rhodesian Creameries (1931).

S.256/11   Cattle Position. Report on by RC (1931).

S.262/12–17   Cattle Route to Walvis Bay (1932).

S.273/9   Beef Chilled – Conference at Pretoria (1932).

S.274/1–3   Beef: Chilled and Frozen Export to UK: Correspondence with Secretary of State (1934–35).

S.274/4   Beef: Chilled and Frozen: Export to the UK (1935–36).

S.274/5   Beef: Chilled and Frozen: Export to Europe: Correspondence with ICS and Principal Farmers and Dealers in BP (1933).

S.274/6   Beef Chilled: Export Overseas from Lobatsi (1936–39).

S.274/7   Beef: Export Overseas to Europe (1939–45).

S.275/4–6   Meat Control Bill 1933 (1933–35).

S.303/7   Meat and Cattle Export Cooperation with Union (1932).

S.306/12   Cold Storage Co: Lease of Approximately 26 Morgen (1938–41).

S.316/7–8   Proposed Meat Extract Factory in BP (1933).

S.316/9	Meat Extract Factory: Proposal to Erect in BP by Bovril Estates (1938–39).
S.370/1–9	Cattle Route to Walvis Bay (1934).
S.372/12	Stockowners Association BP (1934).
S.377/2/1–2	Water Development: Cattle Routes from Ngamiland and Ghanzi (1935–37).
S.388/1/1	Cattle and Meat Export Trade (1935).
S.388/1/2–4	Cattle and Meat Export Trade.
S.388/2	Cattle and Meat Export Trade: Report and Recommendations by Hobday and Walker (1939).
S.388/3/1–3	Cattle and Meat Export Trade: Recommendation (1939–57).
S.389/1/1	Cattle and Meat Export Trade: Legislation (1940).
S.389/1/2–5	Cattle and Meat Export Trade: Legislation (1941–48).
S.403/3	Harding: Sir Edward: Letters re Water Development and Chilled beef Export (1934).
S.420/7	BP-Union of South Africa: Memorandum on Fiscal Relations Between (1935).
S.454/5	Marketing Schemes: Union of South Africa.
S.495/3/2–3	Colonial Development Corporation (1948–51).
S.518/1–9	Cold Storage and Abattoir Facilities (1948–1954).
S.519/1/1–2	Cold Storage and Abattoir Facilities in BP (1955).
S.519/2/1–5	Cold Storage and Abattoir Facilities in BP (1950–51).
S.520/2–4	Cold Storage and Abattoir Facilities (1954–56).
S.521/1/1–4	Cold Storage and Abattoir Facilities: Meat Supply Contracts (1956–63).
S.546/2	Livestock and Meat Industries Enquiry (Purnell and Clayton) (1958–61).

Consultancy Reports

CARL BRO INTERNATIONAL, 'An Evaluation of Livestock Management and Production in Botswana with Special Reference to Communal Areas'. Malervangen 1, 2600 Glostrup, Denmark January 1982.

CHAMBERS R. and FELDMAN D., 'Report on Rural Development', Ministry of Finance and Development Planning 1973.

EVALUATION UNIT, RAMATLABAMA, 'The Management of Communal Grazing in Botswana: Discussion Paper', Government Printer, Gaborone 1981.

EXPERIENCE INCORPORATED, 'The Technical/Economic Feasibility of Establishing Additional Meat Processing Facilities in Botswana'. Minneapolis 1973.

HITCHCOCK R., 'Kalahari Cattle Posts' (Two Volumes). Ministry of Local Government and Lands 1978.

McGOWAN AND ASSOCIATES, 'A Study of Drought Relief and Contingency Measures Relating to the Livestock Sector of Botswana'. May 1979.

ODELL M., 'Botswana's First Livestock Development Project: An Experiment in Agricultural Transformation'. SIDA, Gaborone 1981.

PRICE WATERHOUSE, 'The Livestock Industry of the Bechuanaland Protectorate', 1963.

PURNELL G. and CLAYTON W., 'Report to the Government of the Bechuanaland Protectorate on the Beef Cattle and Meat Industry', 1963.

RYAN G., 'Report to the Bechuanaland Protectorate Government on the Livestock Industry of the Protectorate'. Mafeking, June 1958.

SANDFORD S., 'Dealing with Drought and Livestock in Botswana'. ODI London, May 1977.

SANDFORD S., 'Keeping an Eye on TGLP'. National Institute of Research, Gaborone 1980.

WALKER H. and HOBDAY J., 'Report on the Cattle Industry of the Bechuanaland Protectorate with Recommendations for

Improving its Organization and Assisting its Future Development'. Mafeking 1939.

WILLETT A., 'Agricultural Group Development in Botswana' (four volumes). Ministry of Agriculture 1981.

THESES UNPUBLISHED

BAILEY C., 'Cattle Husbandry in the Communal Areas of Eastern Botswana'. (PH.D.). Cornell 1982.

ETTINGER S., 'The Economics of the Customs Union Between Botswana, Lesotho, Swaziland and South Africa'. (PH.D.). Michigan 1974.

KERVEN C., 'Underdevelopment, Migration and Class Formation in the North-East District of Botswana'. (PH.D.). Toronto 1977.

MASSEY D., 'Labour Migration and Rural Development in Botswana'. (PH.D.). Boston 1980.

PARSON J., 'The Political Economy of Botswana: A Case in the Study of Politics and Social Change in Post-Colonial Societies'. (D. PHIL.). Sussex 1979.

SHILLINGTON K., 'Land Loss, Labour and Dependence: The Impact of Colonialism on the Southern Tswana: C.1870–1900'. (PH.D.). School of Oriental and African Studies, University of London, 1981.

SIMPSON J., 'International Trade in Beef and Economic Development of Selected South American Countries'. (PH.D.). Texas A and M 1974.

SPRAY P., 'The Integration of Botswana into the World Beef Market'. (M. PHIL.). Sussex 1977.

Index

279